Living Life
UNWOUNDED

A Memoir

SYDNEY OLIVER JAMES

authorHOUSE®

AuthorHouse™
1663 Liberty Drive
Bloomington, IN 47403
www.authorhouse.com
Phone: 833-262-8899

*This book is a memoir. It reflects the author's present recollections of experiences over time. Some
names have been changed, some events have been compressed, and some dialogue has been recreated.*

Published by AuthorHouse 09/08/2023

ISBN: 979-8-8230-1161-7 (sc)
ISBN: 979-8-8230-1160-0 (hc)
ISBN: 979-8-8230-1159-4 (e)

Library of Congress Control Number: 2023913039

Print information available on the last page.

This book is printed on acid-free paper.

Dedication

To those who've been hurt by the poor decisions of others and crushed by circumstances they couldn't control, you are not alone. Choose to live your life unwounded and find comfort in the strength and unconditional love of Christ.

For my mom and dad. Thank you for always loving me, especially in life's most difficult moments.

1

By Sunday morning, two mornings after our annual seventh-grade camping trip, I still hadn't recovered from the three days and two nights I spent with over a hundred of my students, but I pulled myself out of bed anyway and drove to church. I knew it would take me the better part of a week to feel like myself again—no matter how much I slept in—and I wanted to meet up with Megan after the service to thank her for taking care of my cat, Izzy, while I was away.

"Thanks, Megan, for checking in on Izzy. I really appreciate all the time you spent with her."

"Oh, it was no problem. It's not like it's a long walk from my apartment to yours. How was your trip? Did the kids have fun?"

As we continued to chat, I noticed Megan's husband, Jonathan, talking with someone I had never seen at our church before.

I wonder who that is.

"Sydney, did you hear me?" Megan asked as she turned around to see what I'd been looking at.

"Uh, no. Sorry. Can you repeat what you said?"

She smiled. "Hey, Jonathan, will you introduce Sydney to Adam?"

Wait, what?

As I got closer, I couldn't help but notice how handsome Adam was. His hair was thick and dark and well cut, and the collared shirt he wore held tightly to his well-toned physique.

1

"Hi. I'm Adam," he said confidently as he offered me his hand.

"Hi. I'm Sydney," I replied. "It's nice to meet you. Is this your first time here?"

"I've been here a few times before when I've been in town to visit my brother, but I just moved into the area about a week ago for a new job, so I'll be attending more regularly from now on. How about you?"

"I've been coming here for almost a year now, but I've lived in the Indianapolis area for the past five years. I moved to the city after I graduated from college, and now I'm a middle school science teacher at a school that's not too far from here."

"And she lives in the same apartment complex that we *all* do," Megan interjected.

I knew she had said *all* on purpose. I don't know if it was for my benefit or for Adam's, but either way, I found myself intrigued by him.

Maybe I should ask him out for coffee. I'd like the chance to get to know him without an audience present. Nah, I'll just wait and see what happens. Maybe he'll make the first move and ask me out.

But after a few more minutes of conversation, he didn't. Maybe I had mistaken his friendliness for something more than it was, or maybe he was hesitant to invest his time into getting to know me, considering everything that comes with a new job and a recent move, but I was left disappointed in myself just the same, wishing I had said what was on my mind and wondering what might have come from a few measly seconds of bravery.

2

By mid-July, three months had passed since I met Adam, and by then, I had nearly forgotten all about him—nearly. We had communicated a bit over Facebook and ran into each other at church one more time, but despite the hint of chemistry between us, nothing came from it. I had hoped our paths would cross at the apartment complex, but they never did, and once school let out at the end of May, I spent most of the summer traveling and visiting with out-of-state family and friends.

When I got back into town, I drove out to my friend Samantha's house in a suburb on the west side of the city. Samantha was one of the first friends I made when I moved to Indianapolis, and because she had grown up in a small, rural town like I had, we hit it off almost immediately. So it was a typical occurrence for us to get together and chat the night away from the comfort of her couch or mine, and considering we hadn't seen each other since our road trip to Nashville at the beginning of the summer, we had plenty of things to talk about.

We filled each other in on the happenings of the past six weeks, looked through the pictures we took from our trip to Music City, and, per usual, discussed our mutual frustrations with being single.

"Sam, you're probably not going to believe this, but I let another friend talk me into signing up for an online dating site."

"Really?" She looked surprised.

"I know. It's completely out of character for me and way out of my comfort zone, but you know how hard it is to meet someone."

"I definitely do," she said as she nodded. "So what do you think? Have you met anyone you're interested in?"

"Well, it's basically what I expected it to be, awful and awkward, but I have been talking to someone. His name is David, and he seems nice enough I guess, but I can't say I'm overly excited about him."

Buzz, buzz, buzz.

Our conversation was interrupted by the sound of my cell phone vibrating loudly on the top of her coffee table. I picked it up and saw that I had a new Facebook message.

"What is it? Is it him?"

"Probably." I rolled my eyes. "He must have seen my recent post about returning home."

Without another word, she hopped off her couch and left the living room, returning quickly with her laptop in hand.

"Here." She handed me the laptop. "Log in to Facebook. I want to see David's profile before you respond to his message."

I was more than happy to indulge her. She could peruse his profile for as long as she wanted to. I was in no rush at all to respond to him, and I was already regretting that I had agreed to meet up with him in person. *Maybe if I'm lucky she'll find a good reason for me to tell him to forget it.*

But when I logged in and took a closer look, my feelings on the matter took a drastic turn. The message wasn't from David at all but from Adam. A brief but robust burst of excitement came over me, replacing the humdrum attitude I had just the second before, and suddenly I couldn't open the message fast enough.

Hey, Sydney. How have you been? Are you enjoying your summer? Would you be up for getting together sometime?

Up for it? Of course I am. So, with some moral support from Samantha, I replied.

Hey, Adam. I've been great. Thanks. I've been traveling a lot and enjoying my summer off from work. How about you? Is grad school going well? I would like to get together. I do have Sunday open, but then I'll be in Chicago for a conference next Monday–Friday. Let me know.

He gave me his cell phone number and wrote back:

My parents are coming into town Saturday and will be here on Sunday, so I'll probably be spending time with them along with my brother and sister-in-law all day Sunday. I don't have anything going on for the rest of tonight or tomorrow night. I know that's kinda short notice. I'm just hanging out at my apartment tonight, so if you aren't busy and it's nice out, we could go for a walk at Lion's Park.

Part of me would have loved to have rushed right over to meet up with him, but the other part wasn't prepared for such a last-minute change in plans. So instead, I agreed to call him after I left Samantha's house, but from that point on, I could hardly think straight. My brain was baffled by the sudden rush of emotions I was feeling. I rarely got that enthusiastic over anyone, or anything for that matter, but something about Adam seemed different.

Not wanting to overwhelm him with this out-of-character exuberance I was experiencing though, I took some time to get it together first. Then, after browsing through his profile for a while with Samantha and discussing every post and picture along the way, I rushed out of her front door and to my car, leaving her with the promise that I'd fill her in on our phone conversation the following day.

I sat in her driveway for a few moments and took several deep breaths. Then I pulled up his name and number on my phone so I could easily make the call with just one click. I backed out of her driveway slowly and into her empty and dimly lit street, and then I hit the call button as I weaved through her neighborhood toward the main road.

My heart thumped forcefully as the sound of ringing filled my ears.

"Hello?" he said after just one ring.

His quick response startled me.

"Hello?" he said again.

"Uh … hi, Adam. It's Sydney. I'm sorry it's so late. Are you still free to talk?"

3

As we drove through the complex and past the clubhouse—a big brick building that looked out of place for a modest, midlevel apartment complex with its faux second-story balcony, ornate white columns, and spired clock tower that rose unabashedly from its rooftop—I folded my hands in my lap and looked out of the window, pretending to admire the flowering trees that lined the street. Unsure of what to say, considering the trip to the coffee shop was too short to start much of a conversation, I sat almost silently once the typical "How've you been?" and "How do you like the area so far?" line of questioning ran dry.

The awkwardness between us was almost suffocating. I had felt so connected to Adam over the phone the night before as we talked for nearly two hours straight, but now that we were together in person, I felt a whole world away from him. *I hope this isn't a bad sign.*

As Adam pulled into the drive-through, I unbuckled my seat belt and reached down to the floor to grab my purse.

"Oh don't worry about it," he said. "I've got it. What would you like?"

"Are you sure? You really don't have to."

"I'm sure," he replied kindly. "Do you need a minute to decide?"

"No, I'd like a tall vanilla chai tea latte with skim milk and no whip. Thanks."

"Of course."

A few minutes later, with the comfort of our warm drinks in hand, we drove onto Zionsville's Main Street, a road covered in well-worn cobblestone that was red at the edges and darker toward the center to mark where the old Interurban rail line once ran through. This brick-laden road was lined with businesses—trendy shops and upscale boutiques, quaint cafés and fine restaurants, art studios and a bed-and-breakfast or two—many of which had taken up shop in historic buildings.

From Main Street, Adam turned onto Cedar and then onto Elm, where he parked the car in front of Lion's Park. Then he hopped out of the car and hurried around to the other side to open my door.

As we walked toward the park's entrance and down a steep flight of stairs, I gripped my chai tea tightly with one hand and the railing with the other, ensuring I wouldn't trip on my way down. When I reached the bottom and looked up, I found Adam staring at me with a grin, and it was then I realized just how slowly I'd been moving. I shrugged and let out a small laugh, and he did too.

I wouldn't have pegged a family park for a good place to go on a first date, with all the noise that running, jumping, screaming, and squealing kids make, but on a Friday afternoon, while most of the adult world was still at work, the park sat quiet and serene. The only sounds I could hear were the cheerful chirps of the birds in the trees above us and the gentle rushing of the stream that flowed nearby.

"So tell me more about your new job and what brought you here," I said.

"Well, my brother lives in the area, and once I finished my military training, he suggested that I look into getting a job here. My new company is a medical device security company. Basically we visit various hospitals across the country and help them better secure the patient information that is gathered by the medical equipment they use."

"And you're liking it so far?"

"So far. It's nice to be somewhere where both my military training as a signal officer and my business degree are being put to good use. Although someday I'd really like to own a business of my own, which is why I've started taking classes online toward my MBA."

His ambition was impressive.

"And the travel is a plus," he added.

"Oh, so you like to travel then?"

"Definitely. I especially like to visit places where I can spend time outdoors hiking, snowboarding, or just sightseeing. And since I double majored in business and Spanish, I'd like to do some more traveling abroad."

"Some more?"

"Yeah. I spent some time in Costa Rica when I was in college."

"Wow. I really haven't traveled all that much, but I'd like to. I'd especially like to visit some ski resorts out of the Midwest. I've been downhill skiing since I was a kid, but I've never had the opportunity to ski at a true mountain resort."

"So if you had to choose then, would you pick a beach vacation or a ski vacation?"

"A ski vacation," I said without giving it a thought, "every single time."

"I like that," he said. "So how did you decide on teaching?"

"I didn't at first. I studied biology in college, with the plan of going onto pharmacy or medical school afterward, but as I neared graduation, my heart really wasn't in either. I moved here with a friend from college and struggled for a year or two to figure out what I wanted to do with my life. There had always been signs that I should go into the education field, but I fought them. I suppose it was a combination of the low pay and my own pride that kept me from giving in, but once I did, it instantly felt right. There's no denying that being a teacher is my calling, and although it can be draining and super frustrating sometimes, I love that I can go to work each day and make a positive difference in my students' lives."

"That's … incredible," he said.

Hours passed as our conversation continued, and all the while we became increasingly more enthralled with each other. It wasn't until I noticed that the sun was going down that I remembered that Abby and Kate were coming over.

"Shoot. What time is it? I wish I had more time, Adam, but I've got to get back. I have a couple of friends coming over tonight, and they'll be at my apartment soon."

"Okay. No problem. Let's get going then."

Five minutes later, we were sitting in his car outside of my apartment.

"It doesn't look like they're here yet," I said as I turned around in my seat. "It's pretty normal for my friends to be running late, so would you like to come in?"

"Sure."

After unlocking my patio door, Adam and I settled into the high-top chairs around my dining room table, and while we talked, laughed, and swapped coy smiles, I traced the lines in the marble tabletop with my fingertips and pretended not to notice Adam inching his hand closer and closer to mine.

"I had a great time, Adam. I wish it didn't have to end."

"Me too," he said sweetly as he placed his hand over mine. "We'll have to get together again soon."

"I'd like that."

Ding-dong!

My doorbell rang out loudly, making us both jump out of our seats and away from each other.

"Come in," I said with a slight inflection of irritation in my voice. *You have such perfect timing.*

The door swung open quickly, and the sound of cheerful chatter filled the room until the girls dropped their bags and saw Adam standing next to me. A look of surprise crossed Abby's face, and then a smirk of satisfaction followed.

"Uh. This is Adam. He lives in the building next door."

"Oh?" Abby said. "Hi, Adam. I'm Abby. It's nice to meet you."

"And I'm Kate," Abby's younger sister chimed in.

"Hi. It's nice to meet you both."

"All right, Adam was just on his way out," I said before either of them could ask him any questions. Then I ushered Adam toward the door.

"Can I call you tomorrow?" he whispered.

I nodded. "I'm looking forward to it."

4

A week later, after suffering through a long five-day conference in Chicago, I found myself pacing back and forth across my living room carpet, waiting for Adam to arrive. We had talked on the phone every night of that conference—generally while I sat surrounded by the dinge of my hotel bathroom so I wouldn't disturb my sleeping roommate—and texted back and forth throughout each day.

Although the conference had come at an inconvenient time for us, considering we were just beginning to get to know each other, it did provide us with a unique opportunity to dig a little deeper, even form a friendship, without the help or hindrance of the other's physical company. In a way, it was kind of romantic I suppose, but that didn't mean I wasn't thrilled to ditch our nightly phone conversations for some more face-to-face time once the week was over.

At the first sighting of his bright blue sports car through my window, I ran to the door and swung it open widely, not giving him a chance to knock. He smiled broadly at my sudden and enthusiastic appearance, then took me straight into his arms.

"I missed you," he said. "Welcome home."

"I missed you too," I managed to squeak out, feeling slightly suffocated by the strength of his forearms.

"Are you ready to go?"

"Yep. I'm ready."

As he drove us in the direction of downtown, the car was filled with lively conversation, each of us taking our turn sharing the highs and lows of our week apart. With Adam by my side, the outside world appeared to be nothing more than a vague blur to me, until we turned down Meridian and the city skyline became visible.

I've always been a bit enchanted by Meridian, as it runs through several historical districts consisting of some of the most prestigious homes in the area—homes designed in such a wide variety of unique and ornate architectural styles that one can't help but stare. I particularly loved to drive down it in the springtime, when the mature trees that bend over the street are covered in new leaves and bright, blossoming flowers. But riding down it with Adam, while we imagined what it would be like to live in such a home, well, that made the experience almost magical.

About halfway down Meridian, Adam turned down College Avenue, which led us into Broad Ripple, one of Indianapolis's most popular cultural districts, especially among the young and unattached. It offers countless local restaurants, bars, and nightclubs to choose from, situated alongside the White River and the twenty-six-mile-long Monon Trail. There we enjoyed a candlelit dinner at the French bistro Petit Chou before continuing onward toward Victory Field, the home of the Indianapolis Indians.

As we neared the field, traffic became heavy, and crowds of people wearing Indians apparel flooded the street. I worried it would take us much longer than we had to find a place to park, but Adam had thought ahead and prepaid for a reserved spot in a garage close to the ballpark. We climbed out of the car and slammed our doors shut in unison to join the mass of Indians fans rushing toward the front gate.

Once in line, Adam pulled the tickets from his wallet and handed one to me. I felt a slight twinge of guilt as I touched it, calculating in my head just how much money he must have spent between dinner and the game.

"Let me give you some money for my ticket. You've already paid for dinner and for parking."

"No, I don't want any of your money. It's my treat."

"Okay, thank you."

After my purse was checked by security and our tickets were scanned, Adam led us toward the concessions to get some drinks, and then we sat down. We had a great view of the field from the first base line, not that it really mattered since we spent most of the time talking and flirting, completely unaware of how the game was going.

"Hey. Would you mind if we took a picture?" he asked.

"Uh, sure, okay."

He pulled his phone from his pocket and wrapped his right arm behind my shoulders to draw me in close. Then he stretched out his left arm in front of us to snap a quick shot.

"Can I see it?" I asked.

He nodded and tilted the screen in my direction.

I could see right away that the picture was awful. Not at all what I wanted our first picture together to look like. We looked out of proportion, as most people in selfies do, and noticeably sweaty and hot.

"Maybe we should take another?"

"Nah. I think it's fine. I just want to text it to my parents."

His parents? I didn't know whether to be irritated or flattered, but it had been such a wonderful night together that I settled on flattered.

By the seventh inning, we had had enough of the blazing sun and nearly 100 degree heat index. The game had been a blowout anyway, with the Indians taking an early lead, so we agreed to head for home ahead of everyone else. Adam filed out of our row first, and I followed closely behind. Then he paused at the top of the stairs and took me by the hand.

On the drive back home, I couldn't stop myself from smiling as I replayed the night over and over again in my mind. I was falling for him already. There was no doubt about it.

Having been lost in my own thoughts for most of the drive home, I didn't realize we had made it back to my apartment until Adam put the car into park and the interior lights came on. I sat and waited patiently as he came around and opened my car door. Then we took a few steps from the parking lot together, up onto my front porch.

The light from the moon illuminated us as we stood facing each other, with both of my hands gently resting inside of his.

"I had a really great time, Adam," I whispered. "I appreciate how much work you put into planning it."

"I'm glad you had a good time," he whispered back. "I did too."

A brief moment of silence filled the air between us. The time had come for us to say good night. Then I watched as his eyes moved downward slowly and settled onto my lips. I knew what he wanted—I wanted it too—so I smiled slightly and stepped closer to him.

His eyes remained locked on my mouth as he leaned in close to me, and I held my breath in eager anticipation of our first kiss. But just before our lips could touch, he seemed to change his mind. He turned his face abruptly to the left and buried it into my neck as he wrapped me in his arms instead.

Wait. What just happened? Did I do something wrong?

I was left stunned and feeling a bit self-conscious, not understanding why he hadn't kissed me. Not knowing what to say, I turned toward my door and unlocked it as soon as he released me, but before I stepped inside, I turned back to face him and said, "Adam, promise that you're not going to break my heart."

"I won't," he replied.

I wasn't convinced.

Then I watched as he turned around and slunk off into the darkness.

5

In one split second, my evening had been ruined. Our attraction toward each other had been so apparent and completely effortless throughout every moment of that date. I couldn't comprehend why he hadn't kissed me. If he hadn't been ready, I could've understood that, but his body language had made it clear that wasn't true. So what had happened? What had caused him to suddenly change his mind?

I supposed it was possible that things between us were moving too fast for him. Although I didn't get the impression that Adam ever did anything slowly. But if that wasn't the case, then I had no other plausible explanation. He'd have to tell me for himself why he had acted the way he had, and if he didn't see the possibility of a relationship in our future, then I was done. I wanted out before my heart got any more involved.

So I turned off my bedside lamp to try to get some sleep, but before I drifted off, my cell phone vibrated, and a text message from Adam lit up its screen.

> I'm so sorry for the way our evening ended. It didn't end at all the way I wanted it to. Would you be willing to come to my place tomorrow night for dinner so I can explain?

"Yes," was all I replied.

I had all night and most of the following day to think about what Adam was going to say to me at dinner, so by the time I started walking down the sidewalk toward his door, I was a complete bundle of nerves. My imagination had been running rampant for hours, taking my mind to all kinds of horrible places, making me afraid to face whatever reason he had for leading me on and then rejecting me.

It's always been difficult for me to let my guard down and let people see what's on the inside, which is why I've only had a handful of meaningful and long-lasting relationships in my life. But somehow Adam had already begun to break down my walls. Somehow his charm and his gentle but full-of-life spirit had won me over, so when he pushed me away, it stung.

Negative thoughts continued to swirl around in my head as I stood anxiously in front of his door, willing myself to ring his doorbell. But when he opened the door and I saw how miserable he looked, those thoughts completely ceased. For the first time since we met, he seemed fragile to me. His usual confident exterior had dissipated, replaced by an uneasiness and an uncertainty in himself. The expression on his face exposed genuine fear—a sign that whatever he was about to tell me wasn't good.

"Hi," he said with a half smile on his face. "Come in."

He led me into his living room, which was well organized but not overly clean. There was hardly a pop of color anywhere, minus the patterned throw pillows his mother had bought for him, nor any pictures that I could see. Each wall was still painted in the standard off-white that the apartment complex provides, and every stitch of furniture—all of which centered around his flat-screen TV and high-tech sound system—was the same dull, chocolate brown. *Okay, so interior decorating is not his thing.*

Under different circumstances, I might have teased him about it, but I sat down on the edge of his faux leather love seat in silence instead. Rather than sitting down next to me, he took a seat on the matching couch adjacent. Then with a slight tremble in his voice, he began to speak.

"Look, Sydney. I want to say again how sorry I am for last night."

I remained silent.

"I wanted to kiss you good night. I really did, but I felt as though I needed to tell you some things first. Some things about my past."

I was feeling queasier by the minute. "Okay … go on."

"Well, I was engaged once before. To a girl I met in college. We had planned to get married the week after my graduation, but I called it off about a month ahead of the wedding. I had been having doubts about us for quite some time and had felt pressured into proposing to her when I did, because of a job offer I had in California. She had made it clear that she didn't want a long-distance relationship, and I didn't want to end things between us either, so I proposed. It was a mistake.

"As you can imagine, she didn't take me breaking our engagement well, and neither did her family. In fact, just a few months earlier, we had flown to India, where her parents lived, and participated in an elaborate engagement ceremony. We shared our commitment to marry in front of nearly five thousand people, and so that only added to the embarrassment they all felt when I went back on my word."

India? Five thousand guests? Really?

"Of course I felt awful for breaking her heart and reneging on my promise to marry her, so I dealt with a lot of guilt. Then, to make matters worse, my father was diagnosed with prostate cancer, my job offer was retracted, and I got into a serious car accident after falling asleep at the wheel.

"My life was a mess, so after graduation, I moved back home with my parents. It was a dark period of time for me for sure, but several months later, I found some direction again when a friend encouraged me to enlist in the army."

I couldn't imagine how difficult that must have been for him. One moment, he had it all—love, his dream job, and a clear direction for his life—and in the next, it was gone. I strained to formulate any coherent words in response to his story, not sure where to start or what was appropriate to say. But finally I said, "Thank you for telling me."

I was thankful. Thankful he had been so open and honest with me before we became any more emotionally invested in each other. But of course I still had to ask, "Do you still have feelings for her?"

"No," he said assuredly. "I moved on a long time ago, and she's since been married to someone else."

"Hmm ..." It was obvious that his past mistakes had been weighing on him. "Then ... okay."

"Okay?" he repeated.

His story was a bit alarming at first, and I felt a bit of jealousy toward this woman he had previously been engaged to, but it had been more than five years since all that happened.

"Yes. I'm okay with it. If you've told me everything and she really is just a part of your past, then it's not a problem for me. I don't think it's anything that should keep us from moving forward—if that's what you want?"

"It is what I want," he said with a smile.

6

Although it hadn't been easy for him, Adam had dug deep and shared some intimate details about his life with me, and that only made my interest in him grow stronger. Because he had been forthcoming about what had likely been the most difficult time in his life, I felt confident that I could trust him wholeheartedly. And as uncomfortable as our conversation had been, it acted as a springboard that propelled our relationship forward—and fast.

During the two months that followed it, we made the most of our time together, spending nearly every day with each other since his travel schedule at work was placed on a temporary hold. It was the simple moments we shared—cooking a meal, working out at the gym, or snuggling on the couch while we watched a movie together—that I enjoyed the most. But I loved the concerted effort Adam always made in planning dates out for us too.

We tried out new restaurants, took in some live music, visited the zoo, hiked, rock climbed, played golf, and went ice-skating. We logged more hours with each other during those two months than most people do in an entire year together, which is why I think our feelings for each other grew so quickly—so quickly that he asked if I'd go home with him as his date for his friend Ryan's wedding.

He wants me to go home with him and stay with his parents for an entire weekend? Am I ready for that? Meeting his parents seemed like an awfully significant step forward, and I didn't think it should be taken lightly. I hadn't planned on him meeting my parents until I was certain we had a long-lasting future ahead of us, but how could I be certain of that unless I knew how he grew up and where he came from?

Two and a half weeks later, on a Friday morning, we left for Ryan's wedding. During the first two-thirds of the drive, we acted as most couples do on their first road trip together—giddy, goofy, and flirtatious. We laughed, teased, and sang to the radio, all the while holding hands. And now and then, I'd lean in close to him and plant a few playful kisses on his cheek. It was an affectionate gesture I knew he loved from the boyish grin that came across his face.

But after stopping for lunch at a little Italian restaurant he had frequented with his family, I started to feel less lighthearted and a bit more anxious. *What if I don't fit in with his family? That could crush our chances of a future together. Or what if I don't like them? If I don't, then I might be forced to end our relationship myself.* It was a thought that made my head hurt and my heart pound.

Once we drove into Springfield's city limits, Adam began pointing out some of the places that held meaning to him. His high school where he claimed to have climbed out of a window during class—for which, if I had been his teacher at the time, I would've gladly locked him outside to rot. The capitol building where he worked as a page. The fields where he played high school baseball and the streets where he and his childhood friends used to live and play.

It was clear that he was thrilled to be sharing his hometown with me, but I struggled to pay attention to everything he was saying, thinking mostly about how differently we had grown up. I hadn't thought much about it until then because we were currently living very similar lives within the same city, community, and apartment complex. But driving through Springfield with him, on my way to meet his parents, I became sure that Adam would be shocked by the little backwoods town I called home, and that made me even more nervous.

So I did what I generally do when I'm nervous; I found something to distract me. I pulled down the passenger-side visor and threw open the mirror. Then I ran a brush through my hair and touched up my makeup. I could feel Adam staring at me as I continued to primp, moving one hair at a time into a new place.

As we neared the end of his parents' neighborhood road and pulled into their semicircular driveway, Adam placed his right hand on my knee, giving it a supportive squeeze, and said, "We're here."

I flipped the visor back up and took a long look at his childhood home. It was a simple, two-story house with an attached garage, dressed in white siding, black shutters, and a bit of brick. The front yard was small, but the grass was green, lush, and perfectly cut. It was bigger than my childhood home was, but seeing how close it sat to the neighbors' houses, without much room to run, jump, build forts, and climb trees, I was thankful to have grown up where I had.

I took a few calming breaths as I waited for Adam to come around to my side of the car and open the door. Then I took the hand he offered to me and climbed out. With my fingers locked firmly between his, we walked toward their front door together, leaving our luggage behind in the back seat of the car.

Just as our feet stepped onto their cement porch, the front door swung open, and there we were greeted by both of his parents. His father was about Adam's height but thinner and had a thick head of gray hair. His mother was a bit rounder and shorter of course, and her smile was friendly and familiar looking, almost identical to Adam's.

"Hi. You must be Sydney," his mother said. "I'm Judy. We're so glad you could come."

"Yes, thank you for having me," I said. Then she gave Adam and me a hug.

"I'm Greg. It's nice to meet you," he said as he shook my hand. "Won't you come in?"

7

After Adam and I settled into the two side-by-side bedrooms at the end of their upstairs hallway, I joined him in his childhood room to talk.

"Adam, I think I'm going to stay here while you go to the rehearsal."

He looked stunned. "You're kidding me, right?"

"I know you've been looking forward to introducing me to your friends, but there's plenty of time for that. It's not like there will be anything for me to do during the wedding rehearsal anyways. I'll just be in the way. I think it's more important that I get to know your parents while I have the chance."

"Are you sure?" He looked concerned.

"I'm sure, and I'll be fine. I'll see you soon when you pick me up for the rehearsal dinner." Then I kissed him on the cheek and left him upstairs to get dressed.

Adam's parents wore a similar expression of surprise on their faces when I joined them in the kitchen to tell them that I'd be staying behind, but from what I could tell, they were also impressed. And I wanted them to be. I hoped that by choosing to sit down with them, alone and without the comfort of Adam by my side, that they would see how serious I was about their son.

"I hope it's all right with you, but I thought it might be nice for us to get to know one another."

"Of course," his mother said. "Let's go take a seat in the family room."

"Okay," I said as I followed behind her.

Initially, Judy and I did most of the talking, discovering a few things we had in common. Then as we got more comfortable, she went on to tell me a few childhood stories about Adam.

"Adam has always been a bit of a daredevil," she said with a grin. "I remember when he was just two or three years old, I found him sitting on top of our refrigerator, which scared me half to death, but of course he was as happy as a clam and very proud of his accomplishment."

I suspected Adam had been somewhat of a handful growing up.

"Oh, and there was another time that he insisted on climbing on top of the roof of our vehicle after preschool one afternoon because something needed to be 'fixed' before we could drive home."

"And you let him?" I asked.

"Well, yes. What else was I going to do? He had already scaled to the top before I could stop him."

I laughed when I imagined the disapproving looks she likely got from the other parents.

"Oh, and did you hear about the time he backed our van out of the garage?"

"No, I haven't."

"When he was eight, he tried to back the van out of the garage to 'help' me. It would be a decision he'd come to regret because he ripped off the side-view mirror in the process and nearly crushed me. It's funny now, but it wasn't then."

"No, I'm sure it wasn't. That had to be frightening."

Hearing her stories about Adam made me feel a bit more connected to his family, and I loved the idea of teasing him about them later, but I didn't learn anything from them. I already knew that Adam was the adventurous type. I already knew that he was thoughtful and that he enjoyed helping others—thankfully now in more appropriate ways that didn't result in the destruction of valuable property. So I turned to Greg.

On the surface, we didn't appear to have much in common, and why would we really? I can't imagine that many twenty-seven-year-old females share the same kind of hobbies or interests with those of any typical sixty-year-old man. But as we began to talk, out on their back deck with a glass of fresh lemonade in our hands, I realized that we were more alike than I expected.

He didn't bother to tell me any cutesy childhood stories about Adam—not that I didn't like hearing them—but he got right down to business, steering the conversation in a more meaningful direction. And that gave us both the chance to compare notes on the important things. The kind of things that can make or break a relationship, like how we view the world around us and what we value most in life.

"When the boys were young, I wasn't a very good father to them," he admitted. "I spent far too much time working and not enough of it engaged in family life. So my relationship with the boys and with Judy suffered. She was left home alone a lot, trying to raise Eric and Adam without much support from me. And as they reached their middle school years, their behavior became more than she could handle. Eventually, we came to a breaking point, and I realized that it was up to me to make a serious change. So I sat down with each one of the boys to ask for their forgiveness and to pray. That day, we all committed to working together to do better."

I couldn't imagine what kind of lasting impression that would have made on an adolescent boy. To see their own father with tears in his eyes, apologizing and admitting he hadn't been the father or the husband he should have been. Adam did nothing but sing his father's praises when he came up in conversation. The respect and admiration he held for him was undeniable, and I have to believe that it was Greg's vulnerability that day that made all the difference in their relationship.

And it was that same vulnerability that gave me exactly what I had been looking for. I knew that Adam and I still had much to learn about each other, but my conversation with Greg gave me the confidence I needed to let go of the parts of my heart I was still holding onto. There would always be risks in letting someone in, and that would always scare me. But knowing that Adam had grown up with a father that loved him as much as Greg did, knowing that he had modeled how to take responsibility for his mistakes and showed him how to put the hard work needed into fixing them, that made those risks worth taking.

8

As soon as I climbed back into Adam's car, I kicked off my shoes, wrapped my arm around his, and laid my head against his shoulder, using his heavily muscled deltoid as a pillow. I must have dozed off immediately because in what felt like just a few seconds, we were back in his parents' driveway, and I could hear Adam whispering my name. My eyes burned as I struggled to peel them open. Then I forced my shoes partway on and slunk toward the front door, where Adam was waiting.

The interior of the house was dark and quiet, solidifying in my mind that it was time to go to bed, just as his parents had done long ago. I willed my aching feet to ascend the stairs and to do so quietly, not wanting to wake his mom and dad. As I neared the end of the hallway, I could practically hear that quilt-covered bed calling my name, but then Adam tapped me on the shoulder and said, "Do you want to watch a movie?"

Ugh. All I wanted to do was sleep. The rehearsal dinner had been a good time for sure, but it had left me exhausted. *How is it even possible that he doesn't look tired at all?*

In truth, the evening had felt much like a marathon to me, one in which I tried to remember everyone's names, occupations, and how they were connected to Adam, all while having to answer the same few questions repeatedly. I appreciated how friendly everyone had been and how eager his friends seemed to be about getting to know me, but it had all been so tiring.

Still, it was hard to say no to him and even harder to pass up on an opportunity to spend time alone with him.

"Sure, just give me fifteen minutes and I'll join you downstairs." I had every intention of cuddling right up next to Adam and letting myself fall asleep as soon as I plopped myself onto the basement couch anyway.

But when I got down to the basement, I soon discovered that Adam had other plans. He spent an absurd amount of time messing with the LCD projector and getting the sound system working to his exact specifications, as if his life somehow depended on us having a perfect movie-quality experience. Then he surfed through hundreds of different channels, looking for a movie we could watch, passing by the same options over and over again.

Finally though—*thank the Lord*—he came across a Jeff Dunham television special and paused on it for long enough that I knew he was interested in watching it. I wasn't fond of stand-up comedy, but I pretended to be so Adam would settle down and I could get some rest. A few minutes into watching Dunham and his most popular puppet, Achmed, do their thing, however, I found myself laughing right alongside Adam at every joke.

But once the show was over and the basement grew still and dark, the mood in the room changed between us. Perhaps it was because the significance of the day and how it had served to advance our relationship was starting to sink in, or maybe it was just the dim lighting and the high endorphin levels, courtesy of our shared laughter, that were responsible for it, but we felt drawn to each other with a force that was impossible to fight.

Without saying a word to me, Adam leaned in close, pulling my body toward his at the same time. Using only his lips as a guide, he placed them onto the side of my neck and gently slid them upward until they met with mine. He let them softly reside there for several seconds before pulling back just far enough to see how I was going to respond.

I placed both of my hands firmly against his chest and used them to push him onto his back with a bit more vigor than I really needed to. Then I eased my upper body onto his, so that we were face-to-face and chest to chest, both of our hearts racing wildly as I kissed him. The intensity of the moment grew and grew until we had no choice but to abandon the couch for the basement floor. But as we neared the point of no return, my brain intervened.

"Adam, we have to stop," I whispered unconvincingly.

"What?" he said as he continued to kiss me.

"I'm sorry, but we have to stop."

It wasn't easy, but eventually we pulled our bodies away from each other. We had committed long ago to waiting, but as we lay on the floor in silence trying to catch our breaths, I knew doing so would only get harder and harder.

9

Adam and I agreed that my first visit to his hometown had gone as well as we could have hoped for, and because of that, we gained a significant amount of confidence in each other. I imagined, though, that once the shoe was put on the other foot, things might not go as smoothly. Not because I didn't think Adam could handle meeting my parents, but because he'd have a few more obstacles to hurdle with them, particularly with my father, who was fiercely protective, not easily impressed, and good at almost everything.

Moreover, my dad and Adam couldn't have been any more different. My dad was a logical man, one who didn't let his emotions guide his decisions. He took the time to think things through and saw the world in black and white. He was mentally strong, smarter than most people I knew even though he didn't go to college, and could build or fix just about anything. He cared about others and would do what he could to help them, but telling them how he felt was a real challenge. He hated crowds, found no pleasure in the arts or culture, and was a true and avid outdoorsman, obsessed with all things hunting.

Adam, on the other hand, was the most emotional man I had ever met. He felt deeply, was more apt to trust his gut, and didn't seem to think twice about taking risks. He was sensitive, sweet, and lavished me with affection, never afraid to tell me he loved me or kiss me in public. He was smart but not in the same ways that my father was, and he liked to spend his time at the gym or playing his guitar while singing. He did enjoy being outdoors but could be just as content going to a museum, a stage production, or a concert.

There really wasn't a single personality trait or hobby that they shared, except for their interest in sports—rooting for different teams of course—and caring for me, but still, I had high hopes that he would win both of my parents over with his charm, passion, and ambition to succeed, just as he had with me. And he got the chance to try the very next weekend—Labor Day weekend—following Ryan's wedding.

My mom and dad arrived at my apartment on Friday afternoon, looking worn out from their early-morning wake-up call and the long drive down. That 450-mile drive—a drive I have made more times than I can count—has a way of wearing on you. It consists mainly of a monotonous stretch of interstate flush with slow-moving 18-wheelers and hotheaded speedsters full of road rage, both of which seem to get some kind of sick thrill out of preventing you from using your cruise control. And the traffic only gets worse as you near the city, making those last twenty miles to my apartment seem longer than all of those that came before it. So, as a general rule, I tried to avoid making that trip unless I had several days to stay and visit, yet my parents suffered through it for just a short weekend, knowing I was eager to introduce them to Adam.

When their truck pulled up, Izzy and I leaped from the couch and stood by the patio door, prepared to swing it open for them as soon as they stepped onto the cement porch. Leaving all her stuff behind, my mom climbed out of the cab first and walked directly toward us, embracing me in a warm hug, while my dad stayed behind to wrestle with their luggage. Izzy meowed at her feet, demanding some attention too, aware of what all animals, wild or domesticated, soon learn, that she was the ultimate animal lover.

A minute or two later, my dad walked through the door and directly into my bedroom with bags in hand and a baseball cap on his head. Then, after setting their suitcases onto the floor, he returned to give me a hug before plopping down onto the couch in front of the television screen, clearly in need of a nap. He rested his eyes while my mom headed into the bathroom to freshen up for dinner, and I texted Adam to tell him he could come over at any time.

As I sat silently looking out the living room window, I could feel my anxiety level rise, more than I thought it should have. I wasn't generally a nervous person, but since I had never introduced a boyfriend to my parents before, the significance of doing so felt overwhelming. I suppose it might seem strange that it had taken me so long to take that step, but there hadn't been anyone else in my life that meant as much as Adam did to me. Adam wasn't just a boyfriend; he was *the* boyfriend—the only one I had ever envisioned sharing the rest of my life with.

So I shut my eyes and said a quick prayer in my head, pleading for the night to go well. I desperately wanted my parents to see Adam the way I did, as an intelligent yet fun-loving person who not only loved me but pushed me in ways that made my life more fulfilling. I wanted them to witness for themselves his extraordinarily exuberant personality and see how it perfectly complemented my typically serious demeanor. And most of all, I wanted them to accept him and welcome him into the family, which was all I needed in order to feel sure that Adam was indeed the one.

Then I opened my eyes to the sight of Adam walking toward the door, so I ran toward it, hoping to lend him some kind of moral support before the introductions began. A peck on his cheek, a hug, or even just an uplifting whisper into his ear to tell him, "You've got this," but he slipped right past me and somehow avoided my touch.

I spun around to face the living room, baffled momentarily by his out-of-character behavior. I couldn't name a time in which Adam hadn't greeted me with the kind of enthusiasm you have for someone you haven't seen in years, but I supposed he was simply focused on the task at hand: meeting my parents. So I shrugged it off and got down to the business of formal introductions.

"Adam, this is my dad."

"It's Dave," my father said as he acknowledged Adam with a firm handshake.

"And this is my mom, Jill."

"It's nice to meet you Adam," she responded with a friendly smile followed by a hug.

After the appropriate amount of trivial small talk, we piled into my dad's truck to head to our favorite pizza place, a local restaurant known for its creative culinary creations. I knew that my parents would likely lean toward their more traditional options, but I still wanted to share a place with them that Adam and I enjoyed so much as a couple.

Fifteen minutes later, we pulled into the parking lot, and Adam led us toward the restaurant, onto their patio and through the side door. It felt good to be out of the truck and moving around in the fresh air. The ride over, although short, was uncomfortable at best, with Adam still refusing to touch me—I think he felt scared to do so in front of my father, even though we had the back seat to ourselves. The conversation in the truck had been noticeably minimal too, but I had high hopes that once we got some food into our bellies and could sit facing one another, the conversation would pick up.

The hostess led us toward our table and left four dinner menus and one beer and wine list in the middle of it. I tensed when I saw Adam reach for the list and flashed him a strong look of displeasure that I'm sure could've been seen from the other side of the room, so he tossed the list off to the side as if he was completely disinterested in it and focused on the food menu.

But I knew better. I knew that ordering a craft beer was exactly what he wanted to do. Most of the time, it took him longer to decide what type of beer he wanted to try than it did his food. He'd read through every description, taking note of the aromas and flavors listed, and then take out his phone to research and read reviews. After that, he'd likely ask for a couple of samples to try before finally settling on his first round, something that was sure to be dark and strong.

I couldn't relate to his infatuation really. All beer tasted the same to me, awful, and if I was going to consume empty calories, I preferred for them to be in something worthwhile, like a decadent dessert. But if craft beer was something he enjoyed, and he drank it responsibly, then it was of no concern to me, except for that night. I had made it clear to him that drinking any form of alcohol in front of my parents was unacceptable. They had grown up in homes where alcohol had been abused, and they were forced to see the problems and pain that it could lead to. So out of respect for them and love for me, it didn't seem like a big ask to refrain from ordering alcohol for a night or two.

With that crisis averted, I looked over the dinner menu and pointed out a few of our favorites to my parents. Typically, we started with salads and chose one of their homemade dressings to put on the side—creamy basil for Adam and creamy cucumber for me—before moving onto choosing a pizza. We both liked a vast array of pizza toppings, but we typically leaned toward their buffalo chicken pizza on a multigrain crust.

Of course it came as no surprise to me that my parents looked disgusted when Adam mentioned it.

"Why don't we stick to something a little more traditional and less spicy," I said. "It might be nice to order differently this time. Right, Adam?"

He nodded.

We settled on a large pizza made with white crust and red sauce, and topped with pepperoni, green pepper, and onion. I could tell from Adam's silence that he was disappointed in the selection, but considering my parents had come so far and deserved to enjoy their meal, I ignored it.

Once our waitress returned with our drinks and I put in our food order, I looked to Adam to start up a conversation, eager to watch him perform. He was always so good with people and never had a problem striking up a conversation with anyone, anywhere, at any time. He was a true extrovert, one who absolutely oozed with charisma and charm.

"So, Dave, you're a builder right?"

"Yep."

"And you've been building for a long time?"

"Since I was a kid."

"Do you have a lot of work right now?"

"Uh-huh, the summer and early fall are always a busy time for me."

There was a brief pause.

"Sydney says you're into hunting too. What do you hunt for?"

"Mostly whitetail deer," my dad said with a bit more interest. "They've got some big bucks where you're from, right? Do you hunt?"

"Well, no, I don't. I'd be interested in learning though. Since I'm in the military, I'm pretty familiar with guns."

"Yeah, that's not really the same thing."

The exchange between them continued to be slow and uncomfortable to watch, so my mom and I did our best to fill in the moments of silence ourselves. But it didn't take long for Adam to shut down. I felt bad for him at first, but the longer he sat without making any effort, uttering hardly a word and staring intermittently at his phone, the more frustrated I became.

I had put a lot of effort into getting to know his parents, and I did so on their turf and without any help from him. I pushed myself hard to make the most of the time I had with Greg and Judy, and after just a few minutes of difficulty, he had given up. I knew my dad wasn't the easiest to talk to, but so what? Make the effort and give my dad the chance to open up.

I knew my dad could be intimidating and that they may not have had a lot in common, but Adam was a grown man and an officer in the military. He was well educated, came from a good home, and had a stable job. He had so many things going for him that there was no reason for him to bow out. So there had to be something more than just the typical first-meeting jitters going on inside of him, but for the life of me, I couldn't figure out what it was.

10

The tension inside the truck on the drive home was painfully apparent to everyone. We were all undoubtedly disappointed with the way the evening had panned out, but no one quite knew what to say to rectify it. And frankly, I was more concerned with trying to figure out why Adam had been acting so strangely.

But it was hard to think clearly about anything, with the indignation that was bubbling up inside of me, trying its best to come pouring out. So I concentrated on holding it inside, not needing an emotional outburst to make the evening any worse than it already was. And I did so as I sat as far away from Adam as possible, refusing to look in his direction, as if he wasn't there.

Despite my best efforts though, I could feel his disappointment in himself radiating toward me, growing with every second that passed. It wasn't typical for either one of us to be angry with the other, and normally I would have jumped at the chance to resolve any problems there were between us, but we couldn't have the kind of conversation we needed to in front of my parents. Aware of that, Adam slid his hand across the seat toward mine to try to build some kind of nonverbal bridge between us, but I pulled my hand away, certain that if we touched at all, I'd lose it.

By the time we neared my apartment though, I had calmed myself down just enough to hash out a plan that I thought might turn our evening around. If I could convince Adam to come in and stay for a while, we could put on a pot of coffee, pull out a deck of cards, and have some fun together. I found that a little healthy competition was a good way to bring people together.

So as my dad put his truck into park, I amped myself up for round two, feeling confident my plan was going to work. I hopped down from the truck and unlocked my apartment door, opening it and then stepping aside so my parents could walk in first. Then I turned around to face Adam, who lagged behind us all, to fill him in on the plan I had concocted.

"Adam, why don't you—"

"I'm heading home," he said flatly.

"No, don't do that. I have a plan. If you could just wait a minute and listen, I think you'll—"

"I've got to go," he interrupted again. Then he walked past me, ducked his head into the doorway, and mumbled, "Thanks for dinner. I'm feeling tired, so I'm going to head home. Good night." And just like that, he was gone, and I was left feeling abandoned, much like I had the night after the baseball game.

Wait, did this have something to do with that night? Did his strange behavior have something to do with that conversation we had about his ex? I didn't know, but what I did know was that he had put me in an awful situation, one in which I'd be forced to try to rationalize his behavior or admit to my parents that he might not be as wonderful as I thought.

Except, I didn't want to do either. I couldn't look my mom and dad in the face and try to rationalize behavior I myself didn't understand, and I certainly couldn't throw him under the bus by admitting I was as appalled as they were by his actions. So instead, I got angry. That same anger I felt in the truck reemerged with a vengeance, and as soon as my parents began to ask why Adam had left so abruptly, I made the mistake of unleashing my anger on them, especially on my father.

"Why did you make things so hard for Adam? You could have put more effort into getting to know him. You could have made it easier if you wanted to, and now you've scared him off. Don't ruin this for me."

I was ashamed as soon as I said it. My dad hadn't ruined anything, but I wasn't ready to admit that Adam had that evening. I felt pushed into a corner, forced to choose who to be loyal to, and I turned on the wrong person. I should've apologized right then and there, but I fled to the bathroom instead and locked the door behind me.

I wanted to scream. I wanted to punch the bathroom mirror and watch the glass shatter to the floor. The whole night had been nothing but a horrific mess, and rather than accepting that and figuring out how to deal with it, I let my emotions get the better of me.

The feeling of regret still lingered inside of me the next morning, but a small beacon of hope made its way in as well when I received a text message from Adam.

> Would your dad be willing to have breakfast with me this morning?

His text was a sign that he was taking responsibility for his poor behavior and trying to make amends for it. I was pleased by his invitation but apprehensive about conveying it to my dad. I had hurt him badly, and it felt wrong to ask him for a favor.

"Have you heard anything from Adam?" my dad asked.

"Well, he sent me a text message a few minutes ago and asked if you'd be willing to have breakfast with him. I wasn't sure I should even ask you after last night."

"What time?"

"You really don't have to go."

"I want to."

He didn't want to, and I knew that, but just as he had done so many times before, he willingly pushed his feelings aside and did whatever it took to make me happy.

A few hours later, my dad and Adam returned from their breakfast together, and as I peered through the window at them, I tried to read their body language. My dad looked as he usually does, serious and expressionless, but seemed to be chatting willingly with Adam about something as they walked in. Adam looked to be much more relaxed than he had the night before, and his upbeat spirit had noticeably reemerged. *I guess their time together couldn't have been all that bad.*

I was certain that it would take an extensive amount of time though, much more than one breakfast together, before they'd come to appreciate their differences and enjoy spending time with each other. But for the time being, I was satisfied with the small step they had made in that direction, and it was enough to keep me moving forward with Adam.

11

Getting out of bed that Tuesday morning, following what had been the longest weekend that I could remember, hadn't been easy. I had come down with a head cold after my parents left, which I attributed to the stress of their first meeting with Adam, so I was slow to get up and get going. Slow because I wasn't feeling well, and unmotivated because Adam was leaving on a business trip to Arizona for the next three weeks and I'd have to face saying goodbye to him.

I hate goodbyes. I've never been good at them. They tend to dredge up emotions—and not the kind that I'm comfortable with. So my plan was to distract and downplay.

How exactly? With handwritten letters, one for every day we'd be apart. I had spent hours writing them. Each one contained a different reason why I loved Adam and the name of a song that reminded me of us.

"Now promise me you won't open these until the dates I have written on them," I said as I handed the stack of brightly colored envelopes to him.

"I won't," he replied.

"And make sure you listen to the songs I've listed inside of them too."

"I will."

"Oh and text me as soon as you land, even though I'll still be at work."

"Of course."

I paused momentarily, still avoiding that inevitable goodbye.

"Well, I guess it's time for you to get going. Have a safe flight."

Adam reached out and touched my face, forcing me to look into his.

"Thank you for the letters. I love you, and I'll miss you."

The sentimental expression he wore was almost too much for me, but it was the sensation of his arms wrapped tightly around me and the warmth left behind by his kiss that made me crumble. I remained silent, but a few tears escaped and rolled softly down my cheeks and onto his shoulders.

"I love you too," I squeaked out.

As I watched him walk through my door and drive away, I let myself shed a few more tears before I continued with my morning. *Stop being ridiculous and toughen up.* It was absurd to be so affected by the sight of him leaving—a sight I'd have to get used to between his business trips and his drill weekends with his National Guard unit—plus I had plenty of things to keep me busy while he was away, and something to look forward to too. In just twelve short days, I'd be flying out to Phoenix to join him, and we'd have an entire weekend to spend together without anything to do other than enjoy each other's company.

When I saw the plane's wing break through the cloud line through my window, a rush of excitement came over me, knowing it wouldn't be long before I'd be back in Adam's arms. I pulled my compact mirror from my bag to touch up my makeup, comb through my hair, and undo whatever damage had come from my in-flight nap.

Then the thud of the landing gear engaging, followed by the loud whoosh of the reverse thrust, signaled me to sit back and hold on for the landing. I tried to anticipate when the wheels would hit the runway, but the jolt exerted still caught me off guard, propelling my body forward hard and fast. I winced in pain from the seat belt digging into my flesh, but as soon as the plane stopped on the tarmac, I was up and out of my seat to stretch my legs.

While waiting for the go-ahead to disembark the plane, I reached for my phone and powered it back on to see that Adam had sent me a text.

> Hi lovey! I'm waiting for you in the baggage claim. Let me know when you're on your way.

I danced in place eagerly, ready to leap over the seats to get off the plane, equally desperate to get to Adam as I was to find a restroom. I don't know if the passengers around me were just exceptionally friendly that morning, or if my joyful impatience was glaringly obvious to them, but I managed to be one of the first people off, despite having a seat near the back of the plane.

Once I emerged from the jet bridge and into terminal 4, I feverishly looked around for a sign that would point me toward the baggage claim. But being shorter than most of my fellow travelers, it was hard to see much of anything, so I followed the crowd until I came across one.

Confirming that I was indeed heading in the right direction, I began to jog, weaving in and around anyone blocking my path. With every step I took, I moved faster and faster, so that by the time I reached the escalators, I was nearly in a full run.

Not patient enough to let the escalator carry me down to the first floor on its own, I hugged the right side of it and dashed down the moving stairs with ease. When I reached the bottom, I rounded the corner and screeched to a sudden halt when I saw the crowd in front of me. *Great.* People were fighting to move in every direction, bumping into one another like a game of pinball, in a hurry to find their luggage so they could get to wherever it was they were going.

How am I ever going to find Adam in this mess? I stood still, up on my tiptoes, bending to the left and then to the right, hoping to catch a glimpse of him, but after a few minutes with no luck at all, I took out my phone to call him.

I held the phone tightly to my ear, barely able to hear my own thoughts, but just as the call was about to go through, a small break in the crowd formed, and I saw him. He was looking down at his phone, likely waiting to hear from me, and was completely unaware that I was standing no more than twenty feet in front of him.

I would have loved to have run toward him—to jump into his arms and plant soft kisses all over his face—but I chose to remain still and wait. After a few seconds had passed, he looked up from his phone and scanned the room for me. And when his eyes finally locked onto mine, he smiled broadly and closed the space between us with just a few long strides.

I dropped my purse on the floor next to him as he swept me up into his arms, so I could wrap both of mine around him. It wasn't hard to tell from how long he held me that he missed me just as much as I had missed him, and I adored him for that. After kissing me firmly, he set me down, grabbed me by the hand, and we were off—off on our next great adventure.

12

After pulling my suitcase from the carousel, we caught a shuttle to the parking lot, where Adam had left the rental car. Since his coworkers had chosen to fly home for the weekend, we were given permission to use the company's rental car and to do so at its expense. Adam hadn't given me any clues as to where we were going, but I was certain he'd take full advantage of the limited time we had together.

I was perfectly content to drive anywhere with him, completely happy to hold his hand and take in the dazzling desert landscape that sprawled out in every direction. But it didn't take long before he prompted me to guess.

"Okay, take a guess where we're headed first," he said enthusiastically.

"All right, let me think," I said while I tapped my temple with my index finger.

I didn't really need to think about it, not very hard anyway. Adam had never been one to do things halfway. He was practically the poster child for the expression "go big or go home," so it wasn't difficult to figure out that he'd choose to drive us straight toward one of the biggest and most beautiful tourist attractions in the country, the Grand Canyon.

"Hmmm …" I pretended to struggle.

I could see the excitement growing inside of him as the grin on his face widened.

"Could it be the … Grand Canyon?"

He looked a bit surprised that I had guessed correctly on my first try but remained thrilled just the same to tell me all about it, along with the other places he had been since his trip to Arizona began. And I happily listened as we drove farther up I-17, interrupting him occasionally to point out a land feature that I wanted to stop and take a picture of.

I became so consumed by the views from the interstate that I was unaware of how far we had traveled, until the flow of traffic suddenly came to a halt. Lanes and lanes of traffic began to surround us, each vehicle competing for their place in line, even though all any of us could do was creep forward a few feet at a time. Adam rolled down all four of the windows so we could breathe in some fresh air while we waited, but the slow movement of the car along with the feeling of a warm, gentle breeze against my skin lulled me into and out of sleep.

When we finally reached the South Entrance Contact Station, Adam grabbed my left shoulder and shook me softly, waking me from an unintended nap. Then he handed his credit card to the park ranger in the booth and was given some brochures in return, which I looked through as the ranger gave Adam his robot-like "Welcome to the Grand Canyon" spiel.

As soon as the ranger had finished his obligatory speech on the do's and don'ts of the park, we continued up the South Entrance Drive toward the Grand Canyon Visitor Center. While Adam looked for a place to park the car, I strapped my digital camera around my wrist, unbuckled my seat belt, and placed my fingers around the door handle.

From the corner of my eye, I could see Adam smirking at me as he swung into an open parking spot, clearly amused by my obvious display of exuberance. I didn't like the idea of inadvertently amusing anyone, especially Adam, but I pretended not to notice and swung the car door open instead.

Just as my right foot hit the ground, I felt Adam tug on my free hand, pulling me back inside. I tried to pull away at first, uninterested in anything other than getting to the rim of the canyon, but he was so persistent that I eventually complied.

I sat back down and spun my body toward him abruptly, with an unmistakable look of irritation on my face. But he remained undeterred by my off-putting body language, leaning in close to playfully steal a kiss. I rolled my eyes, acting annoyed by his flirtation, but we both knew that I loved it.

"Let's go," I said. He didn't hold me back any longer.

Along with thousands of other tourists, we hurried down the stone-laden path, past the visitor's center, and toward Mather Point. When we reached the end of it, Adam handed his camera off to a fellow tourist, who agreed to snap a few pictures of us. Then he climbed up and onto a large, flat piece of limestone that jutted out over the canyon, and I followed suit.

Trembling slightly, I carefully looked down at my feet, not wanting to trip as I neared the edge. With no railing or barrier to hinder our view, the fear of falling was real, but the presence of danger only added to the thrill. With my feet planted firmly in place, I looked up and tried to process the endless vista that stretched out before me. I let out an audible gasp as I looked in every direction. It was truly the most breathtaking landscape I had ever seen.

Enormous formations of sedimentary rock arose from the canyon floor, each one extraordinary in its own right; some appearing as fragile towers, and others as unmovable mountains of strength and stability. The natural elements had been harsh. They had relentlessly and unevenly torn through the earth, leaving the walls of the canyon rough and jagged while exposing the most spectacular shades of red, pink, and brown that would have otherwise gone unseen.

I couldn't help but feel tiny as I stood above such a magnificent tear in the earth's crust. But I felt grateful too—grateful to be standing so close to God's handiwork, alongside the man I loved, in what was the most perfect of moments.

13

It wasn't until I felt a cold sprinkle of rain against my skin that I realized we'd been standing in silence for quite some time. Not wanting to get drenched by the dark rain clouds looming above us, we stepped back down to earth and jogged back toward the car. To give the rain clouds some time to pass, we stopped in at the Canyon Village Market to pick up some picnic supplies, but they never fully dissipated.

I knew it would take far more time than we had to uncover all that the park had to offer, and I was afraid that the rain would ruin the afternoon we had to explore it, but the intermittent rain showers actually served to improve our visit. Each time the sun would peer out from behind the clouds, beams of light would brighten the peaks and platforms within the canyon, causing the rock layers to glisten and reveal new colors. The excess moisture in the atmosphere also worked to bend the sun's rays, stretching numerous rainbows across the canyon, augmenting the splendor of our surroundings even further.

And for the most part, as we drove east along the South Rim, pulling over to take pictures at every scenic viewpoint we came across, the scattered showers remained light and short-lived. Each stop along that twenty-five-mile route provided us with a new angle at which to admire the terrain, and during those few periods of heavy rain, we fled back into the car, making sure to put our time alone within close quarters to good use.

As we neared the end of Desert View Drive, the rain cleared and the temperature dropped, so I asked Adam to pull over so I could use the restroom and change into warmer clothes. And by restroom, I mean some sparse vegetation in an area of the park I could only hope was completely out of others' view.

When I returned to the car, I could see that Adam had laid a blanket down at the perimeter of the canyon for us and was unpacking the food and the bottle of white wine we had purchased at the market. As I watched him lay everything out just so, with the sun beginning to set behind him, I couldn't help but feel so fortunate to have him in my life. It was a picture-perfect view, an exquisitely romantic setting in which we could enjoy the final moments of our time in the Grand Canyon together.

Oddly though, he stood up quickly when he saw me coming, as if he had been caught doing something wrong.

"Is everything okay?" I asked as I began to sit down on the blanket.

He didn't answer. Instead, he took me by the hand and pulled me back onto my feet. Then he got down on one knee and pulled a mahogany box from his pocket.

Is this really happening?

He opened the box and tipped it toward me so I could see the diamond ring that sparkled brightly inside of it. And then, with a slight quiver in his voice, he said, "Sydney, I know we've only been together a short time, but I love you and I want to spend the rest of my life with you. Will you marry me?"

Whoa. I had entertained the thought of Adam proposing to me many times before, imagining when and where it might happen, but in that moment, my immediate response wasn't to say yes. I was *almost* certain that he was the man I wanted to spend my life with, and he had crafted my ideal proposal—the setting was intimate, cozy, and undeniably beautiful—but I wasn't sure that we were ready.

We had worked hard to get to know each other, and quickly. We had been intentional about spending quality time together and had had numerous heart-to-heart conversations as well. But still, we had only been dating for two and half months. Surely there had to be more for the both of us to learn about each other, right?

I could see the fear building in Adam's eyes as he waited for an answer.

But didn't I know enough about him already? Adam was kind and caring, hardworking and trustworthy, courageous and full of life. Although he wasn't perfect, he was everything I had ever wanted in a husband. *Can anyone really know everything about another person anyway?*

There was something else that I needed to consider too. Adam had felt pressured to propose once before, which ultimately led to a lot of pain for everyone involved. I needed to be sure that he wasn't feeling that way about me.

"Are you sure we're ready? Are you sure that *you're* ready, because I wouldn't want you to feel pressured in any way to propose to me before you're *really* ready."

He looked relieved that I hadn't said no.

"Of course I'm ready, and I'm proposing because I want to. I know you are the one for me, and I don't see the point in delaying any longer."

I didn't see the point either. If he was ready, then I was ready.

"Then yes. Yes, I would love to marry you."

Adam scooped me up into his arms and off my feet, kissing me with such a genuine joy that even under the force of his lips, I couldn't help but smile. Then he set me down and slid the ring onto my finger, and we watched the sun set and disappear behind the back of the canyon wall as we toasted to the great love God had given us.

14

Not wanting the magic of the evening to end, we stayed to enjoy the very last of the setting sun's light, holding tightly to each other and admiring how its many hues illuminated every crevice of the Grand Canyon's walls. Then, once darkness completely concealed the canyon, we got back into the car and drove toward Flagstaff, where Adam had reserved a hotel room.

Still flying high from the proposal, we rehashed each wonderful detail of the day and laughed about those few awkward moments it brought. I teased Adam about how nervous he looked, down on one knee while he popped the question, and he retaliated by pointing out how funny it was that I had peed behind a bush just minutes before. Then I picked up my phone and called home, eager to tell my parents the good news.

"Hello?"

"Hi, Mom. I'm just calling to tell you that Adam and I are engaged. He proposed at the Grand Canyon. Can you believe it?"

"Congratulations," she said enthusiastically. "That sounds pretty incredible."

"It really was."

I continued to fill her in on a few of the details but promised to give her more of the story once the weekend was over. Then we said our goodbyes, and I hung up.

"My parents told me to tell you congratulations," I said to Adam, "but I find it strange that they didn't act surprised."

"Well that's because I asked your dad for his blessing to marry you when we had breakfast together."

"You did?"

I was impressed by his bravery but a bit bewildered by it too. Adam shouldn't have put my dad in that position so early on in our relationship. Their first meeting carried enough weight on its own, and based on everyone's erratic behavior that weekend, the added pressure of asking for my hand in marriage was almost too much. I knew our feelings for each other had grown strong at a breakneck speed, but he should've given our families more time to catch up to us. Maybe we both should have.

"How did my dad respond when you asked him?"

"He said that even though he didn't know me well, he trusted you and your judgment, and for that reason, he'd give me his blessing."

"Wow, that's high praise coming from my father."

Adam agreed.

"Why don't you call your mom and dad now. They probably knew that you'd be proposing, right? But you should still give them a call before we share our big news with anyone else."

"Uh …" He shrugged. "I'll call them later."

Later? He had been so proud of how well the proposal had gone, so excited to share the good news with any random passerby the very minute after it happened. Why in the world wouldn't he want to tell his parents?

"Later? Why later?"

He kept his eyes on the road and his head facing forward, not saying anything at first. So I stared. I stared at the side of his head with my eyes fixed upon him, until my laser-like focus made him feel uncomfortable.

"Look, I'm a little irritated with my parents right now, and I didn't want that to ruin our moment. I promise I'll call them later."

"Why? Did something happen?"

He took his eyes off the road and looked at me, searching for a way out of the conversation, but I wouldn't give him one.

"Well, after I bought your engagement ring, I sent them a picture of it, and let's just say they didn't exactly share in my excitement."

My heart sank. I supposed their adverse reaction was somewhat warranted, taking into consideration how fast our relationship had moved and knowing that Adam had one broken engagement under his belt already, but I couldn't help but take their disapproval personally.

I had spent more time with his parents than Adam had with mine, and our time together had gone so well by comparison. I felt as though I had fit into their family so easily, so it was hard to believe that they would have some kind of problem with me marrying their son. *Is there more to this story than Adam is telling me?*

I was sure that there was, but I didn't want to know the details. We were already engaged, and if Adam thought his parents were going to pose any real problem for us, then he wouldn't have proposed. Right?

"Call them," I said with a bit more force. "Call them anyway, even though you're angry with them. It will only make things worse if you exclude them from this."

So he called them, and neither the words they spoke nor the intonation of their voices gave me any clue as to whether they objected to me marrying their son or not. Maybe they felt it was too late to protest, or maybe Adam's silent treatment for the past couple of weeks had made them feel as though they didn't have the right to, but in my mind, the damage had been done. If their concerns had had any real merit to them, then they should've addressed them with me, and since they didn't, I chose to pretend their congratulations were genuine.

15

Our engagement weekend ended on a high note as we spent our last day together hiking among the red sandstone monoliths of Sedona, each one hand carved into its own distinct shape. And even though I had to fly home without Adam that Sunday morning, our last week apart seemed to fly by since my mind was so happily preoccupied with thoughts of our future together.

But once Adam returned home too, I no longer had the luxury of being preoccupied with anything that wasn't on my to-do list. In fact, the very minute Adam walked back through my front door, we hit the ground running in Sedona-red, dust-stained shoes, with more things to accomplish than I felt we had time for, the first of which was planning our wedding.

Some women start dreaming about their wedding day from childhood, thumbing through bridal magazines and scouring wedding websites to find their perfect bridal gown, or floral arrangements, or wedding invitations, but I hadn't. I had always been too practical for that and too distracted by present-life responsibilities to want to waste any time thinking about a day that seemed to be so far off. But now that I was getting married, my lack of forethought made me feel behind. I hated feeling behind.

So on the advice of a friend who pointed me toward a website that she had used to plan her wedding, I found a checklist of items with recommended deadlines. Having such a clear-cut list of tasks to complete was right up my alley, but I couldn't begin crossing off a single item until Adam and I solidified a date and reserved a venue.

I had assumed we would get married sometime in the summer season, like many teachers do for convenience's sake, but circumstances pushed our wedding date months earlier than that, primarily Adam's commitment to the National Guard. His unit had been commissioned to go to Afghanistan the following January, a piece of information he hadn't told me until he returned home.

Being told that my fiancé would be serving in an active duty capacity for at least a year in the Middle East was shocking to hear, but it wasn't like we could do anything to change it. So, wanting to have as much time as possible to settle into married life before he had to go, we set our sights on spring break, which would give us at least nine months together as husband and wife but only six months to prepare.

Can I even find a wedding venue in that short length of time? It wasn't easy, but after several failed attempts, we settled on the Sanctuary, an event space just two miles up the road from our apartment complex. We had walked past the Sanctuary many times before, as we frequently enjoyed eating at the restaurants it was nestled between, but I hadn't paid much attention to what the building was used for.

Its Victorian-style architecture and weathered yellow exterior alluded to its advanced age, and its eye-catching stained glass windows, along with the towering steeple that rose upward from its hunter-green roof, made its original function loud and clear. A sign posted in front of its covered porch, complete with white wooden railings and Victorian-inspired corbels, stated that it had been built in 1894 as a Methodist church and was now designated as a historical landmark.

Nancy Noel, a prominent impressionist painter who studied art at the University of Notre Dame, had bought and renovated the building in 2006 and used it to display her paintings. This updated Sanctuary, as she called it, also housed a French café and tearoom, Ghyslain, named for its head chef, who specialized in fine chocolates and French pastries.

The Sanctuary's vintage flair, local history, and nearby location more than piqued my interest. But our introduction to its striking interior immediately had me convinced that we had found our perfect venue. Noel's extensive million-dollar investment into a ten-month-long renovation had definitely served to impress. Although it had been altered to provide an appropriate space for showcasing Noel's work, the original nineteenth-century charm hadn't been lost.

A twenty-four-foot tall white marble fireplace was the first thing to grab my attention. It sat at one end of the main gallery and ran from the dark-stained hardwood floors up to the ceiling. A large canvas painting of an angel with folded hands was hung just above the delicately carved mantel, bringing my eyes upward toward the balcony that housed a quaint seating area with views of the entire gallery floor.

On the opposite end of the gallery, facing Zionsville's Main Street, sunlight streamed in through three rectangular stained glass windows that rose almost as high as the outer wall of the fireplace. The subtle details of Noel's ethereal oil paintings, depicting images of angels, farm animals, and Amish children, were well highlighted under the pure, natural light. And a one-of-a-kind metal chandelier with candle-like light bulbs hung from the center of the room, rounding out the space.

It seemed fitting to choose a venue just blocks away from the park where we had our first date, and suddenly the thought of planning our wedding day didn't seem quite so daunting to me. I could see us getting married there, standing in front of our family and friends as we recited our vows. So as soon as the event coordinator confirmed that she had a Saturday opening, we jumped at the chance to sign a contract.

16

Putting my time-management skills into practice became more crucial than ever during those last few months of 2011 as I worked tirelessly to plan our wedding day among the busy fall season. With Adam often out of town for work during the week and much of his time at home consumed by an online graduate course, I did my best to handle most of our wedding day details on my own.

I wish I could say that I enjoyed the process, but oftentimes it felt more like a burden than anything else. It also had an annoying way of cutting in on the free time Adam and I did have to spend together. If we weren't thinking about our wedding or talking about it, we were heading somewhere to check another item off our never-ending to-do list. A few hours lost to picking out suits for Adam's groomsmen, an overnight trip to meet with our wedding photographer, a weekend dedicated to our engagement photos, and the list went on and on from there.

Then there were the other commitments we had to tend to— my five-year college reunion, a long weekend away to celebrate Adam's parents' anniversary, and all of the holiday festivities, times two. We were being pulled in so many different directions that we could hardly find a moment to sit and be alone with each other, and at times that really wore on me, even though I knew we had done it to ourselves.

So when Adam revealed that he was searching for houses online, I was completely taken off guard. We hadn't specifically discussed our postmarriage living arrangements yet, but I assumed that I'd break my lease a few months early and move into his larger apartment. That way, we could take our time finding the right home after the fuss of our wedding was over.

"Do you really think looking at homes right now is a good use of our time?" I asked him. "Our schedules are so jam-packed as it is."

"I know, but rent is such a huge waste of money. It makes more sense to invest in a home instead of throwing it all away. Doesn't it? And we have too many things to fit into just one apartment. With the cost of a storage space and our apartment rent, we could save money on a bigger home with a smaller mortgage."

"I see your point, but it's not going to break us financially to wait a year. Purchasing a home is a big deal. Choosing the right one takes time, and we don't have that time right now."

"I'll handle it all. I promise. You won't have to do anything other than come with me to a few showings." Then he looked at me with his bright blue puppy dog eyes. "Say yes … please?"

"All right. If that's really what you want to do, go ahead and look."

For weeks after that, we spent almost every Saturday and Sunday afternoon driving from house to house, hoping we'd find the one that felt like home to us, but every one of them were disappointments to me. I didn't see a single house that came anywhere close to meeting my expectations, and with the exorbitant list prices their owners expected to get, tearing them apart to get what I wanted was completely out of the question, so eventually I told Adam that I was done.

"It doesn't seem like buying a home right now is in the cards for us, and forcing it to happen would be a mistake. The extra stress isn't worth it to me anymore. Please, let's just wait a few more months until after our honeymoon, and then we can try again. Okay?"

"Okay," he said disappointedly.

I thought that Adam had seen it my way and had put the idea of finding a house out of his head as I had, but a few days later, I received a text from him asking me to meet him at another property. I doubted that this house would be any different from the others, but when I found out our Realtor was already there and waiting, I reluctantly agreed to go.

Although the house was located just four miles away from my school, I hadn't driven down that particular street before and was pleasantly surprised by the sudden change in environment. This short strip of city street was left as natural as a residential area within the city limits could be. Each side of the road remained heavily wooded, and a small stream flowed through. The natural ambiance of the area, along with the well-maintained homes, sparked just a bit of enthusiasm inside of me.

But that enthusiasm withered away when I caught my first glimpse of the house. If I hadn't seen Adam's car parked in the driveway, I never would've believed that I'd found it. It probably had been a real gem back in 1977 when it was built, but by the look of its run-down exterior, it had been neglected for quite some time.

Its brick red siding was noticeably faded, and its gray wooden trim was rotten and crumbling. The roof needed to be replaced, as did the garage door, the front porch sagged, the landscaping was overgrown, and there was a large crack in one of the upstairs windows. *What is Adam even thinking?*

The interior was just as bad, if not worse. Everything was dirty, outdated, and in desperate need of repair. Every wall would need to be repainted, every stitch of flooring would have to be ripped up and replaced, and the kitchen and three and a half bathrooms would have to be gutted.

The floorplan was a mess too. The kitchen was too small and would require some major rethinking. The washer and dryer were crammed into the powder room underneath the stairs, inconveniently far away from the bedrooms that were up on the second floor. And the six-hundred-square-foot bonus space above the garage had been modified strangely, as if it had been turned into its own apartment.

"What do you think?" Adam asked eagerly.

I closed my eyes and sighed heavily. "I think it's a disaster."

"Yeah, but think of all the things we could do with it. I know you weren't impressed with the other houses, but with this one, we could start from scratch. We could make it exactly how we want it."

"Hmmm …" I tried to envision it. "I can see what you're saying. I do like the large backyard and the idea of having almost 2,900 square feet to work with, but I'm not sure you get how much work there is to do here. Or how much that work will cost. And there's no way I'd agree to making an offer unless my dad comes to look at it first."

"Okay. Let's ask him."

A few days later, my dad swung through on his way back home from a hunting trip in Missouri. He spent several hours going through each room of the house with us, giving us a rundown on what could and couldn't be done and for how much. And after hearing what he had to say and getting him to agree to do the renovation for us, I gave Adam the go-ahead to make a lowball offer.

Our Realtor practically choked when we asked him to relay it. The house had been valued for over $200,000 before the last owners destroyed it, and had been listed for $170,000 when it first went into foreclosure in August. Since then, the price had been dropped twice, taking it all the way down to $135,000, but still that was more than we were willing to offer.

We had no idea what surprises we might come across once the renovations began, and I knew we'd be sacrificing more than just money to get the house livable before our wedding date. If we were going to take on such an extensive project, I needed to know that it was part of God's plan for us. So we offered $110,000—an offer so low that we referred to it as a faith bid—and a few days later, our Realtor called to tell us that our faith bid was accepted.

17

The new year brought with it an immense amount of hope for a wonderful future together, and the good news that Adam's National Guard unit had been called down from its deployment to Afghanistan, but it also came with a tremendous amount of pressure. We had a lot to accomplish before our life as husband and wife began, and with our newly purchased home sitting in shambles, we had no choice but to shift our focus off our wedding and onto our fixer-upper.

My dad had promised us six weeks to work on the house starting in February, leaving Adam and me with only a month to complete demolition. We knew the more we got done before his arrival, the better the chances the first phase of the renovation would get done before we were married. Highly motivated to help make that happen, we adjusted our morning routine to include a five o'clock wake-up call so we could get our workouts done and out of the way. Then after putting in a full day of work, we'd rush straight home to change our clothes, drive over to the house, and put in another four to six hours of hard labor.

Generally, we wouldn't get back to the apartment complex until well after ten o'clock, and by then, every inch of my body was aching with exhaustion. I should have crawled right into bed when we got home, but instead I'd snuggle up to Adam in front of his television, trying to make a little time to talk with him about anything other than the house. Inevitably, I'd fall asleep in his lap within minutes though, while he finished watching whatever show we had started by himself.

I don't ever remember him falling asleep—not once—and so I asked him about it.

"Why is it that you never seem tired like I do?"

He laughed. "I get tired too, but I guess I'm used to living on a small amount of sleep from being in the military."

His response didn't completely make sense to me. Everyone needs sleep to function, but I didn't question it. He was getting things done, seemed happier than ever, and I knew this phase of life wouldn't last for long. So I made the phrase "if he can do it, then I can do it" my own personal mantra, and that helped push me to keep going during those four long weeks until my dad came.

And by the time my dad did arrive, the two of us—along with the occasional help from our friends—had amassed a whole garage and dumpster full of junk—two heaping piles of musty carpeting, shards of tile, strips of linoleum, worn-out appliances, busted-up cabinets and countertops, old toilets, sinks, and who knows what else. We literally eviscerated our entire home, leaving only the natural stone fireplace in the family room and two of the three upstairs bathrooms untouched, so my dad could use them during his stay.

I felt a strong sense of accomplishment when the demo phase of the renovation was over, but I felt an even bigger sense of relief when my dad pulled up and we could hand much of the responsibility of putting our house back together over to him. And since Adam had to travel for work throughout most of February and March, many of the design decisions regarding the house were left on my shoulders, so I was glad my dad—who tended to think about things in the same way that I did—was there to bounce ideas off.

My dad was a practical person and an efficient one. Someone I could count on to get things done the right way but without a lot of frill. Adam, on the other hand, tended to get a bit carried away with big ideas, ideas that were far from being feasible considering our constraints of money and time. Every time he came back into town, he just loved to walk through the house to see the progress, but he couldn't help but throw out one of his wild suggestions too.

"How hard would it be to rip out part of the upstairs floor so our living room could have a vaulted ceiling?"

"Would it be a big deal to attach a second-floor balcony on the back of the house?"

"I know you are already renovating three bedrooms and bathrooms, but could you turn that bonus space into another master suite?"

It could be frustrating at times to have to explain to him why his ideas were impractical, especially since my dad was already putting in twelve- to sixteen-hour days as it was, but thankfully my dad was always there to help me pull Adam's head out of the clouds and keep our renovation on track. And so, as promised, we were able to say goodbye to our small, drafty apartments and move into our newly renovated home just one week before our wedding.

Thanks to the countless hours my dad put in, along with some help from his best friend, we were able to start our married life in a house that had been built for us, a house that had been completely revitalized—minus that bonus space above the garage—with our specific tastes and needs in mind. To me, it was magnificent. It would be a beautiful backdrop for the lifetime of memories that Adam and I would make together.

On the morning of my wedding day, I awoke to the sound of my cell phone alarm ringing—as I did most mornings—but for the first time in a long time, I had absolutely no desire to hit the snooze button. Instead, I took a deep breath in, filling my lungs with the pleasant aroma of our new home. I elongated my body, stretching my arms and legs, fingers and toes, outward in all directions. Then I propped two pillows against the headboard behind me so I could sit up and take a look through the bedroom window.

Spring had come early. The backyard was lush and green, the trees and flowers were already in bloom, and the raindrops from the night before had been wiped out of the sky, replaced by the bright morning sun. The weather forecast promised an entire day clear of any precipitation and a high in the afternoon of nearly seventy degrees. It was perfect. It was a perfect day to marry the love of my life.

There had been times throughout the years that I thought I'd never get married. I hadn't expected to meet someone who made me as happy as Adam did, but it's funny how quickly circumstances can change. Here I was, less than a year after meeting him, waking up for the last time as a single woman, thrilled to become his partner in life.

And even with the big day I had ahead of me and all the excitement and stress it could bring, I felt completely at ease. Adam was the one for me, and I had put more than enough work into making sure our wedding day would go as planned, so I was determined to do nothing more than enjoy it. I refused to run around in hysteria; instead, I was going to soak up every moment of our big day, making nothing but beautiful memories together.

So I tossed the covers to one side and swung my feet to the newly carpeted floor. Then I showered, dressed, blow dried and straightened my hair quickly, not wanting to start the day off behind schedule.

As I gathered my things, and prepared to meet up with the girls for our hair appointments, Adam appeared at my bedroom door with a flirtatious grin. Knowing my dad was downstairs touching up some of the paint on the kitchen ceiling, I pulled Adam from the hallway and into the bedroom abruptly, closing the door behind us for privacy's sake.

"Adam, what are you doing—"

Before I could finish, he pressed his lips firmly onto mine, kissing me for so long that eventually I had to pull myself away from him just to catch my breath.

I laughed as I said, "There will be plenty of time for that later. I'll see you soon, okay?"

"Okay," he said as he continued to plant playful kisses on my neck and face, clearly not listening to me at all.

"Seriously, I've got to go. I love you, Adam."

"I love you too."

18

I could barely contain myself as I paced back and forth within the bridal suite, waiting for our wedding ceremony to begin. I was glad to have had plenty of unrushed time to prepare and to take most of our wedding photos beforehand, but the long wait of a 6:30 p.m. start time was agonizing. Without a phone or a watch, I listened carefully for the piano music to change. The soft sound of the same few classical songs playing over and over again were beginning to put me on edge, but from all the noise I could hear coming from our guests' conversations, it seemed as though I was the only one aware that our pianist was playing.

When the music stopped and the murmur of voices became silent, I knew the time had finally come. I took one more glance at myself in the mirror and waited to hear the familiar tune of Canon in D, which officially marked the beginning of our ceremony. Although I couldn't see it for myself, I knew Adam's grandmother, then his parents, and finally my mother would be walking down the aisle, fashioned between one hundred white folding chairs. Judy would join my mom at the altar, both lighting a candlestick before taking their seats in the front row.

Adam and Jake would enter from a side door next, queued by the Rodgers and Hammerstein showtune "Edelweiss" from *The Sound of Music.* Even though the song's lyrics were written about a white flower indigenous to the Alps and represented Captain

Von Trapp's love for and loyalty to Austria, I always thought that it had one of the most romantic melodies I'd ever heard.

Once the bridal party began to move down the aisle and take their places on opposite sides of the altar, the wedding coordinator prompted me to join my father at the back of the gallery, hidden behind the floor-to-ceiling satin curtains that hung from the white-trimmed opening next to the fireplace. As I stood there silently, thinking about all the eyes that would soon be focused on me, my heart kicked into overdrive, thumping harder and harder against my chest. I hooked my arm under my father's and held on tightly, hoping his strength would help me relax.

I took a deep breath in, trying to slow the effects of the adrenaline pulsing through my body, but before I could get a handle on my nerves, Jake called out, "All rise for the bride," and the curtains were thrown open.

I felt exposed, then frozen in place, but the power that emanated from the sound of "Here Comes the Bride" compelled me to move forward. Despite my discomfort, I plastered a fake smile on my face and made my way down the aisle, each step slow and unsteady. I looked timidly to my left and to my right, wanting to show my appreciation to our friends and family who had come to celebrate our love with us.

But once I caught my first glimpse of Adam, everyone else simply vanished—their fixed stares no longer of any consequence to me. He looked masculine and strong, standing tall in his military uniform, yet the expression on his face was more boyish and sweet. He eagerly leaned forward on his toes and angled his body to the right, trying desperately to see around those standing in the front row. And when his gaze finally met with mine, his lips upturned in undeniable pleasure, and a genuine smile spread across my face. It was a rare type of toothy grin I'd normally be embarrassed to show.

I kept my eyes locked onto him until I reached the end of the aisle, and Jake opened the service with a welcome and a prayer. I bowed my head and tried to listen intently, but with the distraction of Adam standing nearby, I couldn't help but sneak a peek at him.

"Greatly blessed is the couple that comes to the marriage altar with the approval and blessings of their families and friends. Who has the honor of presenting this woman to be married to this man?" Jake asked.

"Her mother and I do," my father replied.

Then with a kiss on my cheek, he turned and took his seat, and Adam stepped up and into his place.

As practiced, we turned inward to face each other, and Adam extended his open hands in front of him, offering a safe place for mine to rest. I was surprised to feel his hands trembling—it was so unlike him to be nervous in front of a crowd—so I squeezed his fingers tightly and smiled goofily at him, hoping my support would help him calm down. But when Emily, my soon-to-be sister-in-law, began to read from 1 Corinthians 13, tears began to pool in his eyes.

> Love is patient, love is kind. It does not envy, it does not boast, it is not proud. It does not dishonor others, it is not self-seeking, it is not easily angered, it keeps no record of wrongs. Love does not delight in evil but rejoices with the truth. It always protects, always trusts, always hopes, always perseveres. Love never fails … (1 Corinthians 13:4–8 NIV)

Then in the presence of God, and in front of our closest friends and family, we made our promise to love each other, just as the verses described.

"Adam, will you take Sydney to be your wedded wife, to live together in the covenant of faith, hope, and love according to the intention of God for your lives together in Jesus Christ? Will you listen to her inmost thoughts, be considerate and kind in your care of her, and stand by her faithfully in sickness and in health, and preferring her above all others as long as you both shall live?"

"I will," Adam replied.

And after those same questions were extended to me, I said, "I will," too.

Then we exchanged the traditional wedding vows, and after placing a ring on each other's fingers, we walked hand in hand around the altar, taking hold of the candlesticks our mothers had lit. We used their flames to ignite our unity candle, to demonstrate the merging of our separate lives into one. And as the Matthew West song "When I Say I Do" began to play, Adam placed his hands behind my shoulders, drawing me near to him.

With my cheek resting gently against his, he whispered a sweet prayer into my ear, asking God to bless our life together. And then we gently swayed to the music as we remained nestled together, knowing it would take a couple of minutes more for the song to run its course.

We soon found ourselves lost in the moment, as the heartfelt lyrics filled our minds and the sunlight streaming in through the stained glass windows filled the room. When the music ended, silence temporarily took its place. We looked up and leaned into each other, stopping just centimeters before our lips touched.

I smiled sheepishly as we made our way back to the other side of the altar and eagerly waited for Jake to pronounce us as husband and wife.

"Since Adam and Sydney have desired each other in marriage, and have witnessed this before God and our gathering, affirming their acceptance of the responsibilities of such a union, and have pledged their love and faith to each other, sealing their vows in the giving and receiving of rings, I do pronounce them to be husband and wife in the name of the Father, and of the Son, and of the Holy Spirit."

And with a hint of a giggle in his voice, he looked at Adam and said, "You may *now* kiss your bride."

After sharing our first kiss as husband and wife, we were presented to the audience, and the song "God Gave Me You" rang out. We ran down the aisle directly into the bridal suite, bursting with joy and desperate to be alone. Then with our own private bottle of champagne, we toasted to our future together, stealing a few more kisses before our wedding photographer came in.

While we took the last of our wedding photos out on the front porch, the gallery was transformed into an elegant reception space, lit almost entirely by candlelight. Round tables, covered with black linens and silver table runners, were spread across the gallery floor, and the white folding chairs used in the ceremony were rearranged around them. The glow radiating from each table created an intimate and dreamlike setting, while highlighting the room's exquisite architectural elements and drawing attention to the fine details of every painting.

By design, the reception moved quickly, to minimize downtime for our guests and speed up the start of our honeymoon. We transitioned seamlessly from activity to activity—cutting the cake, listening to our maid of honor and best man give their speeches, and clanging our Mr. and Mrs. champagne glasses after the toast. The only time we slowed down all evening was to share our first dance as husband and wife, swaying ever so slightly out on the dance floor all alone, fully captivated by the other.

By ten o'clock, we were back in the bridal suite, gathering our things and saying our goodbyes to our parents.

"Thank you for everything," I said to my mom and dad. "I love you both."

"We love you too," my mom said as she hugged me tightly. "Have a good time, and be safe."

"Text me to let me know when you get to Whistler, okay? I just want to know that you arrived safely," my dad said as he wrapped me in another hug.

"I will, and don't worry. We'll be fine."

Then I turned to Adam's parents to say my goodbyes to them too, and as I embraced Judy, she whispered into my ear, "Please take care of my son."

It seemed like a peculiar thing to say to me—a sentiment better directed toward Adam from my father—but I nodded my head in agreement, chalking up her odd request to the overly protective ways of a mother whose youngest son had just been married.

19

Our honeymoon to Whistler Blackcomb, the largest ski resort in North America and home of the 2010 Winter Olympics, was nothing short of spectacular. Each morning, we woke up to a fresh foot of powder and then spent the day carving through it as we explored a new section of the resort's twin peaks. And every evening, we soaked our sore muscles in our cabin's private Jacuzzi before heading into the village to explore a few shops and sample some of its fine cuisine.

But after four hard days of skiing and snowboarding and an overnight stay in Vancouver where we went to the symphony at the historic 1927 Orpheum Theater, I was happy to get back to our new home to begin our life together. So over the next few months, Adam and I did as married couples do and divided up the household responsibilities. I took charge of the cleaning and laundry, he took charge of the finances and the yardwork, and we shared the responsibilities of grocery shopping and preparing meals.

But since Adam was frequently in and out of town on business during the week, and away one weekend a month for drill with his National Guard unit, the routine I was hoping to build never came. Not having a schedule I could depend on was difficult— although the perpetual cycling between saying goodbye and hello again did a lot to keep our honeymoon phase alive—but it was even harder having to spend so much time away from Adam, until the summer came and brought with it my freedom.

I put that freedom to good use too, sinking as much time into Adam as I could. When he was home, I cooked him new recipes, surprised him at his office with lunch, and greeted him at the front door when he returned home from work in a new negligee. When he had to travel, I went with him if I could, keeping myself entertained during the day and exploring the city we were in with him at night. That summer was the best one that I could ever remember having, until July rolled around and he had to leave for a long military training.

It's typical for National Guard units to train for two weeks in the summer, but because his unit had been set to go to Afghanistan, his training time that summer had almost doubled. Apparently those tax dollars had already been spent, even though his unit had been called down six months earlier. So on July 5, I begrudgingly sent Adam off to Camp Ripley in Little Falls, Minnesota, and I went home to Michigan.

A day or two later, my mom, dad, and I packed up our family trailer and took it up to Mackinaw City. My family had never been big on traditions, since it had always been just the three of us, but one thing we did every summer was camp. Through the years, we had graduated from sleeping in a tent, to a pop-up, and finally into a small travel trailer, but due to its up-close view of the Mackinac Bridge and having over a mile of Lake Huron coastline access, our campground of choice had always been the Mackinaw Mill Creek Campground.

Before I knew about Adam's monthlong training, I had been looking forward to bringing him along with us, wanting him to experience what had been such a memorable part of my childhood. I wanted him to hear the horrid squeal of our car tires as we drove over the green grates of the Mackinac Bridge and get nervous when we drove too close to the edge to avoid them. After riding a tandem bicycle the eight miles it takes to circle the island's perimeter, I wanted him to taste the richness of Mackinac Island fudge and not feel guilty for eating it either. I wanted him to see the vivid pinks and oranges of a Northern Michigan sunset reflecting off the deep blue water of a Great Lake, and I wanted him to smell the fresh, clean air that Up North Michigan summers bring. I wanted him to feel the warmth of a crackling campfire on his skin while we sat side by side, holding hands and admiring the glimmering constellations in a darkened sky. I wanted to do all those things with Adam, but with his military training taking up the rest of my summer, I decided to go on without him.

And while I was there, I didn't get to communicate with him as much as I would've liked to—between the poor cell reception outside of the campground and his hectic training schedule, it was nearly impossible to connect during the day—but he always took the time to call and talk to me for a few minutes before I went to bed.

At first, each call went about the same.

"How's training going, lovey?"

"It's going well, but there is so much to do. I've got to get all of the IT and communications equipment up and running for the unit, but with only four of my twelve soldiers here, I've had to put in some long days so far."

"How long are we talking exactly?"

"Uh, well … maybe eighteen hours or so."

"Adam, that's crazy! You need to make sure you're getting some sleep. You still have a lot of training to get through."

"I know, but I'll be fine, and I'll get some rest once everything is set up. The training can't get started until I do, and since I'm the IT officer in charge, I don't have much of a choice really. Tell me about your day. What did you do?"

"I rode my bike into town this morning and did some souvenir shopping. Then I spent some time lying down by the lake in the afternoon, soaking up the sun. I miss you though, and I wish you were here with me."

"I do too, lovey. I miss you so much."

I didn't like talking to him about the fun I was having, knowing he was more tired and stressed than he let on, but there wasn't much I could do for him except encourage him to make sleep a priority and pray that his superiors were watching out for him. As the camping trip progressed, however, I began to worry more about him. Not only were his calls coming in later and later, waking me up at two and then three in the morning, but they were becoming weird, *really* weird.

"How are things going, lovey?"

"Great. Really, really great. My unit is doing so well and breaking all kinds of records. We are going to be featured on the news."

His speech was so hurried that I could barely understand him.

"Did you say the news?"

That didn't seem right. My understanding of what went on during a military training exercise was practically zero, but I was pretty sure that whatever went on was kept confidential.

"Yep, the national news. We are doing things here that have never been done before, and I've been operating at such a high rate of efficiency that I'm sure I'm going to get some kind of award for it."

"That's great, but are you sure you're okay? You've been calling kind of late. I'm worried you aren't getting enough sleep."

"Oh I'm great. My mission is almost complete, and my sergeant is really impressed with me."

"That's good I guess, but …"

"Okay, I've got to go. I've got more work to do."

Then he just ended the call without telling me he loved me or asking me a thing about my day.

Strange.

But it was the last morning of our camping trip, and day twelve of Adam's training, that my worry for him became actual fear. I hadn't heard from him in a while, no texts and no call the night before, but that morning, I did receive a phone call from his brother Eric, who told me that Adam had been taken to a local emergency room.

"What? Is he okay? What's happened to him, and why did they call you instead of me?"

"Adam doesn't have access to his phone right now, and my number is the only one he could remember. Someone from his unit is going to be calling you soon though, so we need to get off the phone."

"But what's wrong with him? Is he hurt?"

There was silence.

"The officer that calls you will fill you in. I need to let you go." Then he mumbled seven suspicious words under his breath before he disconnected the call. "I knew this was going to happen."

20

It wasn't until three in the morning that I saw a set of headlights shining through our living room windows. Despite the long, panicked drive I made back to Indianapolis, my attempts at getting any sleep up until then had been futile. All I could do was toss and turn, with my unanswered questions and horrifying images of what Adam might look like—bruises, cuts, and broken bones—whirling round and round in my head, so eventually I went downstairs to lie on the couch and wait.

As soon as I saw those headlights turn into our driveway, I ran to the front door and opened it, standing underneath the porch light where I could be seen. A female officer stepped out of the twelve-passenger van that sat idling on our cement approach and walked briskly toward me. Even through the darkness, I could see the weary-worn look on her face. It was the type of look I knew all too well, one that had frequented my face on particularly trying school days.

She stepped up onto the porch and greeted me. Then she gave me her rank and last name. I didn't care in the least who she was. I simply wanted her to forgo the pointless social formalities and get to telling me why my husband had been escorted seven hundred miles home in the middle of the night.

"Adam is suffering from severe exhaustion," she said.

That's it? He's just overly tired?

It wasn't that I thought exhaustion should be taken lightly, but I knew there must've been more to the story than she was telling me. How could anyone with brains in their head think that being overly tired warranted such an immediate drive through the night? And who came to the conclusion that dropping him at my door at three in the morning, when he was already sleep deprived, made any sense at all? Why not leave him in the hospital for a few days so he could get some rest?

I stared at her and waited for more of an explanation, a sensible one preferably.

"Do your best to keep him away from caffeine and help him get some rest, okay?"

"Okay," I said with hesitation.

Then she handed me a pill bottle of muscle relaxants that the emergency room doctor had prescribed for him. I stared at the bottle as I turned it around in my hand, looking for some kind of answer. *Why would I need to keep Adam away from caffeine or help him get some sleep? Wouldn't he be capable of doing those things on his own? And why would muscle relaxants be prescribed for exhaustion?*

"I'm sorry, but I'm not sure I understand what you're telling me."

She repeated what she said before, making it clear that I wasn't going to get any answers from her. Maybe she didn't have them, or maybe she was afraid to tell me the truth. Either way, I didn't push her any further. Instead, I shifted my attention toward Adam and began to prepare myself to see him in whatever vulnerable state he was in.

I expected he'd be tired and weak from all the days he'd gone without rest, and that he'd look beat down too—humiliated that he had been sent home from his training almost two weeks early. Except that wasn't the Adam I saw come hopping out of the van. In fact, the man I saw didn't look or act like my husband at all.

"Lovey! Are you surprised to see me? I accomplished my mission early, so I was rewarded with a personal escort home."

"Uh-uh," I said unconvincingly.

Did he really believe that? Had someone told him that or had he come up with this idea on his own?

A male officer stepped out of the driver's side of the van and joined the three of us on the porch as Adam continued rambling on and on loudly, talking a mile a minute about his mission to no one in particular.

"He talked this way throughout the entire drive," the male officer admitted to me. "He never fell asleep once or even quieted down."

"I'm sorry," I whispered.

I wasn't completely sorry. It seemed to me that the military had been at least partially responsible for putting Adam in the position he was in, but I did have some sympathy for the officers who had to drive him home.

"This seems like more than exhaustion to me," I said.

The male officer nodded his head in agreement. "The doctor in our unit thought so too, and that's why we took him to the ER."

I was sure Adam was exhausted, but I didn't think that it alone could account for his strange behavior. But what could I do about it in the middle of the night? Nothing. What could they do? Nothing either. So I let them go.

"Thank you for bringing him home safely. You should both go get some rest."

Rest. That's what we all needed, and I hoped after a solid night of sleep that Adam would seem more like himself again. Sleep, however, was not on his agenda for the night.

When he left for his training, we had been two exuberant newlyweds, deep in the throes of our honeymoon phase. Typically when he'd return home from a trip, I'd run down the stairs and jump into his arms, eager to fall into bed with him to make up for lost time. But that was the last thing I wanted to do considering his precarious condition. Adam, on the other hand, couldn't see how this particular return was any different from the last.

"Let's go upstairs and get some sleep," I said to him. "I'm tired, and I know you must be too."

As he followed me up the stairs and down the hallway toward our bedroom, his hands were all over me.

"Come on, Adam," I said as I tried to gently push his hands away from me. "I need to get some rest, and the doctor made it clear that you need some too. Can't this wait until the morning?"

"We haven't been together in two weeks," he said with irritation in his voice. "I missed you. Didn't you miss me?"

"Yes, of course I did, but I'm tired, and I'm not in the mood now. It's been a long night. Please, let's just get some sleep."

He didn't reply, acting as if he hadn't heard me, even though I knew that he had. Instead, he undressed himself and motioned for me to join him in our bed. Afraid of how he might react to a more aggressive rejection, I felt I had no other choice than to give in.

I lay completely still on my side of the mattress as Adam slipped his hands underneath me and moved his lips across the surface of my skin. His eyes were wild and unfocused, his movements rough and unfamiliar, and for the first time since we met, the feeling of his body against mine made my skin crawl.

I tried to get my body to respond to his, which had always come so easily before, but I couldn't. Although my brain was telling me that the man before me was my husband, my heart was telling me that he was a stranger, and I had to fight the urge to get up and run.

When it was finally over, I was left with tears in my eyes and a lot of conflicting emotions. I knew it had only lasted a few minutes, but those minutes had been more than long enough to mess with my mind. For Adam, it hadn't been anything other than lust, a way of getting his physical pleasures met. But for me, it had been a sacrificial act—one bred out of my love for him and my newfound fear *of* him.

21

In the hours that followed, I tried to help Adam settle down and fall asleep, but he never did. He was completely incapable of lying still for more than a second at a time, restlessly shifting from the left and then to the right and back again. His perpetual movements tossed me around like a rag doll, making me feel as if our mattress had suddenly been dumped in the middle of an angry ocean.

His mind and mouth were moving a mile a minute, jabbering through the course of the night in military jargon that I pretended to understand. To keep him in bed and away from his phone, I pulled out a notebook from my bedside table and started writing things down for him. He had all kinds of jumbled thoughts he wanted to pass along to his unit, so to keep him from making any phone calls in the middle of the night that he'd likely regret later, I commissioned myself as his secretary and took over that responsibility for him. Of course, I had no intention of doing so.

By the time the sun breached the horizon line, I gave up on the idea of sleeping all together and focused on the day ahead. After the extraordinarily bizarre night I had with him, I was more than certain that Adam needed medical attention and that I wasn't going to get any rest until he did. But I had no idea where to take him or how to convince him to go, so I hoped we'd be able to survive at home until some reinforcements came. It didn't take long though before Adam insisted on getting out of the house.

"I feel like getting in a good workout at the gym. Do you want to go?" he asked.

"Adam, neither of us got any sleep last night. How can you be up for a workout? I'm exhausted."

"I feel great, but if you don't want to go, I can go without you."

"I don't want you to go without me. I want you to stay here and get some rest like the doctor said."

"I'm telling you I'm fine. I haven't been to the gym in two weeks, and I'm going," he insisted. "Where are your keys?"

Since his car was still parked in Springfield where he had met up with his unit before training, he needed my car to get to the gym.

"I hid them," I said nervously.

His father had instructed me to hide both sets of my car keys when I talked to him over the phone on my drive home from Michigan. I wasn't quite sure why Greg had thought to tell me to do so, but it was good advice considering Adam's odd behavior.

"Go get them for me," he demanded.

"No," I responded with a bit of force.

"Okay, if you aren't going to give up your keys, then I'll just run to the gym."

Our gym was only two miles away, so it wouldn't have been hard for him to run there, but I couldn't let that happen. Without a sidewalk or even a shoulder to speak of, he'd have to run down and across some very busy streets, and I was worried that he would get hit by a car.

"All right, you win, but I'm going with you." Then I went upstairs to dig my keys out of the bottom drawer of my dresser and change into some workout clothes. When I got back downstairs where Adam was waiting for me, I said, "I'm ready, and I'm driving."

"I always drive," he replied. "Let me have the keys."

It wasn't like I could physically prevent him from taking my car keys from me, so I handed them over and subsequently found myself clinging to the handle bolted to the ceiling of my car for safety. Adam was generally a good driver, but our short trip to the gym that morning could only be described as reckless.

He drove entirely too fast and far too close to the vehicles in front of him. He jerked the car aggressively when changing lanes or going around even a slight curve. And his response time was slower than normal—most likely because he couldn't keep his eyes on the road—so every stop we made was sudden and abrupt. Yet by God's grace, we managed to make it to the gym in one piece.

As I stepped out of the car, I could feel every body part and internal organ trembling, but what really had me concerned was that I could see Adam's body visibly shaking, and it wasn't from our wild ride over. It was from what he had put into his body—countless cups of coffee and a double serving of his preworkout supplement—a highly stimulating concoction that had put him into some kind of chemically induced hyperdrive.

There was just no telling what was going to happen. Would he collapse? Have a stroke? Get into a fight? Normally we'd separate to run through our own specialized workout routines, but that morning, I knew I wasn't there for myself. I was there to stick closely by his side to monitor him and make sure that nobody got hurt.

Doing so turned out to be more of a challenge than I expected though. A typical workout for us would last around an hour or so, but that day, we hit the gym hard for a long and painful two and half hours, without taking a break at all. And my body throbbed and ached everywhere for every bit of those 150 minutes, because I hadn't slept in over twenty-four hours, nor did I have the superhero level of strength and stamina that Adam did.

Far worse than the physical pain, however, was the public humiliation I suffered. Adam was absolutely bent on counting out every rep we lifted.

"Twenty, nineteen, eighteen," he'd yell. "Come on, push yourself. You can do more."

Then he'd bark out orders at me like a drill sergeant in between sets.

"You need to drink more water."

"You can do better with your form."

"Grab me another towel and fill up my water bottle."

When we weren't lifting weights, he had us running on the treadmill at full speed, or lunging around the perimeter of the gym floor for everyone to see. His behavior was so over the top, it drew all kinds of unwanted attention, until I finally told him that I had had enough. And by some miracle, he agreed to go, and I couldn't get out of there—away from everyone's judgmental stares and gossiping whispers—fast enough.

As the day progressed, Adam's behavior became even more erratic, and while I tried to always keep my eyes on him, I was also dealing with a constant influx of phone calls and text messages from our families and the military.

How's Adam doing?

Any improvements?

What's going on with Adam?

Are you both doing all right?

Keeping up with everyone's inquiries was completely overwhelming to me. I had no idea what was going on with Adam, so I didn't know what to say to them. And finding a minute alone to breathe, let alone answer a phone call or send a return text message back, was nearly impossible since Adam was always in need of something and constantly calling for me.

"What are you doing? Didn't you hear me calling for you? Who are you talking to? You aren't talking about me, are you?"

His paranoia and irritability continued to increase every time he found me hidden away somewhere with my phone, so I tried to keep my contact with the outside world to a minimum, communicating mostly with Greg, who seemed to have more insight into the matter.

"You need to get Adam into a hospital," he said. "I've been talking to Eric, and he's going to drop by after work to help you get him there."

But Eric and I were wildly unsuccessful. Adam downright refused to go anywhere with us to seek medical attention, fully believing that he was fine. So I had at least another night to get through with him. Another long night that I had to be alone with a man who was now a crazed stranger to me.

So once again, I tried to get Adam to sleep, but I couldn't pull him away from his desktop computer long enough to get him to lie down on our bed. In some ways, it was a relief to me, as I was still reeling from my encounter with him from the night before, but I was afraid of the damage he could be doing online without supervision.

Was he carelessly throwing our savings around in the stock market? He had lost over $6,000 just before he left for Las Vegas the month before we got married due to some risky day trading. Was he sending strange emails to his coworkers? His National Guard unit? Or worse, my parents? That was a disaster I didn't want to begin to think about.

I tried to stay awake to monitor him, to keep him from making a mistake that he couldn't take back, but sometime after two in the morning, my body shut down, and I fell asleep while Adam continued to type with a fervor. I awoke just a few hours later though, to the sound of clanging pots and pans coming from the kitchen. And as I walked downstairs and into the kitchen to investigate, I could see that Adam was furiously preparing breakfast for what looked to be an entire army.

"What are you doing, Adam?"

"I'm making breakfast," he said with a smile.

"I see that, but why are you making so much?"

"I emailed everyone in my office to tell them I came back from my training early, and I'm expecting them to arrive around 6:00 a.m. for a business meeting."

Great. What had he written in that email? Had he said anything off the wall or inappropriate that could get him fired? Had he emailed anyone else, and if so, whom?

"A business meeting? Here?"

"Yep. Last night, I came up with a great idea. A business proposition I'm calling 'Mission to Launch.' I'm going to ask my company to invest in it."

I winced as I envisioned the looks on the faces of his coworkers when they witnessed his bizarre behavior for themselves. If anyone showed up, there wouldn't be a thing I could do to protect him, but I had no way of calling off the meeting.

By 6:30 a.m., however, it was clear to us both that no one was coming. Adam was devastated, and I was relieved. He had certainly dodged a big bullet, but I wasn't so sure he'd be able to do it again.

We can't keep wasting time. I have to figure out some way of getting him out of this house and into a hospital. But how?

22

When I opened our front door and saw Greg standing there, I knew that I looked awful, but I was far too desperate for his help to give my haggard appearance a second thought. From the moment Adam had returned home, all I wanted was for someone to help me help him, and finally someone who seemed to know what to do had come. I hugged him tightly and asked, "What do we do?"

"We need to get Adam into a stress center. There is one not too far from here."

I had never even heard of a stress center before and certainly wouldn't have known to look for one. I didn't think Adam's symptoms were solely due to stress, but Greg seemed confident that it was the best place to take him.

"Okay … let's do it. I'll call Adam downstairs."

At first, we tried to play it straight with Adam, pointing out the seriousness of his symptoms and asking him to go with us to the hospital. But in his mind, he was fine. Better than fine actually. He felt happier, healthier, and more full of energy than he had in a long time. So he told us no and then climbed back up the stairs to continue working on his big ideas for Mission to Launch.

It's almost impossible to argue with how someone feels, so I didn't try. Instead, I climbed up the stairs after him to tell him how I was feeling.

"Adam, I'm really worried about you. Could you please come with us to the hospital for a quick checkup? I'd feel so much better if a doctor could confirm you're completely healthy, considering you've just completed some very rigorous military training. Please, can you do that for me?"

If he had been himself, I'm sure that the bags under my eyes and the genuine tears filling them would have been enough to sway him. The Adam I knew would have heard the desperation in my voice and done whatever he could to ease my fears, but that Adam was nowhere to be found. Whoever this new Adam was didn't see the pain I was feeling at all.

So for hours, Greg and I brainstormed new strategies to try to persuade him to seek help, but it wasn't until later that afternoon when Eric joined back in on the effort that we came across a strategy that worked. We could all see how hung up Adam's brain still was on the military, so we convinced him that going to the hospital was a direct order from his commanding officer, and just like that, he agreed to go.

It did take a lot longer than it should've to get Adam into Greg's car though. For some reason, he had to be dressed a certain way, and my outfit had to meet his approval too, before we could go to the hospital. Why he was concerned about my clothing and not the rest of my disheveled appearance I'll never know, but changing my clothes a few times was well worth it if it meant getting him help. Truthfully, I would've walked barefoot, across hot coals, all the way to the hospital, with Adam on my back, if that's what it would've required.

A sense of relief washed over me as the four of us stepped into the stress center's foyer. All I needed to do was check Adam in at the front desk, wait for his name to be called, and then he'd finally be seen by a doctor.

"How long do you think it will be before my husband can see a doctor?" I asked the receptionist behind the desk.

"Oh, honey, he won't get to see a doctor until he's assessed by a social worker."

"So *after* we talk to the social worker, then he'll be examined by a doctor?"

"If he's approved for admittance by the social worker."

Approved? He has to be approved? Anyone in their right mind should be able to see how severely he needs medical treatment. How could someone in Adam's current condition possibly be turned away?

I was appalled that being turned away was even an option, but I didn't show it.

"Okay, thank you." I said to her. Then I took a seat and stewed in silence.

A few minutes later, a social worker led us into a private room to conduct his assessment. After making a brief introduction, he got right down to business and began asking Adam some questions.

"So, Adam, tell me about the circumstances that have brought you here today."

"Well, I returned home from some military training two days ago, and my commanding officer thought I should come in for a checkup."

"Okay, so how did your training go?"

"Oh it went great. I completed my mission so quickly that I was able to come home earlier than planned."

"Wow, that does sound great. Have you been having any problems since you returned home?"

"I guess I haven't been sleeping very well."

Very well? He hasn't been sleeping at all.

"Why do you think you haven't been sleeping well?" the social worker asked him.

"Well, it's not that big of a deal, but I'd say it's probably from consuming too many energy drinks, caffeine pills, and pseudoephedrine while I was away."

"And are you still taking stimulants?"

"No. I was just taking them to get through the training."

Right. He's just drinking multiple pots of coffee each day.

"So that's it? There is nothing else you want to tell me? No other symptoms you might be experiencing?"

"Nope. I think I'm good."

You've got to be kidding me.

Then the social worker turned to me and said, "How about you? Is there anything you want to add?"

There was plenty I wanted to add, so I launched into a much more accurate and meticulous account of the past couple of days, filling him in on everything that Adam had conveniently left out. I rattled off a long list of symptoms that I had observed in Adam—extreme energy, inability to sleep, rapid talking, delusional mindset, irritability, and poor decision-making—and I gave demonstrative examples to further strengthen my case. Adam attempted to interrupt me a few times, but the social worker insisted that he sit quietly, since he had already had his turn to speak.

I also mentioned his compound bow.

"A bow?" the social worker repeated.

"Yes, a compound bow, with broadheads for deer hunting. My dad gave it to Adam last Christmas. He hasn't touched it in months, but last night he pulled it out of our storage room and placed it underneath our bed."

The mention of a weapon seemed to pique his interest, but I could tell the social worker still wasn't convinced that he had enough information to admit Adam.

"Adam, could you wait out in the lobby for a few minutes? I just want to talk to your wife, father, and brother for a few more minutes before wrapping this up."

"Sure," Adam said with a grin on his face.

"Look, I can understand why you're all concerned about him, but I have to have a strong reason to believe that Adam is a danger to himself or to others in order to admit him, and from what I can tell, he's not."

"So I'm just supposed to wait until he does hurt himself or someone else? Because that is just ridiculous!" I said loudly.

It wasn't like Adam was going to come right out and say he was a danger to himself or others. I didn't even believe he had it in him to purposely hurt someone, sane or otherwise, but that didn't mean he wouldn't. The thought of spending even one more night alone with him was terrifying to me because he had become so unpredictable. There was no telling where he would go, what he would do, or what damage he might cause to himself or those around him if he continued to live in this unexplainable state of madness.

Greg, Eric, and I all took our turns trying to explain that to him, but that logical train of thought just wasn't good enough. Even though I knew the social worker felt for us, he didn't feel the legal stipulations had been met.

I was so disappointed. No, it was more than that. I was frustrated, scared, and on the verge of my own nervous breakdown when I realized that Adam would be coming home. I didn't think I could make it through another sleepless night with him.

"I have no idea what I'm going to do with him," I cried. "He needs help and I can't take this anymore."

"I understand," the social worker replied with some compassion in his voice.

Then he called Adam back in to join us and threw a last-minute Hail Mary pass.

"Adam, this is a bit of a sensitive question, but have you ever attempted to commit suicide?"

"Yes, I have," he said point-blank.

He had? When had he attempted suicide, and why hadn't I been told? I looked around the room in horror but was shocked to see that I seemed to be the only one who was surprised.

"When did this happen?" the social worker asked calmly.

"My senior year of college. I was driving down the interstate, heading home after my graduation. My parents were following behind me in their van, and at some point, I unbuckled my seat belt before jerking my car off the road. This caused it to roll numerous times before it came to a stop in a field. My parents saw the whole thing. Right, Dad?"

I felt like I was going to be sick. He had told me that it had been an accident when he fell asleep at the wheel, but it was actually an intentional attempt to end his life. *Do I even know him at all?*

The conversation continued between Adam, the social worker, Greg, and Eric, but I only heard bits and pieces of it on account of the blood pulsing loudly in my ears and the raging headache I had. From what I did hear though, it seemed as if this wasn't Adam's first brush with what the social worker called "manic symptoms." And Greg admitted that there had been some mental health issues that followed Adam's broken engagement, resulting in a few hospitalizations and a diagnosis of bipolar disorder.

23

As I unlocked the front door to our house, I ripped down the paper sign that Adam had taped to it warning others to Keep Out, due to the top secret information he had stored inside. I wasn't sure if he was referring to some imaginary military secrets he had concocted or the big plans he had for Mission to Launch, but either way, I hoped I had taken it down before any of the neighbors saw it.

When I flipped on the entryway lights, I was greeted by the mess Adam had made in his mania. Dirty dishes and uneaten breakfast food filled every surface of the kitchen, his clothes were strewn throughout the entire upstairs, our bedding was ripped apart from two nights of absolute havoc and very little sleep, and most disgustingly, piles of hair from his head, body, and face were left in clumps on his bathroom floor. I had never been so repulsed by his obsession with manscaping.

The pounding in my head and the throbbing in my legs and feet told me I should wait until morning to straighten the house, but I didn't. I wanted the physical evidence of the last two days of chaos wiped away, even though I knew the appearance of an organized life wouldn't change anything. I had a whole new pile of problems to take care of, and they'd be much harder to deal with than washing the dirty dishes or sweeping the floor, but I wanted one thing in my life to feel normal. I needed one small thing to hold onto while everything else in my life had been flipped upside down.

When I was done cleaning and everything was returned to its rightful place, I pulled back the covers to my freshly made bed, turned off my phone, and tried to settle in for the night. Every muscle in my body ached, both of my eyes burned when I blinked, and my brain felt so full of new information that I thought it might explode. I felt weary in ways that I didn't know were possible yet was still afraid the clutter I couldn't clear from my mind would keep me awake. But within a matter of seconds, I was out.

The next morning when I turned my cell phone on, I was immediately forced to face my new reality, one that included the responsibility of taking care of a husband with mental health issues I didn't understand and a dramatic past that I knew very little about. I could see from all the notifications on my phone that I had missed several phone calls, one from Adam's assigned social worker who wanted more information about him—information I was sure that I didn't have—and the rest from Adam himself.

Just hearing Adam's voice in the voice mails he left me made me feel compelled to rush to his side, but my newfound awareness of just how ignorant I was about his illness left me feeling paralyzed too. I understood that my ignorance wasn't my fault of course. I had been thrust into the world of mental illness without warning, as I suppose many people are, but I was afraid that it could hurt Adam in some way and that any mistakes I might make could damage our relationship too.

There were so many decisions that needed to be made. the big and scary kind of decisions that I never expected to be making just four months into my marriage. And there were so many things that needed to be done. Yet I didn't feel equipped to do any of it.

I didn't know how to navigate the mental health care system. I didn't know how to communicate with Adam's employer to request additional time off. I didn't know how to act in front of Adam when I visited him in the hospital, and I certainly didn't know how I was going to balance the roles of both caretaker and spouse. I didn't know how to do anything when it came to Adam's mental health condition—I didn't even have a clue—but there was no time to waste preparing myself.

I just had to suck it up, fight through the shock I was experiencing, and give it my best shot. I relied on the advice of Greg, Eric, and the medical staff attending to Adam as much as I could, aware that my own critical thinking skills were compromised at best. And when they weren't there to help me, I simply flew by the seat of my pants and prayed that God would direct my thoughts and actions.

But one thing I did know for sure was that I was going to show up for Adam in any way I could. I didn't want Adam to ever question my love for him, and I didn't want to look back and regret how I had, or hadn't, cared for him either. I was determined to give him 100 percent, even though he had a lot of explaining to do once he recovered.

So during his stay at the stress center, I visited him as often as I was allowed to, despite having to keep my head on a permanent swivel as we tried to talk. I think every visitor inherently knew that it was wise to keep their eyes open and their backs against a wall as soon as they saw that all the patients, who had a vast array of serious mental health issues, were freely walking around. I answered every one of Adam's phone calls too, which was harder than one might think since he called me incessantly, sometimes more than twenty times in a day. And I tried my hardest to exercise patience and maintain a kind attitude, even though it was anyone's best guess as to which Adam I'd be talking to.

I might get the Adam that was sweet but lonely.

"I just wanted to hear your voice, lovey. I miss you, and I can't wait to get out of here so I can talk to you and hug and kiss you whenever I want. I love you so much."

I could get the Adam that was sad and needy, who would ask me to bring him something he wasn't allowed to have or didn't really need.

"It's so hard being locked in here with nothing to do and no one to talk to. You don't know what it's like to be a prisoner. When are you coming to visit? Can you bring me another pair of socks?"

It was a real possibility that I'd get the Adam that was psychotic and delusional.

"I've been doing a lot of great work here. I've been receiving spiritual prophecies from God that no one else knows. And I've been casting demons out of the other patients too."

Worse, I could get the Adam that was furious with me.

"It's all your fault that I'm stuck here. I'm going to have you thrown out of my house. You're so ungrateful!" Then he'd throw in a few creative expletives for dramatic effect.

For the most part, I was able to let his outlandish behavior and demeaning language roll off my back. I was a middle school teacher in an inner-city school for heaven's sake. I understood that his brain chemistry was all out of whack, which likely led him to say and do things he wouldn't otherwise, but deep down, his hateful comments still took their toll on me.

Before his time in the stress center, he had never sworn at me or even raised his voice for that matter, but considering how much he had kept from me, I couldn't help but wonder if those hateful words had always been there. It didn't seem like too far of a stretch to think that with his inhibitions temporarily dismantled, he could be expressing how he genuinely thought and felt. But I didn't let myself dwell on that possibility for too long, knowing I couldn't handle any more than I already was.

24

It didn't take long for the hospital's psychiatrist to observe Adam's behavior, review his medical history, and confirm Adam's diagnosis of bipolar disorder, labeling it as type 1 instead of nontypical as it had been before. At the time, I didn't fully understand what his diagnosis meant, having only heard people use the word *bipolar* incorrectly, generally when describing a person who they thought to be too emotional or exceptionally moody. Considering how apparent it was that Adam's condition went well beyond that, I went right to work researching bipolar disorder, starting first with the symptoms of bipolar mania.

WebMD, the Mayo Clinic, and the National Institute of Mental Health were the first three websites of over twenty-six million to come up. They described the hallmark symptoms of bipolar mania as such: increased energy, hyperactivity, a decreased need to sleep, excessive talkativeness, rapid speech, racing thoughts, irritability, poor decision-making, distractibility, inflated self-image, and hypersexuality. It was almost as if every website I scrolled through was using Adam as their manic prototype.

I can't believe it. Adam is exhibiting every single symptom on the list. There was no denying that Adam's diagnosis was accurate, and that was a good thing since it allowed his psychiatrist to begin treating him with the proper medications. But as I dug a little deeper into my research, I started to realize just how serious his diagnosis was.

Bipolar disorder, also known as manic depression, is a lifelong mental illness that causes those inflicted with it to bounce back and forth between manic and depressive episodes, due to chemical imbalances in their brains. *Lifelong?* For those diagnosed with type 1 bipolar disorder, the episodes tend to be the most severe when compared to those of the other types. These episodes result in erratic and dangerous behavior that disrupts and can destroy their life, as well as the lives of those connected to them. *That would be me. Can this possibly get any worse?*

There is no cure for bipolar disorder, primarily because there doesn't seem to be one root cause. Instead, it likely results from a combination of different factors that interact with one another. It does tend to run in families, so there is a genetic component, but the pattern of inheritance is unclear.

In fact, there have been documented cases in which one identical twin has displayed bipolar symptoms while the other did not. Therefore, inheriting certain genes—and some researchers estimate there are as many as fifteen—may predispose a person to having bipolar disorder, but other factors must act to trigger the symptoms. Those triggers could be exposure to harmful substances, stress, experiencing a traumatic event, having hormonal issues, or may be hard to pinpoint at all. *So how in the world can we possibly avoid triggering another manic episode?*

In a best-case scenario, all a person can do is attempt to avoid their personal triggers—which is impossible to do all the time— and constantly be on the lookout for the early signs of manic or depressive symptoms, ideally with the assistance of their loved ones. Then when those symptoms appear, they can try to reduce their severity and length of stay by tweaking their medication levels, hoping to find the perfect cocktail of very powerful mood-stabilizing drugs, antipsychotics, antidepressants, and sedatives for their particular set of needs. Of course, they'd already have to be on medication for that to be possible.

All of that heavy information was a lot for me to digest, and I didn't exactly know how to deal with it. What I should've done was reach out to my parents and my closest friends, knowing they would've been by my side in a minute to provide the support I desperately needed. But Greg had advised me to be careful with the information I gave to others.

"I wouldn't share too much with other people. You could end up making things worse for Adam. He could lose his job. He could get in trouble with the military. And I know things are already strained between him and your parents."

Of course I didn't want to make things any harder on Adam, so I made the mistake of trying to deal with everything by myself from the seclusion of my home. I didn't share much of anything with my friends and came up with excuse after excuse as to why I couldn't spend any time with them.

"We are just so busy right now. Our new house is great, but it's so much work."

"You know how much Adam travels and when he's here; I just want to spend time alone with him."

"Once we get through the busy summer months, my schedule should open up a bit. Right now we just have so many things going on."

And I downplayed the entire situation—how Adam was doing and how I was handling it—when my parents called, leaving what I had learned about his illness out of the conversation.

"Adam's recovering quickly and should be home in no time. Then things will get back to normal I'm sure. It's been hard, but I'm really doing fine considering."

But in reality, Adam wasn't recovering quickly, and I wasn't doing fine either. When I wasn't dealing directly with Adam or completing tasks on his behalf, I'd lie in bed for hours, trying to process my feelings on my own. I lost huge chunks of time as I lay there zoning in and out of consciousness, thinking about the ramifications of his diagnosis and how we were going to deal with them when he came home. I thought about my anger toward the military, astounded by how careless they had been when they dropped him at my door instead of checking him directly into a hospital. And I thought about the information that had purposely been withheld from me and wondered how much more there was that I still didn't know.

There was a lot actually. I learned from my sister-in-law that three months after breaking off his first engagement, Adam flew all the way to India unannounced, in search of his ex-fiancée. I can only imagine how terrified she must have been, considering he was completely manic at the time and it took nine full days before her family was able to get him onto a return flight home. I learned that he had started an online office supply company, in which he accrued $17,000 in debt, and then decided to join the National Guard, partially for the signing bonus they offered him so he wouldn't have to declare bankruptcy. And I learned that just before he was set to leave for basic training, he received a DUI and spent a night in jail, which delayed the start of his military career by six months.

I didn't know it then, but with everything that was being thrown at me, I was falling deeper and deeper into a state of shock. I felt tired all the time, donning dark circles under my eyes, no matter how much I slept or how much makeup I put on. I would forget to eat and lose track of when I had talked to my parents last, and I stopped caring at all about the way I looked or felt. Even my hair began to fall out in chunks, but somehow I still didn't recognize how poorly I was taking care of myself. My mental and physical health should have been a bigger priority, but unfortunately, it would take me quite some time to place it on equal footing with Adam's.

25

After a few days in the stress center, Adam's medications began taking hold, and he slowly began to stabilize. But with that, he became more aware of his restrictive surroundings and more desperate to get out of them. When he had entered the stress center, he had been so manic that he was completely incapable of holding in his thoughts—spewing out everything that entered his mind regardless of how it might sound to others—but as the level of neurotransmitters in his brain began to normalize, he started to gain back his ability to read people.

He started paying attention to the medical staff's body language and facial expressions when he talked to them, so he could avoid any topics that made them uncomfortable. Topics such as his plan for his latest surefire, get-rich-quick scheme, the divine prophecies regarding the end-times that God had given to him, and his supernatural ability to fight off witches and cast out demons. But just because he knew to keep quiet in front of those who held the keys to his release didn't mean he stopped believing in them, because he continued to talk about them with me.

He also began making note of the psychiatrist's repetitive questions regarding his symptoms and told the psychiatrist what he thought he wanted to hear in order to be discharged.

"I know that I have bipolar disorder," he told the doctor. "But the medications you've prescribed are really helping me. My mind is no longer racing. I'm not having grandiose thoughts anymore. And I'm sleeping better and better every night."

He might as well have been reading directly out of a mental health textbook. But then when I'd come to visit him, he'd tell me the direct opposite, in hushed tones of course so the medical staff wouldn't overhear him.

"There's nothing wrong with me, and I shouldn't be in here anymore. When I get out of here, I'm done taking all these medications too. They're only pushing them on me because the doctors get kickbacks from the big pharmaceutical companies that make them."

And to my horror, the hospital's psychiatrist began to fall for Adam's act, until I shared what he had been telling me, and Greg and Eric filled him in on Adam's history of charming doctors into releasing him too soon. It was frightening to think that he could be sent home before he was ready, only to go off his medication—as he apparently had done several times before—and slip backward into a full-blown manic state.

There was no telling how much harder it would've been to get him back into the hospital for a second time, or what awful things might've happened in the meantime. None of us wanted to find out either, so the psychiatrist agreed that he should remain in the hospital for a while longer. That was all well and good for a couple of days, but when Adam realized his performance wasn't getting him what he wanted, he threatened to sign himself out, which technically he could do since he had signed himself in. I suppose he hadn't been with it enough to think of that until then.

Fortunately, his threats to do so didn't come until the weekend, and since there wasn't a psychiatrist on duty over the weekend to sign off on his release, he had to wait until Monday morning. Adam's family and I were relieved that he'd have at least another forty-eight hours of protective care, but we all knew that it was far from being enough.

So on that Monday morning, I talked with Adam's social worker over the phone, and based on her recommendation, the psychiatrist agreed to have the hospital's lawyers submit a petition to seek a court-mandated mental health commitment for him. If granted, Adam would be legally bound to any treatment his psychiatrist deemed necessary for the subsequent ninety days following the hearing. If not, Adam would be released and free to do as he pleased but would have to remain in the stress center until the court hearing was over with. It seemed like a win-win situation—one without any major repercussions that I could see—until I had to face Adam on the witness stand a week and a half later.

I found myself sitting in a quiet panic next to my brother-in-law and father-in-law, waiting for Adam's 8:00 a.m. court hearing to begin. Not knowing how the traffic would be downtown, the three of us arrived before anyone else, giving me more time to worry about my testimony and the judge's verdict.

I looked around the room to try to acclimate myself to my unfamiliar surroundings, but the courtroom, which was located on one of the upper floors of the City-County Building, seemed specifically designed for intimidation purposes. The furniture was oversized, uncomfortable, and made of outdated, dark-stained wood. The fluorescent lighting and minimal decor was old, unflattering, and awkwardly formal. And on any other occasion, I would've enjoyed the clear view of the city its picture windows provided, but that day it left me feeling uneasy and acrophobic.

When Adam arrived, escorted by hospital personnel, he looked a lot like the put-together, self-assured man I had married. He sauntered in confidently, dressed in the professional clothing that I had brought to him at the stress center the day before, and happily greeted the three of us before taking his seat. To him, this hearing was nothing but a technicality. All he had to do was get up on the stand, speak his truth, and he'd be free to go home. Greg, Eric, and I were merely there to back him up, which we were, but not at all in the way he expected us to be.

As the judge walked in and the call to rise was issued, a surge of fear swept over me, and negative thoughts filled my head. *What if the judge is fooled by Adam's appearance? What if I bomb up there and he's released to come home because of it? Then we might have to suffer through this nightmare again. And if I don't bomb, is Adam going to hate me? Will that destroy any hope we have of a future together?*

It was then that I realized there was no such thing as a consequence-free outcome in this situation, but I still knew what needed to be done. Even so, the amount of pressure I was feeling was far greater than I had ever experienced before. And it didn't help that Greg had called me the night before to tell me he wasn't going to testify.

"I've decided I'm not going to testify on the stand tomorrow. I think between your testimony and Eric's, the judge will have what he needs to issue the court order. I don't want to damage my relationship with my son."

I said nothing. I didn't argue with him—I never did—and I didn't say that it was okay either, because it wasn't. Greg knew how badly Adam needed that commitment, and he should've been willing to do anything to help him get it, but he let his fear of hurting his relationship with Adam prevent him from doing the right thing. Did he think I didn't have that same fear too?

I had only been in Adam's life for a year and his wife for all of four months. If anyone was at risk of damaging their relationship with Adam permanently, it was me. But I didn't have the luxury of sitting back and watching the chips fall as they may, no matter how I felt about it. I had to get up on that stand, let my voice be heard, and pray that it was enough to get Adam committed because I loved him.

So after Eric testified about Adam's medical past, and Adam's psychiatrist spoke about his diagnosis and progress thus far, I took my turn on the stand.

"Can you please tell the court whether or not you believe your husband is ready to be released from the stress center to return home?" the hospital's lawyer asked me.

"I do not," I said with a quivering voice. "And I'm not ready for him to come home either."

"Can you explain why?"

"Yes I can. I haven't missed a single day of visitation since Adam was admitted, and even on the days that the hospital doesn't allow visitors, I've talked with him over the phone, usually several times a day. He's made it quite clear to me that he doesn't believe he has a mental illness and therefore doesn't need to take any medication. No matter what he has to say today, I know without a doubt that he will not follow through with his treatment unless he is forced to do so."

"And if he is released today, how will that make you feel?"

"Terrified, frankly. The two days I spent with him before he was admitted were awful. I want him to come home—I love him—but not until he's ready. I want Adam to have the best chance possible to recover, and he needs this court commitment to do so."

"Thank you for your honesty. You may step down."

I had avoided looking in Adam's direction as I spoke, but as I walked shakily back to my seat, I could feel him staring at me, following my every movement with his eyes. I didn't want to look, but I felt that I needed to, and when I did, I saw a mix of anger, hurt, and utter disbelief on his face. I wasn't sure how to respond to that, so I smiled slightly and shrugged my shoulders, hoping to communicate to him that I loved him but had no choice.

His expression changed when he got onto the stand though, to one that was determined, confident, and unfazed. Then after he spoke, sharing his side of the story, we were all told to rise while the judge prepared to give us his verdict. Greg, Eric, and I leaned closely together, and I shut my eyes to pray. *Please, God. Please, please, please give us this court commitment.*

And after the judge rehashed his thoughts on the matter, summarizing what had been said by both sides, he granted the court commitment, and Adam was legally bound to comply with whatever treatment plan his psychiatrist put forth for the next three months. *Thank you, God.* It was great news. We had done what we had set out to do, and because of that, Adam would get the help he needed and deserved.

The three of us hugged one another, and the hospital's lawyer turned around to congratulate us.

"Congratulations," he said as he took my hand. "I'm sure it was your testimony that won it for us."

But winning never felt so awful, not when I saw the devastation in Adam's face. Adam had entered that courtroom thinking I was his greatest ally, believing he'd be coming home to me soon. And he left convinced that I had stabbed him in the back, unable to talk to me or even look at me, wondering how much longer he'd have to endure the confinement of the stress center.

26

I had to shake off the residual emotions left behind by the court hearing rather quickly, because the next morning I reported back to school for the start of the 2012–2013 school year. I was looking forward to going back to work and having something else— something I was good at—to occupy my time, but never had I started a school year so beat down.

Teaching has always been a very important part of my adult life. It's one of the few things that I know for sure God put me on this earth to do, and although it's a profession that is often underappreciated, I love that teaching matters. It's such a great feeling to make a positive difference in a child's life. Witnessing them love what they're learning and accomplishing things they never believed they could is the greatest perk of the job.

And school was somewhat of a second home to me, especially after that summer. It was a safe place to land when my own home wasn't. A place where I was surrounded by caring people who dedicated their time and efforts toward helping others succeed, and that effort often extended beyond the student body. So I refused to let the difficulties I was facing in my personal life ruin that for me or disrupt the education of my incoming seventh graders. That's why I chose not to share anything about Adam's illness with my coworkers, acting as if my summer had been completely normal instead.

When I walked into the school building every morning, I shut that part of my life off entirely and focused on my responsibilities as a teacher. Then when I walked out of the building each afternoon, I switched that part of my life back on again, resuming my responsibilities as Adam's wife and caretaker. Compartmentalizing my life like that wasn't too difficult to do while Adam was still in the hospital and hardly talking to me, but a week later, twenty-two days after his admittance, Adam called me to tell me that he was being released.

"Lovey, can you pick me up from the hospital after school today? My doctor said that I'm finally ready to go home. Isn't that great news?"

"It is, and of course I will. I'll be there as soon as I can. I love you."

I was glad to hear happiness in his voice again—opposed to the defeat that dripped from his words ever since the court hearing—still I was uneasy about him coming home. I knew it was a necessary step back toward normalcy for us, but for me it was a scary one. I didn't know if Adam would really abide by the rules of his court commitment, and I was nowhere near strong enough yet to deal with more manic behavior if he didn't. And with me being back at work, I knew I wouldn't be able to monitor his every move either, and I'd have to trust him to make good decisions when I wasn't home. The problem was I didn't trust him at all.

Before his manic episode, I believed that Adam told me everything. The only lie I had ever caught him in occurred the month before he left for his summer training, when a can of chewing tobacco fell out of the pocket of his jeans after I picked them up off the floor. I was upset that he was using it—we had discussed my hatred of tobacco products early on in our dating relationship, and he had promised not to use them—but I was far more upset that he had been hiding it from me, and I made that abundantly clear to him.

After that, I didn't think he'd have the nerve to lie to me again, but that was before I learned he had bipolar disorder and hadn't told me. Adam had let me down by not telling me the truth about his past. He hadn't just lied about small, insignificant things but big, life-changing things that I deserved to know. Every conversation we had, every moment we shared, everything I thought Adam was, was tainted by his lies. And worse, he had asked for my hand in marriage under completely false pretenses, taking away my right to know who I was giving my heart to. So I confronted him about it soon after I brought him home.

"Adam, now that you're home, I need to ask you an important question, and I need you to answer it honestly."

"Okay," he said hesitantly.

"I need to know why you didn't tell me that you'd been diagnosed with bipolar disorder."

He swallowed nervously, taking a moment or two to respond.

"Well, I didn't think I'd have another manic or depressive episode again. I thought they were just flukes because so much time had passed without incident. And when I made it through boot camp and then officer candidate school without any problems, I was sure they were just a part of my past."

I don't know how anyone could have thought that months of mental health issues were just a fluke. Mental illnesses don't generally disappear into thin air.

"All right, even if that's true, you still should have told me. Don't you think I deserved to know?"

"Yes. I do. I should have told you, and I was going to tell you. I was going to tell you over dinner the night after we went to the Indians game, but I got scared."

Now I know why he looked so nervous that night.

"I was falling fast for you, and I was scared I'd lose you. I was worried that you'd run screaming in the opposite direction if you knew everything about my past."

"You're right. I might have, but I should have been given the choice to do so. You took that choice away from me by lying to me, and lying to get what you want, even love, is wrong."

"I know, and I'm sorry. Do you think you can forgive me?"

His lies were cruel, and they were selfish. He placed his own desires above my well-being, and so did his family when they helped keep his secrets. It was an ugly dose of reality, but it didn't negate the love I had for him.

"It's going to take some time for me to forgive you and probably even longer before I can trust you, but I love you, and so I'm going to stay and help you fight this."

27

Adam didn't return home in a fully normalized state. His most blatant manic symptoms did subside quickly. His speech had slowed, his energy levels weren't as excessive, and he no longer struggled to focus on one task at a time. But his more inconspicuous symptoms clung to him for much longer, especially his convoluted way of thinking and obsession with becoming a successful entrepreneur.

Instead of concentrating on what was important, like his recovery or repairing our relationship, he spent most of his time acting as if his manic episode had never happened, while locking himself away in his home office for hours on end. A home office that didn't exist until I came home from work one day to find that he had thrown everything out of our spare bedroom and replaced it with newly purchased office furniture and an obnoxious amount of wall decor with inspirational sayings on them. Sayings such as "Find a passion and pursue it," "Follow your dreams," and "Believe in magic." *Please, how about "Take your medication," "Go to the doctor," and "Listen to your wife."*

While in his office, he worked primarily on putting together pitch decks to show potential investors, hoping they would throw money at his feet so he could get one of his zany business ideas off the ground—a nonprofit company that would deploy the National Guard on international, humanitarian missions and a web-based company that would allow companies to donate services and goods, instead of money, to charities in exchange for tax breaks. And when he wasn't working directly on his business plans, he was sending emails and making phone calls, hassling everyone he could think of who might have a connection he could utilize.

He did follow through with his treatment plan, however—taking his medication each day, attending doctors' appointments, and participating in outpatient group therapy three times a week—but his heart wasn't truly in it.

"How'd therapy go today, Adam?"

"Fine I guess, but it's basically just a waste of time. A room full of people with all kinds of problems that don't have anything to do with me."

"I know it might feel that way now, but you might as well give it a chance."

"I guess. I don't really see the point though. I wouldn't even have had a manic episode if I hadn't been so stressed and had been more careful with the amount of caffeine I was taking."

"I know the stress, lack of sleep, and caffeine certainly helped trigger your manic episode, but ultimately you had one because you have bipolar disorder. People get stressed all the time, including me, and they don't become manic. That's why you're going to therapy, to learn how to accept your illness and how to manage it."

"Whatever. As soon as my ninety days run out, I'm done with it. I'm done with it all."

It was evident that his compliance was only superficial, having nothing to do with a desire to get better and everything to do with wanting to avoid legal problems. So when the end of his court commitment approached, and his bad attitude still hadn't changed, I tried harder to convince him that his illness was real, hoping he'd choose to continue managing his illness after the legal constraints were cut. But I couldn't.

Every time I'd initiate a conversation about his treatment plan, he'd either get mad and storm out of the room or act so hurt that he thought I'd give up. But I never gave up. I kept pushing and pushing until that dreaded ninety-first day came and Adam stopped taking his medication. I knew that the consequences of ignoring his bipolar disorder could be catastrophic and that those consequences would undoubtedly blow back on me as well, but there wasn't anything left for me to say.

Adam had to make the choice to face his illness himself, and no one, not even me, could twist his arm hard enough to get him to do so. I was tired of fighting with him. I wanted to have fun with my best friend again, and I wanted the romance between us to return. So for the sake of my own well-being and the survival of our marriage, I stopped.

I stopped sinking all my energy into thinking about his illness. I stopped trying to control something I had no control of. And I started enjoying our life together again, even though I believed it was just a matter of time before his next manic episode would come crashing down on us. When? I wasn't sure.

And for a while, our life together did get a bit better, and we began to feel more like a newlywed couple should. We gradually slipped into a routine more typical of regular married life, and we did some traveling together too—a hiking trip in Colorado, a beach vacation with his family in the Florida Keys, and a first wedding anniversary celebration at the SnowShoe Mountain Resort in West Virginia, where we relived our honeymoon. But soon after the first of the year, the military came calling, and Adam could no longer pretend that his manic episode had been a horrible dream.

The National Guard needed answers from him about what had happened during his summer training, so they launched an investigation to determine if and how he should be discharged.

I was almost certain that Adam's discharge was inevitable. The military is no place for a person with a mental illness, considering it's a hotbed of high-stress situations and provides access to powerful weaponry, but it didn't keep me from worrying about what might happen if he wasn't discharged, especially since Adam was confident that he could explain his incident away.

Following numerous interrogations, however, Adam slowly began to change his tune and came to realize that his military career would soon be over. I wanted it to be over—it needed to be—but what I didn't want was for his discharge to be dishonorable. A dishonorable discharge would not only bring shame and embarrassment with it, but it could make finding future employment difficult for him.

"When will you be informed of the National Guard's decision?" I asked him.

"Soon I think."

"And how do you feel about it?"

"I'm worried."

"I know you are, but you need to be prepared for whatever the outcome. And I'll be here to support you no matter what happens."

"Thanks, Syd, but I don't know what I'll do if I can't serve in the military. And there's a possibility that I might receive a dishonorable discharge too."

"Really? Why? It's not like you meant to have a manic episode."

"Because technically my enlistment paperwork was fraudulent. One of the questions asked is whether you've ever been hospitalized for a mental health issue, and I answered that I hadn't."

"Adam!"

"I know. I know I shouldn't have."

Once again, Adam had lied. He had lied to get into the military by not disclosing the truth regarding his medical past, and neither the military nor I took lying lightly. So he deserved to be dishonorably discharged, but he wasn't. Adam was extended a generous amount of grace and granted a general discharge, partly because he had friends in the upper ranks of the army who spoke on his behalf and partly because his recruiter, who knew some things but not everything about his medical history, had advised Adam to keep it hidden.

It was about the best outcome we could've asked for, considering the circumstances, and even though it made him ineligible for veteran benefits, it didn't result in any real-world consequences. But the shock of his discharge left him devastated just the same. The army had been a big part of his life, and through his hard work and dedication, he had excelled in it. He loved everything about being in the military—the honor of serving his country, the pride of leading and helping develop the young men under his command, and the camaraderie he had developed with the rest of the soldiers in his unit. His identity was deeply connected to his military position, and to have it ripped away, fairly or not, took a real toll on him.

So for the next year or so, he struggled off and on with depression, not major bipolar depression but situational depression. When he chose to set his mind on the good things he had—a loving wife and family, a beautiful home, a job that provided much more than we needed—he was happy, attentive, and fun to be around. But when he chose to set his mind on the bad things— his military discharge, his unsuccessful attempts at starting his own business, his dissatisfaction at work—he let the feeling of failure consume him, turning him into a constant complainer somedays and a withdrawn, apathetic shell of himself on others.

28

In May 2014, I was given the answer to the long withstanding question that had been eating away at the back of my mind for quite some time—*when would Adam's next manic episode appear?*—when I started to notice some early warning signs that it was on its way. At first, the signs were subtle, small changes in his behavior that weren't necessarily odd but were odd for him. Things like leaving his dresser drawers wide open, not finishing his morning cup of coffee, or using jargon and silly catchphrases I'd never heard him say before.

These behavioral aberrations were so minute that most people wouldn't have noticed them at all. Thinking I was letting my paranoia get the best of me, I reasoned them away for a while, wanting to avoid an unnecessary confrontation with him. *Everyone can be absent-minded from time to time, right? And maybe he's just picking up these new words and phrases from someone at work. My language has certainly changed from all the time I spend surrounded by middle school students.*

But it didn't take long before his warning signs developed into more pronounced symptoms—symptoms that made it clear to me that Adam had drifted into a state of hypomania—the stepping-stone state sandwiched precariously between stability and full-blown mania. And I knew that if he didn't address them immediately, it would only be a matter of time before we'd have another crisis to deal with. So on the morning of Monday, May

12, I crossed my fingers and cautiously told Adam about the symptoms I had observed.

"Adam, I know you probably don't want to hear this, but I've noticed some changes in your behavior that are starting to worry me. You seem a bit more energetic than normal and forgetful at times too. I also noticed that you've been tossing and turning in bed more than usual and struggling to sleep all the way through the night."

"Honestly, I have been feeling different lately, and I have been having trouble sleeping as well."

"So would you consider making an appointment with a doctor?"

"Yeah. That's probably a good idea."

Did he just say going to a doctor was a good idea?

"But it will have to wait until I return from my business trip to Baltimore. I'll make an appointment with one of the doctors the stress center recommended as soon as I get back. Okay?"

"Well, I'm not sure waiting is a good idea. I'd feel better if you made an appointment now."

"I can't do that, Syd. You know I fly out later this afternoon, and it's too late to change my flight. I'll only be gone for four days. I'll be fine."

I was frustrated that he didn't grasp the urgency of the situation like I did. A lot could change in four days' time, and with him traveling completely alone, there would be no one looking out for him. I knew that he was choosing to play with fire by waiting to seek help until after his trip, but from previous experience, I also knew that Adam couldn't be coerced into doing something he didn't want to do.

"Okay then … I love you and please be careful. Call me every night."

Then I hugged and kissed him goodbye and left for work without another word about it. Of course, I had to tell myself over and over again that it was going to be all right.

But by day two of his trip, I began to think that it wasn't going to be all right because each time we talked over the phone, his speech was noticeably more pressured and harder to follow. And when his father called me on that Wednesday afternoon to tell me about a call he had received from Adam, I became certain of it.

"Sydney, I just got off the phone with Adam, and I think we have a problem."

"What? Is he okay? Did something happen to him?"

"He's physically fine, but he called me for help because he couldn't find his way back to his hotel."

"But he's usually so good with directions, and if he had his phone, why didn't he use Google Maps?"

"He tried to, but he sounded so disoriented that I don't think he could follow it. Don't worry though; he's back in his room now safe and sound."

Right, don't worry. My husband is just several states away, completely alone, and obviously manic.

"What's more concerning to me is that he sounded scared, and he admitted that he was fighting spiritual attacks."

"What do you mean by spiritual attacks?"

"I can't really say for sure, but he told me that he had been experiencing those same types of spiritual attacks the day he intentionally drove his car off the interstate."

"What? He was?"

At the time, I still didn't have a complete picture of the day that Adam attempted to commit suicide, and I didn't know what he meant by spiritual attacks either. Were these attacks an oppressive feeling? Did they cause him to visualize doing violent things? Did they come in the form of negative thoughts, or was he hearing some kind of voices? I had no idea, but if Adam was scared, then I knew I should be.

"Should we hop on a plane and go get him?" I suggested.

"I don't think that getting on an airplane now is practical, but I do think we should plan on meeting him at the airport tomorrow night so we can take him directly to the hospital."

Greg was right; it wasn't practical. But thinking about him being alone in a strange city, with his mind jumbled with confusion and filled with dark thoughts, was almost too much to bear. There was no telling what his misguided thinking might lead him to do.

"Okay. I'll be ready."

29

On Thursday night, Greg and I drove to the airport together, bound and determined to grab Adam as soon as he stepped off his flight to take him directly to the stress center. But, as I feared before he left, those four days in Baltimore robbed him of his previous insight. He was too far gone—lost so deeply in his own delusions—that he couldn't be convinced to get into the car, let alone sign himself in for treatment. So against my better judgment, I told Greg to meet us at the house, and I climbed into Adam's car with him.

Adam took the longest, most convoluted route imaginable to get home. Not because he wanted to but because he kept forgetting where he was and where he was going. His driving was negligent at best; his speed was way too fast, his reactions were way too slow, and his eyes were everywhere but on the road. I've never ridden in a car with a drunk driver before, but I imagine it would be much like it was that night with Adam.

As we drove aimlessly around the city, I tried to keep myself calm by making use of the time Adam was otherwise wasting. While he rattled on and on about how he had miraculously landed his plane using only his mind, and how excited he was to have brought home "the relic"—which turned out to be nothing more than a stolen hotel ice bucket he had stashed away in his luggage—I recorded his bizarre, one-way conversation on my phone, hoping to use it later as evidence to demonstrate to him just how real his illness was.

Eventually though, we did make it home safely, although it took at least twice as long as it should have. And while I was upset that I hadn't been able to get Adam to steer his way toward the stress center, knowing that every hour without medication could lengthen his recovery time by days, I was more thankful than anything to be out of the car and safely on the ground again, no longer at the mercy of his malfunctioning mind.

But after another long, sleepless night spent trying to keep Adam in the house and out of trouble, my thankful attitude had completely vanished. Adam needed to get back into the hospital immediately, not only for his sake but for mine. I certainly couldn't make it through another day with him, trying to force him to stay at home and out of the public eye, but without his willingness to seek treatment or the military card to play as I had before, I had no idea how I was going to make that happen.

So when morning broke, I went downstairs to brainstorm with Greg, who had slept on our couch that night. We agreed to try reasoning with Adam again before attempting anything more assertive, hoping to keep him calm and cooperative.

"Adam, I think it would be wise for you to get evaluated at the stress center—"

Before Greg could finish his statement, Adam got right up in his face and started screaming and pointing at him.

"I don't need to go to the stress center. This is none of your business. Why are you even here? Nobody wants you here. Get out!"

His belligerent reaction to his father's advice shocked me. I hadn't thought that Adam was capable of violence, especially against his own family, but if Greg hadn't backed away from him when he did, I'm almost certain that it would've come to blows.

"Adam, stop it!" I yelled.

He paused and stared at me.

"Please, stop," I begged.

Suddenly realizing how outrageous his behavior had been, he stepped away from his father and went upstairs to cool down.

"I think we should call the police now," Greg said to me. "Instead of trying to handle this on our own."

"I don't know …" I replied hesitantly.

Looking back now, I should've known. I should have gone along with Greg's suggestion, but at the time, calling the police on my husband seemed like a nuclear option. I was exhausted, desperate to get Adam help, and scared to be in his crosshairs while he was so easily provoked, but I was also worried about the consequences that might follow if we got law enforcement involved.

"Give me a little more time to talk with him, and if I can't convince him to go back to the stress center, we'll call the police. Okay?"

I took a deep breath in, trying to calm my nerves. *I can do this. I have to do this.* Then I walked quietly up the stairs toward Adam's office. The door let out a high-pitched creak as I swung his office door open slowly, causing him to look up from his computer screen at me.

As I took a few slow steps toward him, I could see that his eyes were still burning with anger—a clear warning that I should tread lightly. He stood up abruptly from his black leather office chair, with a look of intensity on his face. He was prepared for battle, prepared to refute whatever it was I had to say.

But I didn't say anything. Instead I fell into his arms and sobbed hysterically. I was so worn down from another night of no sleep and frustrated to be back in the same awful position I had been in just twenty-two months prior that I completely lost control over my emotions and let them explode all over Adam. I had intended on begging and pleading with him, but I couldn't get an intelligible word to come out of my mouth with all my tears getting in the way. All I wanted was for my husband to hold me tightly and tell me everything was going to be okay, and strangely enough, my outburst stopped Adam dead in his tracks.

His eyes softened, his focus momentarily shifted off himself and onto me, and he did exactly what I had hoped for, only it was far from being a comfort. He should've been the one person in my life who could ease my pain, but instead he was the source of it, and sadly, he didn't even know it. It was a heartbreaking thought for sure, but amid my temporary breakdown, while I pathetically clung to Adam, an idea came to me.

Adam's father had told me that he'd faked a heart attack once to get Adam into a hospital, so why couldn't I do the same thing? Why couldn't I fake a panic attack? It would be easy enough to pretend, considering I really was an emotional wreck. Would Adam buy it though, or would he connect the dots and realize I was trying to deceive him? Did the answer to that question even matter to me?

Honestly, no, it didn't. So I went for it without thinking any further.

"Adam," I squeaked out between sobs. "Please take me to the stress center."

"You want me to take *you* to the stress center?"

"Yes. I've been having thoughts of harming myself, and I'm scared. Please take me. Take me right now."

Without any hesitation or argument, he said sweetly, "Yes, I'll take you. You're going to be okay. It's all going to be okay."

Then he yelled down the stairs to his father and to his brother, who had dropped by sometime earlier to join in on the effort, "Come on. Grab your keys. We need to take Sydney to the stress center."

30

When we arrived at the stress center, the drizzle of rain falling from the sky gave Eric reason to drop me off at the front door before parking the car. Trying to stay in character, I climbed out of the car slowly—as if I was in physical pain—and slunk pathetically into the building with my head facing downward and my arms wrapped tightly around me. As soon as I got inside, however, I rushed straight toward the front desk and frantically tried to explain to the receptionist what was really going on.

"Hi. I don't have a lot of time, but my husband, who has bipolar disorder, will be coming in soon. He thinks we're here for me and that I'm having some type of anxiety attack, but that was just an excuse to get him here. Can you get a social worker to talk with him as soon as possible? He's manic and needs treatment right away."

I could tell by the skeptical look on her face that she didn't believe me. She'd likely heard all kinds of off-the-wall stories over the years, and based on the way I looked—no makeup, black circles under my eyes, and still in pajamas—I didn't blame her for doubting my reliability.

"Uh huh," she said in a sarcastic tone. "Do you have your identification and insurance cards?"

Of course I do, lady, but I'm not the one who needs medical help.

Knowing that Adam could walk through the entrance doors at any time, I chose not to argue with her. I dug through my purse to find the cards she asked for, took the clipboard she placed in front of me, and found a seat in the waiting room. Seconds later, Greg walked in, somehow managing to arrive a minute or two ahead of Adam and Eric. He hurried to the front desk, just as I had, to corroborate my story.

Then the four of us sat together and waited nervously for my name to be called. Naturally, Adam was worried about me, but the rest of us were worried about our precarious situation. It had been a small victory getting Adam to the stress center, but how was he going to respond when he realized that I'd deceived him?

Guilt had started to bubble up inside of me during the short ride over to the hospital, while Adam held me tenderly in the back seat, truly concerned about my safety. It's a horrible thing to think that the person you love the most in the world is in danger, and I felt awful for making him think that I was, because I knew exactly how terrible it felt.

But I could handle the guilt. It was a small price to pay in exchange for Adam getting the medical attention he needed. But could I handle the ramifications that might follow? And would just getting him into the building even be enough? It hadn't been the last time.

The more I thought about it, the more I regretted my actions. I just couldn't see how the situation could work itself out. *What was I thinking?*

When a social worker finally called us into a private room for an evaluation, I quietly started to panic. I desperately wanted to disappear, or at least plug my ears and close my eyes, so I wouldn't have to witness Adam's reaction when he found out we had been lying to him.

"So can someone tell me why you all came in today?" the social worker asked.

"We're here for my wife," Adam chimed right in. "I think she had a panic attack and has been having thoughts of harming herself."

While looking in my direction, the social worker said, "Is that true?"

"Well, somewhat. I haven't been having thoughts of harming myself, but I have been anxious and scared."

"Why?"

"Because my husband has bipolar disorder, he refuses to take his medication, and he's currently manic. He needs to be here to get some help."

Greg and Eric agreed.

"What?" Adam exclaimed. "You tricked me? How could you do that?"

Feeling betrayed and literally backed into a corner, he stood up and fled, running out of the building on foot, leather flip-flops in hand, with a look of disgust on his face. It was the response I had expected from him, but it wasn't at all the one I had hoped for. And from my last experience at the stress center, I knew my conversation with the social worker was over.

Even though I was sitting in an incredible facility, full of all kinds of knowledgeable medical professionals who could provide Adam with the proper medications and therapies to get him back on track, all I could do was wait for more mayhem to ensue because the mental health care system is broken. It's only designed to help *after* a crisis has occurred and not before, so I had no choice but to walk out with nothing, leaving worse off than I was when I came in.

Not knowing what horrors I had ahead of me, I didn't rush to get up and leave. I knew I needed to find the inner strength to press on for Adam, but I wasn't ready to face the bedlam quite yet. Instead, I would have preferred to climb into bed, curl up into a ball, and cry myself to sleep.

"Maybe I should check myself in," I joked.

It wasn't a funny joke, but Eric, Greg and the social worker chuckled out of pity, realizing it was a poor attempt at masking the anguish I was feeling.

"Well, I guess there's no point in staying any longer. Let's go ahead and drive back to the house."

But just as I willed myself to stand, Adam made a most unexpected reappearance. Two police officers, who had been driving by the hospital at just the right time, saw Adam running barefoot through the rain and away from the stress center, the sight of which prompted them to pull over to make sure he was all right. I was never told how their interaction with Adam played out, but whatever happened, it resulted in his apprehension and return to the hospital. And his escorted return was even more dramatic than his departure had been.

He came through the doors shouting at the top of his lungs and fighting the police officers the entire way, despite being handcuffed and held firmly by the arms.

"Let go of me! You have no right! I didn't do anything wrong. Just wait until I get out of here."

And when he passed by the intake room we were still in, he threw his body against the doorjamb to buy himself some time, which he used to explain to us how upset he was.

"You are all liars, and I hate you. I can't believe you would do this to me. I'll never talk to any of you again. And you," he said as he pointed directly at me, "you are completely ungrateful."

It wasn't until the police got him upstairs and behind closed doors that I felt the hot tears rolling down my cheeks and noticed that I was trembling. Under normal circumstances, I would've been embarrassed, but there wasn't anything I could do to control it. My body was simply doing what it was created to do in response to immense stress.

It was the first time in my adult life that I felt frail, like even a gentle breeze would be enough to knock me off my feet and down to the ground. Adam had taken me to the brink. He had burnt through every line of defense I had worked so hard to build, leaving me exposed and vulnerable, a feat that only someone I truly loved could accomplish.

But through the trauma of it all, God had given me what I had come for. And he had given Adam exactly what he needed too: another chance to gain some perspective on his illness while safely under the care of the stress center. Certainly this would be the wakeup call he needed to change his ways and start taking care of his mental health.

By the next afternoon, I felt strong enough to visit Adam on my own and bring along some of his clothes and toiletries. I had avoided any conversation with him since his involuntary psychiatric hold began, knowing I needed the break to rest and he needed the time to cool down, so I wasn't sure how our first visit would go. Based on our last interaction though, I thought it was best to keep my expectations low.

If he was still furious with me, and chances were he still was, he'd either let me have it all over again or refuse to see me altogether. Neither scenario was preferable, and I wasn't sure that I could handle another emotional blow so soon, but I made myself go anyway. Not because I loved being publicly humiliated or even because I felt obligated to, but because I couldn't bear the thought of him having to endure visiting hours alone.

I refused to let him sit in a deserted corner of the day room, watching other visitors come in and out, wondering if I still loved him. I had seen that exact same scenario play out for many of the stress center's patients. It's far too common for patients seeking treatment in any mental health care facility to spend their entire stay without a single visitor. In some cases, such as with Adam's mother, the visit is just too hard on their family members, but for others, there simply isn't anyone left in their lives to visit them. Years of destructive behavior, coupled with a compounding pile of poor decisions, have a way of destroying relationships and pushing loved ones away.

Adam had already started down that lonely path, but I didn't believe it was too late for him to turn back as long as he had someone to turn back for. That someone should've been himself. He should've cared enough about his own well-being to make the necessary sacrifices to manage his illness, regardless of how inconvenient or burdensome they might've been, but I was willing to step up and be that person for him until he figured that out on his own.

31

A few minutes before visiting hours began, I climbed up the steps to the second floor where the adult mental health unit was located. At the top of the stairs, to my immediate left, was the check-in desk with a binder placed open on top. I signed the visitor's log it contained, with my first name and relationship to Adam only, and whispered his private patient identification number to the staff member standing behind it. Then I stashed my cell phone in the bank of lockers next to the desk while I waited for the bag of Adam's personal belongings I'd brought with me to be examined for prohibited items.

I learned early on what types of items were on the no-go list: food, medications, technology, and of course any kind of weapon. Most banned items were easy to identify, but as ridiculous as it might sound, it wasn't always easy to determine what the hospital would deem as a weapon. Obviously I wasn't attempting to bring in a gun or a knife, but at first I didn't think much about everyday items like belts, shoelaces, writing utensils, or fingernail clippers. Even a church program I brought in for Adam one Sunday afternoon was flagged as contraband, until one of the nurses removed the three tiny staples holding its pages together.

After Adam's bag was approved to be taken in, I found an empty space to lean against the wall and wait, alongside a few other visitors. Unlike most other waiting rooms, people completely avoid making small talk with one another. Maybe it's because they can't think of anything positive to say considering their situation, but it's more likely that they're just too busy giving themselves their own internal pep talk, like I always did, to worry about social niceties.

Whether or not that's true, my own observations of visitor body language over the course of a dozen or more visits made it apparent to me that everyone who comes to visit a loved one in the stress center is apprehensive about it. The rigid limbs, the empty and unfocused stares, the crossed legs and tightly folded arms; they're all dead giveaways that the stress center puts people on edge, and I was no exception. Although I had visited Adam numerous times before and knew the drill like the back of my hand, I never really got used to it.

The stress center is a far cry from the horror scenes depicting mental hospitals in the movies. There are no bars on the windows or torture devices hidden behind closed doors. The medical staff doesn't neglect or abuse their patients—I've personally witnessed countless examples of their employees going above and beyond to show Adam kindness even when he's been at his worst—and patients are provided with safe activities to pass the time and help them recover, like individual and group counseling sessions, yoga and art classes, and movie and game nights.

But that doesn't mean that it is a welcoming environment either, especially when you're sane and fully aware of your surroundings. Every time I was ushered through that heavily secured door—quickly, so no patients would attempt to squeeze out—my body would automatically tense up, and my mind would go on high alert. Then I'd instinctively take a glance behind me to watch my only exit door close, leaving me feeling trapped—trapped in a confined space with a dozen or more freely roaming patients who had all kinds of issues I didn't understand.

I didn't want any of them to feel judged by whatever nervous facial expressions I wore, but I was also afraid to make eye contact or to give them a friendly smile, thinking that might invite a conversation or confrontation I didn't want to have. So I chose to keep my head facing downward as I made my way directly to the nurses' station, unless I saw Adam first. Then we'd attempt to find a quiet area in the cafeteria or day room to sit together, where I'd count down the seconds until Adam said I could go or visiting hours were over.

This particular visit wasn't much different from the rest. Although admittedly I was a bit more apprehensive than usual, since I was so uncertain of how our time together would pan out. But as Adam often did, he surprised me, as he seemed genuinely happy that I had come.

"Hi, babe," he said as he hugged me. "I'm so glad you came."

"Uh, hi. Of course I came. You know I wouldn't miss a visit."

I wondered if the mishmash of medications and neurotransmitters in his brain had somehow caused him to forget the pandemonium from the day before, but that theory was soon squelched when I noticed the memento left on his bicep—a dark, grapefruit-sized bruise.

"Hey, what's up with that bruise? It looks awful."

"Oh this?" he said as he proudly pointed at it and laughed. "I got into a little disagreement with one of the guys that works here. It's no big deal though. He's really a great guy, and we're all good now."

I didn't find its existence to be quite as funny as he did, but I let it go, not wanting to push my luck.

From there, I let Adam do all the talking, even though the redundancy was utterly mind-numbing and his delusions began to grate on my nerves. I would've given anything to discuss something worthwhile, like our relationship or his illness, but I held my tongue, thinking a serious discussion about our new plan of attack would be better had during a later visit. Except there didn't end up being many more visits that go-around, because Adam was released just five days later when his seventy-two-hour hold came to a close. Remember, weekends don't count.

There had been no question in my mind that the hospital would file for another court commitment, especially with another manic episode and a brush with law enforcement to add to his thick medical file, so to say I was taken off guard by his quick release would be an understatement. So why? Why wasn't a court commitment pursued?

Because Adam was admitted to the hospital earlier into his mania than he had been the last time, so he was recovering more rapidly too. Coupling that with the fact that the mental health care laws had gotten even stricter than they were in the two years prior, the hospital's lawyers didn't think they had a strong enough case to spend the time and money seeking one. So with all that had happened, they just let him go.

32

I knew it would be up to me to figure out how to attack Adam's illness differently this time if we were going to avoid another major manic episode. Staying on medication and working regularly with a psychiatrist to fine-tune his dosages were a given, but I wanted to find a counselor as well, who could help Adam accept his illness and hold him accountable for following through with his treatment plan.

Adam had complained in the past that the outpatient counseling sessions that the hospital offered were unhelpful, since they took place in a group setting similar to that of Alcoholics Anonymous. He claimed that there were too many people in the same room, all having their own unique set of problems to tackle, making it impossible for anything constructive to get accomplished. As far as I knew, that could've been the case, yet I had my own suspicions that he was only using it as an excuse to avoid giving counseling a real shot.

But after he finished his court-mandated sessions during his previous manic episode, he made it clear to me that he would never go back, so I took it upon myself to find something that suited him better. I started by talking to my sister-in-law about the counseling program at our church.

"So what do you think about the church's counseling program?" I asked Emily. "I was thinking that Adam might feel more comfortable working with someone who shared the same beliefs and values as him, but I wasn't sure he'd be able to get in."

"I think he'd be able to get in, but I'm not certain that our church's counseling program is the best fit for him."

"Really? Why?"

"Because after I talked with the director of the counseling program, I got the feeling that Adam might be advised to stop taking his medication eventually."

"What? You've got to be kidding me. Why would a trained counselor even think to suggest that?"

To my knowledge, there isn't a single reputable doctor on the planet, who understands all the ins and outs of bipolar disorder, that would describe a consistent regimen of the proper medications as anything but essential to a patient's success. Nevertheless, there are people out there—generally uninformed people who have no real personal experience with mental illness—that believe that mental illnesses are not illnesses at all. Meaning, they don't believe the root cause of their symptoms is a biological one but instead a result of their own transgressions. Never mind the overabundance of scientific evidence that proves otherwise.

Now Adam had made plenty of poor decisions, which had exacerbated his symptoms, and he let his pride prevent him from sticking to his treatment plan. I knew that medication alone wasn't going to be enough to manage his illness, which is why I was looking for a counselor in the first place. Living a healthy lifestyle by exercising regularly, eating nutritious foods, avoiding drugs and alcohol, maintaining a consistent sleep schedule, and keeping his mindset right by focusing on God's truths were all important components of his mental health as well. Even so, the last thing he needed to hear from someone he trusted was that he should stop taking his medication, which he didn't want to take anyway.

"I don't know whether or not a counselor would actually suggest that, but I do think it's a possibility," Emily replied.

"And I can't afford to take that risk. Adam needs to stay on his medications, permanently."

"I know you can't, and I wouldn't take that risk either. I'll do my best to find someplace else. Okay?"

"Thanks, Emily. I appreciate it."

With Emily looking elsewhere for a counselor, I directed my attention toward the parts of Adam's recovery I thought I could control. I started by keeping track of everything: how much he was sleeping each night, when and how much medication he was taking, what he was eating and drinking, the amount of exercise he was getting, and how he was spending his time. I also tried to keep a pulse on his attitude toward his illness, paying close attention to his words and his body language to gauge where his level of acceptance really was. And wanting to be completely in the know this time, I demanded to be part of every one of his doctor's appointments, not trusting that he'd be honest with his psychiatrist about his progress or that he'd share what they had discussed with me.

I knew he didn't like having me tag along every time, asking questions and putting my two cents in when I felt he was withholding important information from his doctor, but he tolerated it.

"Do you really need to come to another one of my doctor's appointments? You'll have to take some time off from work."

"Yes, I do. It's not been that long since you were hospitalized, and I think I've more than earned the right to be there. Don't you?"

"Yes, you have, but you won't be able to keep this up forever. Eventually you're going to have to trust me."

He was right. I couldn't keep looking over his shoulder forever, constantly trying to monitor his every move. But until I gained more confidence in him, I was going to try to. Until he provided me with proof, over an extended period of time, that he would continue taking his medication, working with his doctor, and living a healthy lifestyle, all on his own, then I couldn't let up.

"I know, but it's going to take some time and a lot of hard work on your part."

33

A few weeks into Adam's recovery, my dad drove down to work on phase two of our house renovation, residing and retrimming the exterior of our home. I had been more than eager to remove the rotted wood trim and faded red siding from the day we took ownership, so as soon as we'd saved enough money to do so, I made plans with my dad, months ahead of time, to do the work.

Typically, his work schedule was jam-packed, especially in the summertime. It wasn't uncommon for him to have jobs booked back-to-back for six months or even a year in advance. And with him living so far away from us, I was hesitant to cancel when Adam became manic again, although I figured I might eventually have to. My dad had never witnessed Adam manic before—and I hoped he never would—but since Adam had been making such big strides toward stability since his release, I decided not to cancel.

In the time since his release from the stress center, Adam had done everything I asked of him and with very little grumbling. Each day, his attitude toward his illness seemed to improve, and so did his level of responsibility toward managing it. When I asked him about his medication or his next doctor's appointment, he no longer answered in an irritated tone or with an eye roll.

"Did you take your medication today?"

"Yep, I took my medication this morning, and I called in another refill because I noticed the bottles were getting low."

"What about your next doctor's appointment? Do you have one coming up?"

"I do. I made the next appointment on my last visit. You'll see I've added it to our shared calendar if you'd like to come."

But soon after my dad arrived, I noticed some small signs that Adam might be regressing. *Maybe he's not doing as well with all of this as I thought?* I knew that Adam had a special knack for telling people what they wanted to hear, and with the growing number of disappointments I had piling up, I certainly wanted to hear some good news for a change. *Is it possible that he's doing that to me? Am I falling for his good boy act just like everyone else?*

I didn't want to believe that I was. I was his wife, his best friend, and his caretaker. It had become my job, and my obsession really, to pay close attention to him and to get to know who he was and what he struggled with deep down inside. I thought I'd become good at seeing through his clever smoke screens, but maybe I'd been deceived by him again.

As much as I wanted to believe that I'd become immune to his deceptions, I couldn't ignore what my gut was telling me, that somehow Adam had managed to mislead me again. So on the morning of June 13, after Adam left for work, I opened the kitchen cabinet where we stored our medications and fitness supplements and pulled out two of his pill bottles to look for tangible proof.

One bottle contained Depakote, an anticonvulsant used to treat seizure disorders, as well as the common symptoms of bipolar mania. The other bottle contained Zyprexa, an antipsychotic used to treat the manic phase of bipolar disorder, along with the more aggressive symptoms of schizophrenia. Both medications act as mood stabilizers, but as Adam's psychiatrist explained, they do so in different ways and thus are more effective when taken together.

Zyprexa works by increasing the levels of gamma-aminobutyric acid, also known as GABA, in the brain—a neurotransmitter that relaxes the neurons and prevents them from firing as often. Whereas Depakote weakens the effects of dopamine and serotonin by blocking their corresponding neuroreceptors. These two neurotransmitters are often found to be elevated during bipolar mania, leading to feelings of euphoria, heightened energy levels, increased aggression, and an intense interest in sexual activity.

Adam's doctor intentionally prescribed them to be taken collectively. So if he was taking his medications correctly, as he had led me to believe he was, each bottle should've contained an equal number of dosages inside.

But they didn't. I counted their contents multiple times, hoping I had made an error in my haste, but I hadn't. From what I could tell, Adam had skipped at least seven days of his Zyprexa, and that was based on the assumption—a poor assumption I'm sure—that he hadn't missed a single dosage of his Depakote. *How could I be so naive?*

A flurry of negative emotions—anger, fear, and sorrow— flooded my mind and sent me into a panic. Out of sheer desperation, I called the church's counseling line and left an urgent message, begging for someone to come and try to persuade Adam to go back onto his medication before he lost all control again. Then I sat down to think and take some calming breaths, knowing I'd need a well-thought-out plan and a level head when I confronted him with my findings.

A couple of hours later, still without a word from the church or much of a plan to speak of, Adam pulled into the driveway on his lunch break, wanting to check in on the progress my dad had made on the house. With the muffled sounds of their conversation outside filtering through the front door, I paced back and forth in the living room, trying to prepare myself for what was bound to be the quarrel of the century.

Maybe this won't be as bad as I think. There could be a reasonable explanation for the excess medication I found in his Zyprexa bottle. Although I can't think of one right now. And if not, Adam might own up to his mistakes this time. I can work with that.

The sudden rattle of the doorknob and whoosh of the door swinging open caused me to jump backward, but before Adam could utter a word, I rushed straight toward him with the courage I had mustered up and asked him point-blank about his medication.

"Can you please tell me why your Zyprexa bottle has more pills in it than it should?"

I could tell by the bewildered look on his face that I had caught him off guard.

"Uh, what do you mean?" he asked, acting as if he was baffled by my question.

"I mean, there are at least an extra seven pills in this bottle than there should be." Then I shook the bottle in front of him. "I counted them, more than once."

"You counted them?" he said angrily.

"Sure did. I could tell that something wasn't right with you, and so I compared the number of pills in both of your medication bottles. I know you haven't been taking your medication like you should be. Why do you keep lying to me?"

When he realized that he'd been caught red-handed, and there was nothing he could say or do to escape the truth, he became irate.

"I'm not the problem. You're the problem. You have no right to go behind my back and look in my pill bottles," he shouted.

Normally, I would have backed down from the argument when I realized just how out of control Adam was becoming, but not this time. I was sick and tired of him doing whatever he wanted to, despite how it was hurting me, and I wasn't going to put up with it any longer. He was getting all too used to bulldozing over me, and I was getting all too used to letting him. So not thinking at all about the possible consequences, I stood up for myself and yelled right back at him.

"Don't put this on me, Adam. I have every right to count your pills, because you do nothing but lie, and your illness affects me too. When are you going to get it? Wasn't another hospitalization and an arrest enough of a wake-up call for you?"

Our collective screams at each other became so loud that my dad rushed in from outside to pull Adam away from me and into our backyard. Then after a brief but poignant conversation with my father about Adam's inability to take care of himself, let alone me, Adam sped out of the driveway with a squeal, and I sprinted up the stairs to pack.

34

The drive up to Northern Michigan had been a long one, but I was afraid that the 450 miles I was placing between Adam and me still wouldn't be enough. There was no telling what he would do when he came home to find that I had left, and the last thing I needed was to have him show up on my parents' doorstep in the middle of the night, filled with a particularly terrifying kind of rage that was unique to his current manic situation.

By God's grace though, that didn't happen, but the sheer possibility of it was enough to keep me tossing and turning all night long. So by the next morning, when the ugly reality of all that had happened began to sink into my weary brain, I couldn't see anything but darkness in my future.

I was thankful to be somewhere safe and to be temporarily removed from the bedlam Adam's unbridled illness and incessant dishonesty brought, but the torture he inflicted on my mind from afar was just as destructive. Countless questions—questions no one other than the good Lord himself had the answers to—spun around and around in my head, until I thought the tangled mess of doubt and confusion they spawned might strangle the life right out of me.

Would Adam hurt himself or someone else without me there? Would he be able to stabilize again, and if so, when? Did he ever truly love me, or had his feelings just been an illusion bred out of a bipolar mind? Would our marriage be able to withstand this? Did I even want it to?

Truthfully, I didn't know if I wanted the answers to those questions, but that didn't keep me from speculating. And with very little to occupy my time, other than an online graduate course I was struggling to wrap up, I speculated a lot, generally coming to the frightening conclusion that I needed to prepare myself for the worst-case scenario. Which at that point in time was losing Adam and the life we had built together, even though that life was currently in shambles.

Only I couldn't prepare myself for a future without him. I couldn't even hold it together when I tried to imagine it. Every time I did, my legs would buckle underneath me, and hot, heartbroken tears would pour out. *What can I do to fix this? How can I salvage what is left of our relationship? Is there anything I can do that I haven't already done?*

There wasn't. Whether I liked it or not, I was at the mercy of Adam. Until he started taking control of his own mental health—not only because it was the right thing to do but because he saw value in it—our marriage had no chance of surviving. And since I wasn't ready to give up on us yet, I had no other option except to sit in my childhood home and prayerfully wait.

Praying, that was the easy part. Not only did talking to God bring me comfort, but because I did it so often, it became as effortless as breathing and blinking. Waiting on the other hand, that was a whole different story, especially considering Adam's proven track record of unreliability. And as day after day ticked by without any noticeable improvement on Adam's end, I started to feel more like a caged prisoner than an escapee. *Will I ever be free again?*

In moments of weakness, I considered giving in and going home, knowing full well that doing so would've been a mistake, and probably a dangerous one. Those moments generally came after enduring one of Adam's hate-filled phone calls.

"This is ridiculous. You need to come home now. Stop being such a child. You're acting like your fifteen. Was running away your dad's idea? You need to start thinking for yourself."

And sometimes they came following a guilt-laced conversation with my father-in-law, who seemed more interested in my return than my well-being.

"You've been gone for a while now, Sydney, and Adam needs you here. We need you here. When do you think you'll be coming home? You're still part of our team, right?"

Fortunately, I had Tanya to keep me from giving in though. She was the counselor my sister-in-law had suggested I contact just before I confronted Adam about his medication. Not only was she a certified marriage counselor, but she was a registered nurse, a member of our church, and a strong, levelheaded woman who helped me develop and stick to a plan. And I reiterated the conditions of that plan repeatedly, to Adam and his family, no matter how angry or pathetic they sounded over the phone.

"Adam, I understand that you want me to come home, but I'm not coming home until you do as I ask. You need to go back to your doctor, start taking your medications consistently, and agree to go with me to counseling once I return. When I feel confident that you are doing all of these things, and you provide me with proof that you are, then I'll consider coming home."

At first, Adam didn't hear me. It's difficult to hear someone, let alone understand their point of view, when you're constantly yelling over them. And he did that a lot. He also called me names, shifted some blame, and abruptly hung up on me. But to be fair, I hung up on him sometimes too.

With time though, my message started to get through to him—whether that was due to my persistence or the voice of someone else I'll never know—because the tone and content of our phone calls finally began to change. And fourteen days into my unwanted sabbatical, after a solid week of civilized conversations, multiple confirmations given by Adam's doctor and his family that he had been taking his medications, and a sworn promise to attend a counseling session with Tanya, I apprehensively made the decision to drive home.

"Mom, Dad, I've decided it's time for me to head home."

"Are you sure you're ready?" my mom asked.

"You know you can stay here for as long as you need to," my dad added.

"I'm sure, and I know I can, but it's time. Adam has done everything I've asked of him, and I can't hide out here forever."

"Well, if you're really set on going, do you want me to come with you?" my dad asked.

"No, but thanks for the offer. Adam and I have a lot of things to work out between the two of us, and I can't see that happening with you there."

I may have sounded confident in my decision when I broke the news to my parents, but I was far from it. Although Adam had seemingly met all my demands, I had no guarantee that he wouldn't go back on his word the moment I stepped through our front door and he had what he wanted. Then I'd find myself in the same horrific position I was in before, but I'd be there alone, without the protective presence of my father.

A big part of me knew I wasn't ready to leave the shelter of my childhood home, and in the grand scheme of things, staying another week or two would've given Adam a better opportunity to demonstrate whether his dedication to self-care, and ultimately our marriage, was real. It would have provided me with some more assurance that it was indeed safe to return too, but with another school year vastly approaching and the countless number of surprises I expected to encounter upon my return, I decided to rip the Band-Aid off, ready or not, and just go.

35

On my drive back home, I had more than enough time to think about all the different ways in which my reunion with Adam could go. I practiced what I would say to him, thought through who I would call if I needed help, and lined up a safe place to stay for a while if my own home wasn't an option. But even after having hours in the car to prepare, I still didn't feel ready.

At the sight of our neighborhood sign, I broke into a nervous sweat, and the uneasiness that had been residing in the pit of my stomach intensified further, becoming a deep, take-you-to-your-knees kind of pain. Maybe I was a complete fool for coming home so soon, especially by myself. *Why hadn't I let my dad come with me when he offered?* It had been a combination of things really—wanting to spare my dad from any more heartache, wanting to protect Adam from any more shame, and feeling as though I needed to face Adam alone, even though I was afraid to.

I gripped the steering wheel tightly to subdue the pulsating waves of fear that were taking ahold of my body and to keep myself from turning the car around. *This is just pitiful. I shouldn't be afraid to return to my own home or to be alone with my husband.* But I was. Adam had given me more than enough reason to be.

Even so, there was still a small flame burning inside of me that was pushing me to face my fears and try to repair some of the damage Adam had done. And when I saw the extent of that damage for myself—which included much more than the crippling blow our marriage had suffered—that tiny flame was instantly set ablaze and transformed into a raging inferno.

As I walked in through our front door, I was greeted by Adam with a hug and a kiss, which was a real relief until he said, "I'm so glad you're home, babe. I want to show you what I did upstairs."

Oh no. What did he do?

I followed behind him up the stairs and into our laundry room.

"What do you think?" he said cheerfully. "Now you have the extra storage you've been asking for."

"Uhh, it's nice," I fibbed. It wasn't nice. Without talking to me first, he had repainted our laundry room an awful, bright red color, which stuck out like a sore thumb in our otherwise tastefully neutral home. "Did you do this by yourself?"

"I had a little help from a friend I met at the stress center. He was a big help when it came to installing the cabinets."

Some friend.

I could tell by his enthusiasm that he thought his surprise laundry room makeover would please me, and I was glad that pleasing me mattered to him again. So even with the red splotches of paint he left on the floor and trim, and the crookedly hung cabinets that remained shelf-less for almost two years until my dad finished the job, I said, "It's great, Adam. Thank you."

I couldn't, however, hide my feelings about what he did to the outside of our house.

"Adam, why does it look like there is water seeping in and around this window?"

"That's probably because I tore off all our old siding while you were gone."

"You did what?"

"Well, I was getting impatient, and I thought I'd take it all off to save some time for your dad."

"Adam, my dad isn't going to be able to come back anytime soon to work on our house. He set time aside for us, and you blew it when you stopped taking your medication."

"I know. I'm sorry."

"Yeah, well we can't leave our house unprotected. That's why my dad was only tearing off a small amount at a time."

"I'll fix it. I'll find someone else."

"No, you won't. I'll take care of it."

And if that wasn't enough to deal with, my blood pressure shot through the roof when Adam came home a few days later to tell me that he'd been fired. I wasn't shocked that he'd lost his job. I can only imagine what inappropriate behavior went on in his workplace while he was manic, but with all the money we had flying out of our accounts, the timing couldn't have been worse.

There were medical bills, the extra cost of having to pay another contractor to finish siding the house, and all the frivolous things Adam had bought while I was away. While manic, he tended to waste money on things we didn't need. For example, he bought dozens of new bathroom and kitchen towels, even though ours were practically new, and hundreds of dollars' worth of fitness clothes, all of which were a size too small for him.

"Adam, I'm not upset with you, but I am worried. We have a lot of things to pay for, so we're going to have to tighten things up for a while until you find another job."

"Oh we'll be fine. We have plenty of money. I was sick of that job anyways."

"We're okay for now I guess, but you can't go without medical insurance. You need to start looking for another job, and in the meantime, I'll talk with HR about adding you to my insurance plan. I'm sure it won't be cheap though."

"See, it's no big deal."

It's not a big deal to you, because you know I'll take care of everything, just like I always do.

Adam didn't seem to be bothered by the loss of his job, despite the extra pressure it put on me; instead, all he wanted to talk about was his latest business venture, his third since we'd been together. While I was away, he had opened a business account, purchased promotional items—business cards, ballpoint pens, and T-shirts—and roped a few unsuspecting individuals, who clearly had no idea that he had bipolar disorder, into serving on his board of directors.

"Getting fired is actually a good thing for me. Now I have all kinds of time to work on developing my new business. And you'll see. We are going to make so much money from it."

Apparently, he hadn't learned anything from his past entrepreneurial failures.

"I'm glad you're happy, Adam, but getting a new company up and running takes time. It could be months or even years before you make any money from it."

Personally, I didn't think Adam would ever become a successful entrepreneur, nor did I want him to. It wasn't that he wasn't smart enough or that he couldn't come up with promising ideas, but his mental instability made him irresponsible. He had no business trying to manage a company of his own when his mood and reasoning skills were all over the map. Adam making decisions that would affect the health of a company, and the lives of the people working there, was just another disaster waiting to happen.

I couldn't tell him that though. It would have crushed him and ultimately pushed him harder to prove me wrong. Instead, I discouraged him from placing all his eggs into one basket, or should I say *our* eggs into one basket—something I had been doing since he started grumbling about how unfulfilled he felt in his current position months before.

"Adam, I know you really want this new business idea of yours to take off and that becoming an entrepreneur is your dream, but you can't force it to happen. You shouldn't rush something that's so important to you. So I'd like you to look for other jobs in the meantime. I think it's only smart."

"I guess it is."

"It is, and you never know what connections you'll make if you find another job. Maybe you'll meet some people who can help you with it."

"That's a good point."

"Right? I wouldn't think you'd want a big gap in your résumé either."

"All right, I'll look online and submit some résumés, but I'm not going to take a job just to take one."

"I can live with that."

Just days after he was let go, Adam got an interview for a project manager position at a trendy software development company that focused on helping start-ups.

"Babe! I got the job, and I think it's going to be perfect for me."

"That's great. It really is, lovey. I'm so proud of you."

It was great news and a huge blessing to have avoided long-term unemployment. And I was genuinely happy that Adam was excited about his new position, a position that was nearly a perfect fit. Not only did it allow him to work in the business field alongside all kinds of successful entrepreneurs, but it also satisfied his fierce desire to be in a position of leadership—just as he had been in while serving with the military.

And the best part of all, other than the steady paycheck and medical insurance it provided, was that he'd no longer have to travel, except locally. Which meant less worry for me and a safer working environment for him. As far as I was concerned, his new job was a gift sent straight down from the heavens. A gift I prayed he would protect and care for.

36

Once I got the house taken care of and our finances back on track, I focused on what was most important to me—my marriage to Adam—and scheduled our first counseling session with Tanya. At the time, counseling was a foreign concept to me. I had never participated in counseling before, other than in a few premarital sessions over Skype with the military chaplain who performed our wedding ceremony, so I wasn't particularly comfortable with the idea.

I felt self-conscious enough just shedding a few silent tears in the back of a dark movie theater, so I imagined airing out my personal problems and discussing my deepest, darkest feelings with Tanya would be a thousand times worse. But because our marriage was riddled with problems, problems that were so intricately entangled with one another, I knew that we needed someone to help us unravel it all. And if spilling my guts in front of a near stranger was what it was going to take for that to happen, then I was all in. But would Adam be?

I doubted it. It's difficult for anyone to put their heart into something they've been forced into, and since Adam had only agreed to attend counseling as part of my ultimatum for coming home, I didn't expect him to do much more than walk through the motions. During our first session, however, he openly answered every question Tanya threw at him, giving her an intimate and up-close look into his struggles with bipolar disorder, as if it was nothing at all. I don't know if it was the overabundance of manic neurotransmitters still floating around in his brain, or if he was being fueled by a genuine fear of losing me for good, but either way, his A+ effort made me believe that counseling could work for us.

And in some ways, it did, by providing us with the push we needed to divulge how we had both been hurt by his illness.

"Sydney, can you share how Adam's illness has impacted you?" Tanya asked.

"Well ..." I took a deep breath. "Being married to someone with bipolar disorder is overwhelming to say the least, but because Adam hasn't been properly taking care of himself, it's turned me into someone who is always exhausted and overly anxious. I'm constantly watching and waiting for the next catastrophe to strike."

"So when Adam doesn't choose to take care of himself, how does that make you feel?"

"Scared, obviously, but also unloved. When he doesn't take his meds, or prioritize sleep, or limit his alcohol consumption, he is knowingly putting himself at a higher risk for another manic episode, and that puts us both in danger. It also pushes more responsibilities onto me, and that isn't fair."

"Okay, so what about you, Adam? How has your illness impacted you? How does having bipolar disorder make you feel?"

"It's been hard to accept my diagnosis because people with mental illnesses are often held back by negative stigmas, and I don't want to be held back. I have things I want to do and goals I want to accomplish. I know what I'm supposed to do to help manage my illness, but those things aren't easy. The medications come with side effects, and those side effects make it difficult for me to live the life I want to, but my intention has never been to hurt Sydney."

Gaining some perspective from the other's point of view was certainly beneficial and inspired us both to show more compassion for each other. But no amount of empathy or understanding was going to make Adam's illness disappear. It was likely that he'd always feel held back by his responsibility to manage his bipolar disorder and that I'd always be on the lookout for potential fires that needed to be put out. So instead of wallowing in self-pity over the difficulties we couldn't change, we worked with Tanya to develop a plan that would help shape our future together into one we could both live with and maybe even enjoy someday.

Essentially, this plan was based around two goals, the first of which was helping Adam to become successful at managing his illness. Adam agreed to work closely with his doctor to monitor his mood and behaviors, to keep taking his medications and notify his doctor when changes needed to be made to them, and to avoid his manic triggers whenever possible. To help with this, we removed all alcohol and tobacco products from our home, we committed to sticking to the same workout and sleep schedule, and we put some financial safeguards in place, so I could monitor his spending, since frivolous spending often occurred on his way up to, down from, and in the middle of his manic episodes.

The second goal was about rebuilding trust—specifically, my trust in Adam—and we knew that it wasn't going to come easily. It goes without saying that Adam had a lot of work to do to make up for all the lies told and promises broken. He'd have to show some long-term consistency with his treatment and be fully transparent with me about his progress before I could even begin to believe him as trustworthy, but that didn't mean that I was completely off the hook either.

Just as Adam had to push himself to step up each day, I had to consciously make myself step back, even though my bruised heart was begging me not to. It wasn't that I didn't want to relinquish some control—I was more than ready to drop some of the extra weight I had been carrying—but I had become so accustomed to being the only responsible party in the relationship that I was afraid Adam couldn't do what needed to be done. Afraid or not though, I knew that I had to, even if that meant letting Adam fail. It was the only way I could give him an opportunity to prove to himself, and to me, that he could do better.

After several weekly counseling sessions with Tanya and a lot of hard work, our relationship began to strengthen, and Adam's mental health began to improve. Although it was a struggle at times to follow through with the plan we had made, our shared desire to save our marriage compelled us both to fight hard for it. But it wasn't too long after Adam and I finally began to find our footing together again that I received an unexpected phone call from Tanya.

"Hi, Tanya. How are you?"

"Oh, I'm fine. You?"

"I'm good. Are we still on for this week's counseling session?"

"We are, but it will have to be our last one."

"What?" I was genuinely shocked. "Why?"

"I think it's time. I don't think the two of you can get much more out of our sessions together."

I can't believe this. We need her. I need her. We were just starting to move in the right direction. How can she possibly give up on us now?

It didn't make any sense to me. She had put so much effort into us, providing us with exactly what we needed—emotional support

and blatant honesty, practical solutions and accountability—
so dropping us seemed like a cruel, coldhearted, push-me-to-
the-ground-after-I-had-just-gotten-up kind of thing to do. The
kind of thing that was completely out of character for her. She
had been the only person who managed to make me feel like I
wasn't alone in the mess that my life had become, and one of
the few who had even the slightest grasp on how complicated
being married to Adam could be. I just couldn't imagine moving
forward without her.

"Please, Tanya, give us a little more time," I begged between
panic-stricken sobs.

"I can't, Sydney. I'm sorry. The truth is the real root of your
problems is not marital in nature, and I'm a certified marital
counselor, not a psychologist. There are other couples, with true
marital issues, that need me."

She was right. Our life together hadn't been falling apart
because of personality conflicts, or financial disagreements, or
Adam's addictions to nicotine and alcohol. They weren't due to
poor communication either, or even the lies Adam had told. These
were simply symptoms of one core problem, and that problem was
Adam's defiance toward his bipolar disorder.

"Look, I have witnessed the two of you making progress as
a couple for sure, and Adam seems to be following through with
the promises he has made, but I don't think he's truly convinced
that his mental illness is real. Or at least that it requires as much
attention as we both know it does. Until he pushes himself out of
that well-worn rut of denial, any work done in marriage counseling
is simply futile."

I said nothing in response.

"I'm only a phone call away, anytime you need to talk. I'll
be praying that Adam continues to take care of himself, and of
course I'll be praying for you. I'll see you at our last session, okay?"

"Okay."

The longer I let her words set in, the more I understood her decision, but I still couldn't help but feel abandoned by her, which is why I didn't do much other than cry and blow my nose at our last session. Adam, on the other hand, was more than pleased to say goodbye to Tanya for good.

"It's been a pleasure, Tanya," he said with a smile as he shook her hand. "We both appreciate your help. Thank you."

He wasn't fooling anyone with his words of gratitude, least of all me. His interest in the counseling process had started to wane sessions ago—grumbling about the book we were asked to read together, complaining about the time counseling required of us, and even accusing Tanya of showing favoritism toward my point of view every now and again. It was obvious that he was more than ready to be done with counseling and thrilled to be rid of the extra accountability it provided, which was both irritating to me and worrisome. So I communicated those feelings to Adam by giving him the cold shoulder on our car ride home.

Despite not understanding why I was upset with him exactly, nor comprehending the vast number of fears and insecurities that leaving Tanya behind brought to the surface for me, he did recognize that I was hurt and needed comforting. So after several minutes of tension-filled silence between us, he tried to be the bigger person by being the first to break it.

"It's going to be okay," he said as he squeezed my knee. "Even though we're done with counseling, you have no reason to worry. I'm still committed to carrying on with my treatment plan and upholding the promises I've made to you. I can take care of myself, with or without counseling, and I will, for the both of us."

I had been desperately waiting to hear those words come out of his mouth for the better part of two years, and if they had, even a few months earlier, I would've gotten down on my hands and knees and thanked the good Lord above for finally answering my most fervent of prayers. But with all that had happened between us, specifically that which led to our recent separation, I had a hard time believing that his self-proclaimed commitment was anything more than talk.

"You aren't just saying that because you know I'm upset, are you?"

"No. I'm saying it because it's the truth. I can do this without Tanya."

"We'll see," I mumbled under my breath.

37

I stumbled into our en suite bathroom, as I did most mornings before work, with my eyes still closed and my mind in a drowsy, disorienting fog. A fog that often lifted slowly, lasting throughout most of my morning routine, until its last remaining remnants could be chased away by taking a few sips of hot, fresh-brewed coffee as I hurried out to the car.

I had no reason to expect that that particular morning would be anything out of the ordinary. The day ahead was planned out like every school day had been before it: an hour to get ready, fifteen minutes to drive to work, another twenty minutes to set up my classroom before the first rush of kids blew in, followed by eight straight hours of teaching, policing, counseling, and whatever else the job threw my way. But while using the bathroom that morning, I caught a glimpse of something that startled me, something I hadn't seen in over three years—blood.

It's funny how just a few unexpected spots of blood held enough power to jerk me right out of my sluggish state as I tried to reconcile what I was looking at. *This can't mean what I think it means, can it?* I hardly ever missed taking a birth control pill and hadn't remembered missing a single dose in months. *But why else would I suddenly spot bleed like this? Maybe it's just stress induced.* Stress had been a constant fixture in my life after all. *But what if it isn't? What if I'm …*

There was no point in trying to speculate any further. The only way I'd be able to go about the rest of my day was if I knew the actual reason for this unforeseen occurrence, so I found the number to my gynecologist's office and called right away. As the phone rang and I waited for someone to pick up, I paced my bedroom floor in double time, trying to release some of the nervous energy that was rapidly growing inside of me.

After being transferred to a nurse and explaining my situation to her, I was placed back on hold to wait for my doctor. While I continued to wait, I continued to pace. I shuffled my stocking feet faster and faster across the carpeted floor, generating more static electricity in those few maddening minutes than I likely had in an entire year.

"Hello," my doctor said. "What can I do for you, Sydney?"

"Hi," I said nervously. "As I was explaining to your nurse, I'm experiencing a bit of breakthrough bleeding."

"Has this ever happened before?"

"No, it hasn't. I haven't seen a drop of blood in the past three years. I stopped taking the placebo pills long ago, to avoid having a period all together."

"Okay. Have you missed taking any of your birth control recently?"

"No, not that I can remember, and I'm pretty good about taking it at the same time every night too."

"All right, that's good. Have you been taking any new medications?"

"No, I haven't. Could stress be the cause?"

"It could, but I doubt it."

"I couldn't be pregnant, could I?"

"Well, it's a possibility. Birth control isn't 100 percent effective. I'd suggest you start by taking a pregnancy test, and then we can go from there. Why don't you call my office once you've taken one, and we can talk about your next steps."

"Uh, okay," I said faintly.

She hadn't told me anything I didn't already know, but somehow her candid words still stunned me, so I stopped listening to anything else she had to say after that. All I could think about was getting to the nearest drugstore to purchase a pregnancy test, so I would know for sure if I was among the anomalous 1 percent of women who end up pregnant even while they are consistently taking their birth control. But looking at the time, it had to wait. I was already running late and had no choice except to hang in suspense until the workday was over.

And that workday seemed to drag on at a snail's pace, but my mind raced at a breakneck speed. Any second that it wasn't fully occupied with the needs of my students, and sometimes even when it should've been, all I could think about was the possibility of being pregnant and what that would look like, considering the copious array of difficulties we were already fighting as a family of two.

Babies are a lot of work, and they can cause a lot of stress. They're loud, they're demanding, and they don't often sleep through the night. In essence, a baby would be the ultimate trigger for Adam's manic episodes. How could I possibly divide my attention between a baby's needs and his?

It would've helped if I could've talked to Adam about it, so I could place some of my apprehensions onto him and begin preparing for what I was sure was inevitable. But each time I found a few free minutes to send him a text or give him a call, I stopped myself. He deserved to be told such life-changing news in person, and honestly, I wasn't ready to open Pandora's box with him until I knew I was pregnant.

So I toughed it out on my own, checking my classroom clock countlessly throughout the day, until finally the time read 4:05 p.m. With five minutes left in the school day, I gathered my personal belongings, put on my jacket, and slung my purse over my shoulder, fully prepared to run out of my classroom, right on the heels of my last student.

"Come on, everyone. Pack up your supplies, put your stools up on your desks, and line up at the door," I said loudly, not wanting to wait an additional second for those who liked to lag behind.

At the sound of the final bell, I ushered everyone through my classroom door, whether they were ready or not. And I made my way through the hall, down the stairs, across the student center, and out to the staff parking lot in record time, weaving in and around hundreds of students wearing oversized backpacks like an NFL running back. So by the time the buses were filled, I was long gone, already halfway to my neighborhood drugstore.

I continued moving at my frantically fast pace all the way home and up into my bathroom, slowing down only momentarily as I selected from the pharmacy's vast supply of pregnancy tests, looking for one that was reliable and easy to read. Then, with the bathroom door closed and locked behind me, I broke open the box, ripped open one of the interior packages, and did my thing.

Two minutes later, after asking God to help me handle whatever was about to come my way, I took a deep breath, pulled the test off the bathroom counter, and with one eye just slightly open, I peered down to see the results displayed in the test window. It was negative. I repeated the process again with a second test, to be sure the results were indeed accurate, and once again, it read negative. *Thank you, God.*

I sighed in relief as my heart rate began to normalize, until I heard Adam's heavy footsteps coming up the stairs and down the hallway toward our bedroom. Not having any time to think about how I was going to tell him, I just blurted out an explosion of hurried words as soon as he stepped through the bathroom door.

"This morning when I went to the bathroom, I found a few drops of blood, and so I thought I might be pregnant. I called my gynecologist, and she told me that I needed to take a pregnancy test. So I had to wait all day before I could go to the pharmacy and get one. I wanted to tell you, but I decided it would be better to wait until I knew for sure."

He said nothing as I momentarily paused to take a breath.

"So I went to the drugstore as soon as school was over. I took two pregnancy tests just before you came home, and they were both negative."

I had expected him to feel a bit ambushed by the news— having children wasn't something we had talked about much, not since before we were married—so I assumed he'd feel relieved, as I did, when the shock wore off and he learned that I wasn't pregnant. But as soon as he heard me say that the tests were negative, a short-lived but hard to miss look of disappointment flashed across his face. A look that quickly turned my feelings of relief into sadness because the possibility of having a baby should've been cause for celebration, not a reason to fear.

Up until that moment, we had been operating under an agreement we had made as an engaged couple, that we would wait at least three years before trying to have a baby, wanting to establish a solid marriage relationship first. And with all that we had been dealing with as a result of Adam's illness, I hadn't given the idea of having kids a second thought, even though that three-year mark was only a few short months away. Circumstances had forced me to now though, and my new thoughts on the matter were nothing short of heartbreaking: we couldn't have kids, not now, not later, not ever.

I wanted to have kids, and Adam did too, but doing so wouldn't be right. Our home was too chaotic, and Adam, no matter how hard he worked on managing his illness, would always be unpredictable. Fearing for my own safety was one thing, but putting a child at risk would be criminal.

And there was always the possibility that any biological children we had could end up with bipolar disorder too. I couldn't purposely do that to a child, and I couldn't imagine taking care of a child with a mental illness while trying to support a husband with one as well. So as sad as it was, I came to two important conclusions that day: first, staying with Adam meant sacrificing having children, and second, getting pregnant, despite doing everything in my power to prevent it, would likely mean I'd have to leave him.

38

Cracks—eventually the truth always finds a way to create cracks, and in Adam's case, his true feelings about managing his bipolar disorder began to create hairline fractures in his fortitudinous facade as another holiday season approached. His attitude had been souring as he grew tired of his safer and more subdued way of life. And eventually, those promises he had made so easily just a couple of months prior became burdens to him, burdens he griped about almost daily.

"I'm sick of feeling tired all the time. I can't work out like I used to. I have a hard time waking up in the morning, and I'm putting on weight because I'm always hungry. This medication is wrecking everything."

"It's not wrecking everything, Adam. It's preventing you from having another manic episode."

"So I guess I'm just supposed to sit around here, getting fatter and being miserable then?"

"Obviously I don't want that, but your priority needs to be your mental health. If you think your medications are too strong for you, then you need to go see your doctor again and work that out with him. Going off your medications is not an option."

"I know. I know," he said indignantly.

His attitudinal shift toward the plan we had put in place to preserve our future together came as no surprise to me. Living a life that is so carefully controlled and saturated with restrictions wouldn't be easy on anyone, but for the free spirits like Adam—those who thrive on spontaneity and thirst for the freedom to do as they please—it can be downright disheartening.

"Let's go out for a drink tonight. We never go out anymore."

"You know you aren't supposed to mix alcohol with your medications, Adam."

"Come on. I'm just going to have one. You need to stop worrying all the time, Syd."

"I don't think it's a good idea."

"You can't expect me to never go out again. I need to have some fun once in a while. You do too."

"I'm not saying you can't have any fun, but I don't see why alcohol must be involved. It shouldn't be that important to you, but your health should be."

There are always hurdles to jump when pursuing something of value, so it was just a matter of time before Adam's perpetual pursuit of healthy living would force him to face an obstacle that would make him stop and question whether the effort needed to overcome it was worth it to him in the end. I had hoped that by the time that day came, he'd be able to come to the conclusion that it was, in fact, worth it.

I hoped that he'd believe in his own heart that his illness was undeniably real and undoubtedly dangerous when not cared for. That he'd recognize that our safety, our well-being, and our marriage were not only dependent on his commitment to managing his illness but were exponentially more important to him than his desire to be unhindered and unconstrained. And most of all, I hoped that the very second he saw that figurative brick wall in front of him, he'd jump at the chance to scale it, so he could continue pushing upward and onward toward what he knew for himself to be a better life, despite the sacrifices he'd repeatedly have to make.

But for some reason, a reason only God Himself knows, Adam still wasn't there yet even though we had suffered through so much in the aftermath of his manic episodes. Still, I believed that the scales would fall from his eyes eventually, and he'd finally see things for the way they truly were. So in the meantime, I refused to let him quit, no matter how many times he protested loudly in frustration or grumbled under his breath.

"I can't do this anymore. I'm done taking these medications."

"Yes you can, and you're not going off your medications. We can go to the doctor together if you want and see about reducing the dosage."

"It probably won't make a difference."

"Maybe not, but you'll never know if you don't try. You promised me that you would stay on medication, and breaking that promise is not only irresponsible but completely unacceptable."

"Ugh! Fine!"

Remaining calm but steadfast in my pursuit to keep him on track with his treatment plan prevented a lot of outward strife between us, and the very real threat of losing me seemed to keep Adam motivated to stay on his medications as well. But what it didn't do was prevent him from harboring resentment toward me. Resentment that generally made an appearance in the form of nasty little, passive-aggressive behaviors, which personally stung more than his usual and more conspicuous ways of communicating anger.

"Where have you been, Adam? I was starting to worry about you."

"Work."

"Okay. Why didn't you send me a text to tell me you were going to be late?"

"It wasn't planned. I just forgot."

"Well, I sent you a couple of texts, because I was trying to figure out what to do for dinner. You could have responded on your way home at least."

"All right. I will next time. It's not that big of a deal. Stop being such a helicopter wife."

"A what?"

"A helicopter wife. You know, because you're always hovering."

"Adam, letting me know you're going to be late is just the polite thing to do."

"Fine. I'm sorry. If you must know, I stayed after work to have a drink with one of my coworkers at the bar next door. It was just one, so don't freak out."

Despite how much his snide comments and inconsiderate behavior hurt, I chose to let them roll off my back, expecting his resentment to diminish over time. One day, the vital importance of caring for his illness would become clear to him, and he'd realize that I wasn't the one standing in his way but the one standing solidly in his corner, fighting hard for him while facing my own set of adversities.

And I was right; his resentment toward me did dwindle with time. Not because he acquired the insight he had been lacking for so long but because the dark clouds of bipolar depression came swooping over him, numbing all feelings he had for me and pretty much everything else. For months, I hardly saw him do anything other than lie in bed, although he managed to hold onto his job despite frequently going into work late, often coming home early, and sometimes not going into work at all.

He had no interest in anything, not even the things that normally excited him, like lifting weights, playing his guitar, watching a college basketball game, or even his business ventures. He neglected his personal hygiene—showering, shaving, and brushing his teeth were viewed as optional—and he abandoned all of his responsibilities at home, leaving our cars unserviced, our yard full of leaves, ice, and then snow, and his clothes—which I washed, dried, and folded for him every week—spread throughout the spare bedroom, some in heaping piles on the bed and others randomly tossed on the floor.

I tried everything I could think of to pull him up and out of the deep pit of sadness he had fallen into, but nothing, even momentarily, helped to raise his spirits. I tried cooking him nice meals, but he wouldn't get out of bed to eat them. I tried planning special events out, but he refused to go. I tried turning on some romantic music, lighting a few sweet-smelling candles, and slipping into a new negligee to entice him, but still he remained aloof and apathetic. Even lying in bed next to him, so he wouldn't feel so alone, proved ineffective. He'd just slide to the very edge of the bed and face the opposite direction, unwilling to talk or even touch.

It became all too common for days to go by without Adam uttering a single word to me, and the little conversation we did have only served to hurt and terrify.

"Adam, sit up and look at me. I want to talk with you."

"Leave me alone," he said as he turned over in bed and covered his head with his pillow.

"Please, Adam, you've been feeling down for months, and it's not getting any better. We can figure this out together. I'm worried about you, and I miss you."

"You never should have married me. Just go live your own life and forget about me."

I can't say I completely disagreed with him. If I had been told the truth about Adam's illness and had been given even a clue as to how difficult life would be with him, I likely wouldn't have married him.

"Maybe I shouldn't have married you, but you asked me to, and I did. There's no going back on that now, so I can't go live my own life as if you don't exist. I don't want to. I love you, and I hope you love me too."

"Honestly, I think everyone would be better off if I was dead."

"Don't say that, Adam. That isn't true."

It was hard to hear him talk like that, and even harder to know that he meant it. But what was worse was realizing that this wasn't just a small bout of discontentment and self-doubt like before. This was an exceedingly cruel and abundantly ruthless depressive episode that no one had the power to coax him out of. One that could've easily taken him away from me permanently if he didn't choose to get professional help.

Getting help, however, means seeking help, and considering he hardly had enough strength to lift his head from his pillow, leaving the house to do so was completely out of the question. So, without the support of his doctor, who could adjust his medications to meet his new set of needs, or a counselor he could trust, to help him clear the dark thoughts and sinister lies from his mind, he kept slipping deeper and deeper into the doldrums of despair, and I was forced to sit by and watch. And the longer I watched and the further he sank, the greater the crevasse of separation between us grew, giving rise to some intense feelings of loneliness on my part, which only worsened with all the time I spent alone.

I left the house only when I absolutely had to, afraid of what Adam might do while I was gone. So I became more desperate to connect with others—with friends who could take my mind off my troubles, bring a little joy back into my life, and remind me that I was still loved and valued by someone—but I didn't. I had become so secluded from the outside world that no one really knew how bad it had gotten, and not wanting to pull anyone else into the vortex of misery that seemed to be permanently residing within our home, I didn't reach out to tell them either. So I found myself following in Adam's footsteps, down into my own dreary chasm of depression.

For me, life became nothing more than a vicious cycle of monotony and dread. There was no happiness, no laughter, no love, nothing to look forward to, and sadly no sign that things would change. There was just work, household chores, and an inanimate and unresponsive husband who was fading right out of existence in front of my very eyes. So eventually, as one might expect, it became too much for me to handle. Every day, it felt like another hundred-pound plate was being added to the tall stack of weights sitting on top of my chest, and I could feel my sternum and ribs cracking under all the pressure, warning me that sooner or later it would be too late if I didn't find a way to escape.

But how could I escape? Could I run? I could run and run and run until I finally felt like I could breathe again, but I knew that wouldn't work. I couldn't start a new life with my current one left completely up in the air, and I couldn't deal with the guilt I'd surely have felt for leaving Adam behind. So instead, I entertained the awful thought that the only surefire way I could be free from the life I hated, the life that was slowly killing me anyway, without having to endure the self-fabricated guilt and the guilt inflicted on me by others, was to end it.

And I thought about it a lot, especially about how I'd choose to do it. I'd call in sick but get ready in the morning as usual. Then I'd drive around town until I was certain that Adam had left for work, the only place he ever went. Once he had, I'd pull my car back into the garage, close the garage door, and let the car run for a while, while I swallowed a bottle full of sleeping pills. Then, when I started to feel groggy, I'd put my earbuds in to listen to some soft, calming music while I lay comfortably in the back seat.

And as my lungs and bloodstream filled with carbon monoxide, I'd drift off slowly, taking my last breath on earth and my first in the presence of the Almighty God above.

It seemed simple, peaceful even, but I'm glad to say that I never attempted it, and I know I can thank the Lord for that. In my weakest moments, when my mind would fixate on this plan, God always found a way to direct my thoughts in the opposite direction. It could've been through an unexpected text from a friend, an unplanned phone call from my mom, or a kind word from a coworker, but no matter the means, God always reminded me that I was loved and that He had a better future planned for me.

39

By the end of January 2015, I finally began to see some small rays of hope shining down on us, as Adam's dark clouds of depression slowly began to break up and dissipate. I didn't know why his mood was starting to improve—maybe his depressive episode had simply run its course—but the reason behind it really didn't matter to me. I was just thankful to see a light at the end of the long, dark tunnel we had been crawling through for months, grateful to be crawling out of it with both of us still alive.

And I found myself feeling uncharacteristically optimistic, even though the possibility of a relapse was always on the table. I knew, too, that even if he didn't relapse, it would take a while longer before he'd fully make it out of the woods—several more months actually—but seeing Adam trending in a positive direction for the first time in a long time felt like something to celebrate. So after almost three years of saying no to Adam's pleading, I decided to surprise him with a yes. A yes I knew would likely put more work on me but would give him something to look forward to. Something tangible that would say thank you for hanging in there, and that's how we ended up with Max.

"Adam, I've been thinking about it for a while now, and I'm finally ready to get a dog."

"Really?" he said enthusiastically.

"Really," I said with a smile. "You've suffered through a tough couple of months—we both have—and I think getting a dog is a great way to celebrate us getting through them. I also want to tell you how proud I am that you've continued taking your medications."

"Thank you," he said sincerely. "You won't regret this. I'll find us the perfect dog."

I had been leery about adding any living thing into our chaotic mix for obvious reasons, but from the very moment I told Adam I was ready to get a dog, my misgivings disappeared when I saw how excited he was. Within seconds of hearing the news, he ran into his office and glued himself to his computer screen, surfing the internet for hours, eager to find our new puppy. It was magnificent to watch, not actually watching him scroll through and click on countless websites about the friendliest dog breeds or online ads with puppies for sale, but seeing him happy and full of ambition again, like he was when I first met him.

And after days of internet research and numerous conversations about our allergy issues, my repulsion toward loose dog hair, the size of dog we thought we could handle, and our personal preferences in doggie personality, we settled on a sweet-natured, curly-haired, miniature Goldendoodle named Wiggles that was born the day after Christmas. Wiggles is a ridiculous name—hence the immediate name change over to Max—but he truly did wiggle his way into my heart well before I met him.

Max was the absolute best the Goldendoodle breed has to offer—a breed known for its intelligence, affection, vivacity, and teddy bear–like appearance. Better still, he gave us a much-needed distraction from the suffering and sadness we had been through, and he gave us the opportunity to strengthen our bond as we worked together as a couple on something that was fun and normal.

I'll never forget the day we went to pick him up because everything about that day was nearly perfect, and days like those were hard to come by at that point. On the morning of Saturday, February 21, we climbed into the car with our back seat full of all kinds of new puppy things—a travel carrier, a soft blanket, some toys, a couple of treats, a tiny harness, and a leash—and our hearts filled even more so with a shared feeling of exuberant anticipation.

During the two-hour car ride north, we held hands and cheerfully chatted about our big plans for Max.

"I can't wait to take him for walks," I said. "We'll probably have to start with short walks around our neighborhood first, but when he starts to walk well on a leash, I'd like to take him down the Monon Trail."

"Definitely," Adam agreed. "I've already researched some dog-friendly parks we can try out as well. And I can't wait to show him off at work. Almost everyone brings their dogs with them, which will be great for his socialization and potty training."

We were so absorbed in the moment, so preoccupied and present for a change, that it felt like old times again, like we didn't have a single care in the world other than safely bringing our new baby home.

"There it is," I said, pointing toward a long, dirt driveway. "Turn here."

As we drove down the driveway, past a small, slightly run-down mobile home, a beautiful two-story barn with bright red siding came into view.

"I think I know where all of their money goes," Adam joked.

I rolled my eyes but grinned.

After parking the car, we were greeted by a rush of warm air, lots of friendly barking, and the breeder's husband as we walked through the barn doors.

"You must be here for Wiggles," he said in a low, monotone voice.

"Yes we are," Adam said.

"Okay, this way," he replied as he directed us toward the far end of the barn.

"Is Michelle here?" Adam asked.

"No she isn't, but she has everything in order for you, and the paperwork is ready to be signed."

While Adam handled the paperwork and tried his best to make friendly conversation, I squatted down next to the kennel to get a closer look at Max, his mother, Sophie, and his last remaining sibling. His mother looked strong and alert, standing protectively over Max and his sister, who was just half of his size. His sister had a beautiful mahogany-colored coat and a fiery personality to match. But Max, although not as flashy or outgoing, was far more special.

His blond coat was fluffy, wild, and soft to the touch, with golden highlights that shimmered brightly in the afternoon sun. And his big brown eyes, which he used to expressively look up into mine without lifting his head, could've melted the most callous of hearts. I could tell right then that he was a sensitive soul, the kind of dog that would become much more than a pet—a true and loyal friend.

"We're all set here. Let me get him for you," the breeder's husband said as opened the kennel door. Then he placed Max into my arms.

At first, Max seemed terrified to be separated from his mother, his little body quaking as he let out a few high-pitched cries. Then Sophie stuck her paw through the holes in the kennel fencing, as if she was reaching out for him, not wanting to let him go.

"Shhh … it's going to be all right, Max," I said as I rocked him in my arms.

"Oh, don't worry about them. It will only be a couple of minutes before they forget," the breeder's husband said.

I gave the breeder's husband a dirty look in response to his insensitive comment, then whispered to Sophie, "I'm sorry. I promise we're going to give Max the very best home."

And that's exactly what Adam and I did. We gave Max all kinds of love and affection, and he gave us even more back. He was a wonderful addition to our family, and having his smiley face and perpetually wagging tail around every day did a lot to help us both stay positive and keep us moving in the right direction.

In fact, throughout most of Max's first year with us, Adam appeared to be psychologically stronger than I had ever seen him, postmarriage anyway. He finally seemed to have a good grasp on how to successfully manage his illness, and he learned to appreciate the good things he had in his life. And that gave me just enough breathing room to enjoy some of things I used to as well, like spending time out with my friends and being his wife.

We even took a trip to California together that June, which was a big step forward for us, considering it had been a long time since Adam felt well enough to travel and I felt safe enough to go with him. It wasn't a perfect trip of course, but it was an exceptional one for reasons both known and unknown to me at the time. It included two nights in Vegas, a drive through the stunning desert landscape of Death Valley, numerous treks up and down the granite cliffs of Yosemite National Park, a casual stroll through the ancient Mariposa Grove of Giant Sequoias, a romantic outdoor wine tasting at a quaint family vineyard in Arroyo Grande, complete with friendly locals and roaming peacocks, and an exciting yet nerve-wracking ocean kayaking adventure, where we encountered the magnificence and sheer power of surfacing humpback whales.

40

After returning home from our summer vacation together on a high, our life continued to positively progress together, becoming about more than just survival, as it had been for so long. Instead, we worked toward making all aspects of our existence fuller and more vibrant. We got involved in a small group to not only strengthen our spiritual relationship with God but also to build new relationships with couples our age—relationships I surreptitiously hoped would help keep Adam on the up-and-up. We recommitted to working out at the gym together, shopping for and cooking nutritional meals together, and spending as much time out of the house as we could, enjoying an active lifestyle instead of sitting in front of the TV or lying in bed. And at Adam's insistence, we set every Thursday night aside as a date night, to purposely carve out time each week to communicate and connect.

I felt as though we were doing everything we could do to keep Adam's bipolar extremes at bay and to safeguard and enhance our relationship. But as another Thanksgiving drew near, I began to wonder if Adam might be flying a bit *too* high.

"Adam, I hate to bring this up, because we've been doing so well lately, but I've noticed some small changes in you that make me think it might be time to talk with your doctor about tweaking your meds."

"What changes?"

"The biggest thing I've noticed is that you've been sleeping less and less, and yet you still seem to have a lot of energy. It could be nothing, but I think it would be wise for you to check in with your doctor just the same. It's better to be safe than sorry, don't you think?"

"Yeah. I agree. I'll call and make an appointment."

Making adjustments to his medications were simply a part of managing the complexities of his illness, so I wasn't particularly nervous that I had seen slight shifts in his mood and behavior. The bipolar brain is a sensitive and dynamic one, and an infinite number of factors can easily throw it off-balance. The key is recognizing early on when the scales are starting to tip and then following through with immediate changes to one's lifestyle and medication plan, to tip the scales back in the opposite direction before becoming so out of control that isolation in a mental health facility becomes one's only hope for recovery.

Up until then, Adam had never been able to accomplish that goal, but his willingness to stay on his meds and make an appointment with his doctor, along with all the work he had put in since his most recent depressive episode, made me think that this time he'd find success. My confidence wavered, however, when he returned from his doctor's appointment.

"Hi, lovey. How did your appointment go?"

"It was fine, but I had to see a new doctor because mine retired."

"Retired? When?"

"The receptionist told me that it was a few months ago."

"A few months ago! Why weren't you informed?"

"I guess it's been a while since I've been in."

Apparently, it had been a lot longer than I realized since Adam had connected with his doctor, and that made me wonder whether

Adam had been as devoted to his treatment plan as he had led me to believe.

"Okay, that kind of scares me … but tell me what happened with this new psychiatrist."

"She didn't make any changes to my medications, but she did draw my blood and prescribe me some sleeping pills."

"That's it?"

"Pretty much, but when she gets the results back from the blood draw, she said she might make some changes to my medications then."

I wasn't happy with that. Sleeping pills would only serve to mask some of the symptoms of an upcoming manic episode. And although I knew his new doctor needed time to evaluate just how much medication was flowing through his veins before she felt comfortable making any modifications to them, I was afraid that by the time his results came back, he'd be too far gone for that to matter. So I talked to his father about it.

"Greg, I'm starting to get worried about Adam. He's been sleeping less and less, his energy levels have been climbing, and he seems more upbeat than normal. I know he's been doing well, and I'm glad he's happy, but I think he's working his way up into another manic episode."

"I haven't noticed anything out of the ordinary with him. I think you're seeing things that aren't there because you still haven't forgiven him for his past episodes."

Wow! I didn't know how to respond to that. I probably did have some work to do in the forgiveness department, but that didn't mean I was wrong. I had been the only one by Adam's side every single day and every single night for the past four years, so I knew him and his illness better than anyone else did—better than his father did.

"I don't think that's true, but will you please keep your eye on him anyways? Can you talk with him and see if you see what I see?"

It bothered me that Greg didn't take my concerns seriously and that he accused me of letting my feelings about the past cloud my judgment about the present. I had proven long ago that my love and loyalty for Adam were strong. I had worked hard to maintain a level head and to learn from his previous episodes. Why couldn't his father just support me and take me at my word?

He should have, but he didn't, not until he was forced to do so on December 20. That night, Adam attended an evening church service—a worship-centered service our church held just once a month—and I chose to stay home. Adam's hypomanic symptoms had been worsening since the conversation I had with Greg, so I told Adam to go without me, so I could stay home and think.

Christmas break was only a few days away, and Adam and I had made plans to spend the holidays with my parents. We had been talking for months about the trip, and Adam was looking forward to using it as an opportunity to build a better relationship with my mom and dad. But with Adam well on his way into another manic episode, going on that trip—a trip that would take place in a small Northern Michigan town far from the type of serious medical care that he would need—was nothing but a disaster waiting to happen.

And unless he was physically prevented from getting into his car, I knew no amount of reason would stop him from making that trip, even if I refused to go with him. So I had to devise a plan to get him back into the stress center, *again*, before that trip came. I wracked my brain to come up with a plan that I thought would work, but I couldn't. Then help came in the form of a phone call as soon as the church service let out.

"Hi, Sydney. It's Emily."

"Hey, Em."

"We've all been talking." By *we*, she meant Greg, Judy, Eric, and herself. "And we want you to meet us at our house. We've told Adam that we're getting together for dessert and coffee, but we really want to talk to him about checking himself into the hospital."

"It's about time," I mumbled to myself.

I don't know what went on at that service—although I could make a good guess—but evidently Adam's behavior was bizarre enough that it caught the attention of others. It caught the attention of the other people attending the service. It caught the attention of the church's security team, and it finally got Adam's family to see what I had been seeing all along.

"All right. I'll be there."

41

I was astonished by how easy it was to convince Adam to go to the stress center. In fact, it went so smoothly that I would've described it as an outright miracle. But helping Adam manage his illness, something I had been trying so hard to do for so long, never could be that easy. Even though Adam marched right into that hospital ready and willing to succumb to their care, and they had a thick, medical file documenting the severity of his illness at their fingertips, they turned him away without hardly a thought.

"I think it's great that you're here, Adam," the social worker said. "You've obviously come a long way since your last visit. But if you're well enough to ask for help, then I don't think you need to be admitted."

Adam nodded along in agreement. I did not.

"You've got to be kidding me," I said angrily. "After everything that Adam's been through and all of the documentation you have on him, you aren't going to give him the help he's asking for?"

"Well, our facility only has so many beds."

"And you don't have one open?"

"We do, but ..."

"But nothing. This is ridiculous. I imagine there is nothing I can say that's going to change your mind though, is there?"

"No, but if things get worse, you can always come back."

"Sure, because it's so easy to just come back."

I would have loved to have completely let go of my self-restraint and let my frustrations explode out onto everyone who worked there by yelling and screaming at the top of my lungs about everything that was wrong with their poor excuse for a hospital. And it would've felt so good to demonstrate my disgust and outrage about their dim-witted rationale by shoving my fist through a wall or throwing a chair through one of their windows, but I knew no level of tantrum—no matter how over the top—would've gotten me what I wanted.

Not only were they used to seeing people have outright conniptions in their lobby, but they weren't really the people responsible for the broken mental health care system we have in this country. They weren't the ones who had enacted such ineffective and callous mental health laws; nor were they responsible for the endless supply of red tape I had come to know and abhor. So I kept it together, as I always did, and walked out quietly, leaving my dignity intact.

But my heart was burdened with resentment and full of fear about what was to come. Adam hadn't just been denied the care he needed; he had been sent out into the world where he could easily hurt himself or harm someone else. And worse, he was provided with the justification he needed to believe that he was perfectly fine and had no reason to listen to us.

I awoke early the next morning, not by choice but by the loud sounds of Adam's heavy footsteps and the frenzied opening and closing of his bathroom drawers.

"What time is it?" I said wearily as I sat up in bed and found Adam scurrying around our room.

"Just before five," he said hurriedly.

"Five? Why are you up so early?"

"I'm meeting someone for an early breakfast. I want to talk to him about my business plan before he goes to work."

"Who's he?"

"Not anybody you know."

Normally I would've tried to stop him, knowing that this morning meeting of his was likely nothing more than a last-minute invitation he had forced onto some unsuspecting acquaintance he hardly knew, but I didn't dare do anything to aggravate him. Not after the promise he had made when we returned home from the hospital the night before.

"Okay, but you're still planning to see your new psychiatrist this morning, right?"

"Yep. Just like I promised."

"All right, well good luck at your meeting then. Call me right after your appointment is over."

"I will, but I've got to go now. Love you."

I had been pleasantly surprised that he had agreed so readily to take the morning off from work to meet up with his psychiatrist again, especially after having one of the hospital's social workers tell him that he was fine. But when I asked him to go, just to make sure he was in tip-top condition before we left on our trip to see my parents, he conceded without much of a problem. I knew I had manipulated him by bringing the trip into the conversation, even though I had no intention of going, but I had learned that his illness didn't fight fair, so I couldn't always afford to either.

It was likely that a visit to his psychiatrist wouldn't result in much anyway, but I clung to the hope that his doctor would somehow see his need for medical care and that she'd do something to help him. Maybe she'd even use her medical connections to get him into the stress center, without the need to jump through all the typical bureaucratic hoops like I had to. *A girl can only hope, right?*

After an hour of tossing and turning, I gave up on trying to go back to sleep and began scrolling through my unopened emails on my phone. As per usual, most of them were promotional in nature, making sure I was aware that my favorite stores were offering free shipping or having another big sale. But then I came across an email that was forwarded to me by my brother-in-law—an email written by Adam and sent to several of his friends at 4:22 that morning—and it made it clear that mania was no longer coming; it was already here.

Subject: 40th Jubilee First Quarter Report (TOP SECRET)

Jon,

Shalom and blessed Monday to you. I hope you and Tammy had a wonderful, worshipful weekend! I was on a 24-hour wilderness camping trip last night with the Lord but he brought me home early because he revealed the next steps in His plan to me after 6 hours of prayer and meditation.

I wanted to let you know what YAHWEH is doing behind the scenes as we have just completed the first quarter of the 40th Jubilee since our LORD Jesus' Crucifixion.

1. I have adopted my spiritual name Yahosua Tsebaote that was given to me in a vision back in May of 2014 while on a business trip to Baltimore. While I will remain to be Adam behind the scenes I will be operating as Yahosua Tsebaote. Social media profiles for Tsebaote will soon be created but will not have my photo because I am called not to draw attention to myself.

2. On January 1st I will start to strategically unlock an investment fund that dates back to when I was in High School and I took the money from my various jobs

and invested in companies like Google, Apple, Yahoo, Netflix, Tesla, etc. This account has grown to well over $1 million, however, I have kept it hidden for the past 12 years from everyone.

3. I will be starting a few new companies in January along with the two companies I currently own and my nonprofit company. I have included my business plans and Pitch Decks in this email for you to study in case you have any ideas on how to make them more perfect. My next company will be called NHOEN, LLC NHOEN = New Heaven on Earth Now. All of my companies will be under a holding company called "New Genesis." NHOEN LLC is a Real Estate Investment and Construction Firm. I will start to strategically buy houses around my Church to GIVE to families within our body of believers paid in full.

4. Our first Investment / Renovation House is the "White House". This will be the headquarters of J.P., whom the Lord has gifted me as my right hand brother for our Mission of ushering in the eternal Kingdom of God here on earth. I went and did an outer inspection on the house yesterday. It looks great and is actually priced at about 60-70% of market value. I believe J.P. will use the resources the Lord has blessed him with to purchase this property because it is important for him to start owning pieces of this new world as well. However, if he doesn't, I will buy the property myself for him to live in and operate out of. Would you be available to meet me at the café at 96th and Meridian at 11:30 and then we can go look at the inside of the house together since you are a licensed realtor and have "keys to the kingdom" so to speak? Perhaps J.P. could join us if his schedule allows.

Attached are my Business Plans. Please pray over them and report any ways to perfect them to me. I would also like to formally extend an offer to you to be an Elder to sit on the Board of Directors for New Genesis.

As clearly stated in the title, keep this email TOP SECRET. It is imperative that it does not fall into the hands of believers that do not fully understand Biblical prophecy and how it is now being fulfilled. I have Cc'd others that have been a part of this plan for many years so they have situational awareness into what is happening.

In Him, Through Him, To Him

Adam

It was a common occurrence for Adam to believe he was a prophet in times of mania. He believed wholeheartedly that he was receiving special messages from God, many of which were directing him to use money he didn't have and obsess over companies that didn't exist to further God's plan. Or should I say the plan that Adam's misfiring mind had fabricated haphazardly. This was bad of course. It could lead us—and anyone else he had sucked into his fictitious entrepreneurial world—into financial ruin. But what was far more terrifying was thinking about how far he might go, or what he might be willing to sacrifice, in order to fulfill this plan.

Please, God, help his doctor see how badly he needs help!

42

I was still lying in bed when Adam's phone call came through—a phone call he shouldn't have made for at least another hour or two—and I knew right then and there that I had been duped again.

"Hi, babe, did you need something?" I asked, knowing that wasn't the case.

"No." He laughed. "You told me to call you after my appointment was through. Don't you remember?"

"Of course I do, but I didn't think you'd call me so early. Did you already meet with your doctor?"

"Yep. Sure did."

I knew he was lying.

"And how did it go?"

"It went really well. We talked about how I was feeling, which is great actually, and she said that I should just keep doing what I'm doing. Basically, she gave me a clean bill of health, so I'm all set to go to Michigan for Christmas."

"She didn't have any concerns at all?"

"Nope. You've been worrying over nothing."

"Adam, I don't—"

"I've got to go now, lovey," he interrupted. "I've got a lot of things to take care of before I go to work. Bye." Then he hung up.

Now it all made sense to me. There was a reason convincing him to see his doctor felt too easy. I hadn't coaxed him into going; he had just told me what I needed to hear to get me off his back, and I fell for it. How stupid could I be?

Ugh. I'm so sick of all this.

I jumped out of bed and hurried to pull myself together. Then I took a trip over to his psychiatrist's clinic myself.

"Hi. I need to know if my husband was here this morning," I said to the receptionist sitting behind the plexiglass window. "He called me to say he met with his doctor, but I don't believe him. He has bipolar disorder and has become manic again. And before you ask, yes, my name is on his paperwork, so you can release his information to me."

After giving her his name, she typed a few things into her computer. Then she looked up at me with a look of pity on her face and said, "I'm sorry, but he wasn't here. He never had an appointment."

"He never had an appointment?" I exclaimed.

"No. I'm sorry, but he didn't."

Was I really surprised that Adam hadn't made an appointment? No. I'd been afraid that the small window of opportunity I had to talk him into seeking medical care had closed when those of the stress center had, and in that moment, I knew I'd been right.

Why hadn't that social worker just listened to me? If he had admitted him last night, I wouldn't be going through this now.

Hot tears began to stream down my cheeks, but I wiped them away and pushed my emotions aside so I could try to formulate another plan to get Adam help—plan C, since plan B had just gone up in smoke.

But plan B wasn't the only thing to blow up in my face that morning. After calling my father-in-law to give him the bad news about Adam from the clinic parking lot, my car battery died. What perfect timing.

I hit my steering wheel with my fists a few times and let more angry tears slip down my face. *What else is going to go wrong today? I can't just sit here and wait.*

After making a couple of phone calls and realizing that it would be some time before anyone was free to pick me up, I opened and slammed my car door shut. Then I made a mad dash through the rain to Eric and Emily's house, which was just a quarter mile away from the clinic.

"Hi, Emily. Thanks for letting me barge in like this," I said as I gasped for air.

"Oh, it's no problem at all. I'm just here watching the kids. Come in so we can get you dried off."

Despite how horrible the morning had been, I was thankful that Emily lived close by and had been home taking care of her seven-month old daughter and two-and-a-half-year-old son, a niece and nephew I hardly knew thanks to Adam. Emily and I rarely got to spend time together, but under normal circumstances, I think we would've been good friends.

"Can I get you something hot to drink?" she asked.

"Sure, that would be nice. Thanks."

Eric and Emily had distanced themselves from Adam and me long ago, generally only seeing us in times of emergency or when forced to at the occasional awkward family get-together, where everyone went to great lengths to avoid talking about Adam's illness. Especially if his grandmother was present, because she was unaware that he had bipolar disorder, and Judy was determined to keep it that way.

Their reasoning for detaching from us wasn't lost on me, but it still hurt. I understood that they wanted to have a life of their own, one that wasn't consumed by all of Adam's problems. They wanted to travel. They wanted to spend time with their kids. They wanted to celebrate the milestones, both big and small, without being eclipsed by the constant needs of Adam. They wanted normalcy, and I didn't blame them for that, but it was hard not to be resentful knowing I'd never have any of that with Adam.

"So tell me what's been going on," she said as she sat down on the opposite side of the kitchen island from me.

"A lot," I said as I sipped the hot coffee she'd placed in front of me.

"That's all right. I'm here to listen. I've got the time."

An hour or so later, Greg pulled up and helped me get my car into a nearby dealership for repair. Then he hatched a plan to meet up with Adam for lunch at the café across the street from his office to ask him to go back to the stress center, just as we had the day before.

Personally, I hated the plan, and I was fairly certain it would fail. It wasn't like there was anything new for us to say to Adam, and I was worried about how he would react to another confrontation, particularly a public one taking place in front of numerous onlookers. Were the possible consequences for Adam, and anyone else in that café, even worth risking for the highly unlikely chance that he would agree to go back to the hospital and that the hospital would take him in?

I wasn't sure. But I knew I didn't have it in me to walk into that restaurant and watch whatever was about to happen unfold. I needed a break from all the turmoil, a time-out from the immense pressure I always felt to perform, an intermission from the inevitable public humiliation I would have to suffer. I wanted

Adam to get the medical care he needed, but I had reached my limit. How was I going to tell Greg that though?

I had always tried so hard to be strong in front of him, wanting him to feel confident that I could care for his son no matter how much pain doing so inflicted on me. I shouldn't have felt that way. I didn't have anything to prove to him. I hadn't been the one to lie or let him down. And I hadn't been the one to place my own desires in front of the well-being of others either.

Putting on a brave face for Greg and the rest of the family was foolish, and I know that now. But at the time, I still let the need to do so control me. That need partially stemmed from my own pride because I wanted Adam's family to think highly of me. It also stemmed from my love for Adam because I felt I had to be strong when he was weak, which was most of the time.

"Are you ready to go inside?" Greg asked as he placed his hand on the driver's side handle.

I took a few deep breaths and looked at the café through the windshield.

Just say yes. You can do this. Say yes.

Greg stared at me as I tried to psych myself up to go inside.

"I can go in alone, Syd, if you're not up for this."

Ordinarily, I would have put up a fight. I would've felt ashamed for even thinking about stepping back while someone else stepped forward to help Adam, but not this time. Instead, I chose to listen to my gut and conserve some strength, strength I'd no doubt need in the near future.

"I'm not, Greg. I'm not up for this."

"It's okay. I can handle it."

While I sat and waited from a safe distance, I kept my eyes fixed on the café doors, praying that Greg's plan would somehow work.

A few minutes later though, Greg emerged from the café and made a beeline for the van while he conspicuously avoided looking in my direction. It was a telling sign that things had not played out as he had hoped. Then when he opened the driver's side door and peered in, his face exposed a wide range of emotions that he was fighting hard to hold back. It was a mix of feelings I knew far too well—anguish, terror, exasperation, among others.

"It didn't go well, did it?"

"No. He didn't get upset, but I couldn't persuade him to go to the hospital either. And I can tell that he's worse than he was last night."

"I know he is. What do you think we should do now?"

"I don't know."

Maybe it was finally time to give up, go home, and let the nature of the bipolar beast do its worst until something horrible enough happened that someone with authority was forced to take notice. It was advice we'd both been given on numerous occasions. Advice that made my skin crawl every time I heard it.

"Let's call 911," Greg suggested.

"I don't know. That might just be asking for more trouble."

The idea of calling 911 was terrifying to me. Doing so could have easily turned what had been a relatively mild confrontation with Adam into a total newsworthy spectacle. I wasn't even sure if a 911 call was an appropriate course of action to take. (It was, by the way; law enforcement and first responders are specifically trained to handle mental health crises like the one Adam was experiencing.) And even if I didn't make that call myself, agreeing to let Greg do so seemed an awful lot like an act of betrayal, one that could've easily led to some dangerous ramifications for me if it didn't result in an immediate hospitalization for Adam.

"I don't think we have any other choice," Greg replied.

I was caught between a rock and a hard place. I didn't want to go home just to have to wait and worry. I didn't want Adam to go back to work where he'd be free to say and do whatever off-the-wall thing came into his mind, and I definitely didn't want to regret taking the easy way out later.

"You're right. I don't like it, but go ahead. Make the call."

Within minutes of Greg's call, the café was surrounded by police cars, ambulances, and even fire trucks.

What on earth have we done?

With all the noise and commotion, everyone in that restaurant had to have been terrified, and I felt awful for that, but once Adam realized that this sudden infiltration was set in motion by us and noticed all those strangers' eyes focused on him, I thought for sure he'd become so enraged that he'd put on an even bigger show for them. A show I personally didn't want to witness but one I hoped would lead to a police escort to the stress center with a mandatory psychiatric hold.

But Adam didn't walk out of those doors in handcuffs or even try to flee the scene. Instead, he calmly greeted the police officers who approached him, and after having a rather civilized conversation with them, he agreed to drive himself to the hospital to seek treatment after he responsibly finished the second half of his workday. Now who could argue with that?

No one could, not even the police officer who vividly remembered apprehending him from the side of the road during his infamous 2014 barefoot run away from the stress center. Yet we all knew that even though he agreed to check himself into the hospital later, there was absolutely nothing holding him to that promise. In fact, he might not even remember making that promise by the time his workday was through. Anyone who genuinely knew Adam or had any real experience with the behavior of the mentally ill would know we still had plenty of reason to worry.

That police officer knew. He had seen for himself how wildly unpredictable Adam could be when manic, and he had a career full of experience interacting with the mentally ill, so he took the time to come to my passenger-side window to apologize.

"I'm sorry we couldn't do more to help," he said kindly. "We both know he needs to be admitted to the hospital, but he hasn't broken any laws, and he hasn't given us any reason to believe he is a danger to himself or others. I can't imagine how hard this is on you, but if you need anything, please call."

"Thank you. I appreciate everything you've done. I just hope he shows up at the stress center."

"Me too."

43

At 4:45 p.m., I drove to the hospital to meet up with Adam after work, fully expecting to be stood up and disappointed again, but instead I was left stunned when I saw his car pull into the parking lot. Even more surprising to me was how composed and amiable he was. After the highly dramatic incident we had experienced just a few hours earlier, I could have hardly blamed him for becoming unhinged.

I wasn't sure why he had decided to show up. The stress center hadn't exactly been a source of fond memories for him. Maybe the police officer he had talked to at the café made him believe that he had to. He did generally respect legitimate authority figures, due to his time serving in the military. Or maybe he thought it was best to keep the peace between us, feeling guilty for lying to me about going to see his doctor and confident that he'd be turned away again anyway.

I'll never know what his true motivation was—although I'm certain it wasn't because he believed he needed medical help—but whatever the reason, I was grateful that he had come under his own free will and that I had one more opportunity to get him the care he needed before anyone got hurt. But would the social worker conducting his intake interview recognize his need for admittance?

"Adam, I'd like to admit you here for a while. Of course you'd have to agree to sign yourself in," the social worker said to him after a thorough round of questioning.

"You really think I need to be admitted?" Adam replied with a look of bewilderment in his eyes.

"Yes, I really do."

I sat on pins and needles as I stared closely at Adam's body language, looking for some kind of hint as to how he was taking this unexpected news. Would he become combative or try to flee, as he had back in 2014? I braced myself for that, remembering clearly how ugly things had gotten then, as he was dragged past the very room we found ourselves in now, handcuffed, belligerent, and completely out of touch with reality.

"But we're supposed to be heading up to Michigan soon," he said to me. "I could just take a higher dose of my medication so we can still go."

"Adam, I don't want to go up to Michigan while you're unwell. You need to sign yourself in and get the help you need. We can go up to see my parents another time."

He sat silently, probably regretting his decision to come to the hospital as promised.

"What if we delay our trip by a couple of days then? That would give me some time to work with my doctor on getting my medication levels right."

"No, you should have done that a long time ago. I think you're well past that point now anyway."

The social worker agreed.

"All right," he said with an air of sadness I could hardly take. "I'll sign myself in."

It's funny how getting what I wanted, even after fighting such a hard-won battle to get it, had such a ruthless way of leaving me heartsick. It's not a pleasant thing to witness your husband get locked away from everyone and everything he loves, being stripped of his freedom, his dignity, and his life, even temporarily.

I hated seeing Adam hurt. I hated leaving him there. I hated watching him climb that long set of stairs up to the adult unit, which I knew felt an awful lot like a prison to him, but I had learned over the course of our years together that doing the right thing for someone you love doesn't always feel good, and it doesn't always come without judgment either.

Every hospitalization I had been through with Adam had brought with it its own unique set of challenges and heartbreaks for me, but I knew they were necessary for his long-term well-being, so I accepted them. This hospitalization, however, which lasted the full two weeks I had off for Christmas break, wreaked havoc on my state of mind more so than any other.

I had a long night alone to think about all that had transpired over the past forty-eight hours. And as I sat on the couch, completely oblivious to the TV show I had streamed, I ate more than I should've from the foam takeout container I held in my hand, while I tried to decide how I was feeling. I was tired, of course, and relieved to finally have Adam receiving the treatment he needed, but more than anything else, I was angry. I was so angry with him.

I had no way of knowing whether Adam's manic episode could've been avoided, but I was upset just the same with him for not doing more to prevent it. *I'm not going to put up with any more of his lies. I'm not going to tolerate any more of his messing around or only caring for his illness partway. I'm not going to stand for any more self-adjusting of his meds or self-medicating with alcohol. I'm not! I absolutely refuse.*

If time had proven anything, it was that his illness was exceptionally severe, so his management of his bipolar disorder had to be too. I planned to march into our first face-to-face visit together boldly, with the mission of making all that clear to him, because I couldn't, and wouldn't, keep following him down the proverbial rabbit hole his lack of effort kept throwing us into. Soon after I arrived at the stress center for visiting hours, however, my plans were derailed by a new and completely unforeseen problem.

"Hi, Adam. How are you feeling?" I asked upon seeing him.

"I'm fine," he said without giving my question any thought. Then he pulled me into a quiet corner of the day room and pointed toward a small table with two chairs around it. "Sit down. I have something important I want to tell you."

"Okay," I said as I followed his orders.

"Now I don't want you to get upset, because I've been thinking about this for a long time, but when I get out of here, I'm moving out."

"What?" I said loudly.

"I'm moving out. I'm going to get my own apartment so I can focus on running my businesses without the distraction of our marriage getting in the way. I think it will take me about six months to get them up and off the ground, at which point I'll move back into the house with you. It will be just like I was never gone. I promise. You like to spend time alone anyways, right? And all of it will be worth it, because I'm going to make us so much money. We're going to be rich!"

Now I knew that this horribly insensitive and wildly preposterous idea had been constructed inside of a deeply delusional mind, but hearing him toss our marriage to the side, like it didn't mean a thing to him at all, was devastating. I had practically destroyed myself for him—sacrificing my hopes and dreams, my relationships with friends and family, and my physical and mental well-being. And now he just thought I'd—what … wait? Wait happily at home for him for the next six months while he tried to pursue his impractical dreams? How could he be so selfish? How could he be so ungrateful?

"You can't be serious, Adam. I don't care about being rich. I care about you. I care about us. We're married. We're supposed to be together."

"I'm moving out, and there's nothing you can do about it. You'll thank me for it later."

If I couldn't get him to change his mind before he was released from the hospital, there would be no way for me to protect him. If Adam insisted on separating from me to foolishly chase after his entrepreneurial fantasy instead of spending his time at home tending to his illness, it would be the beginning of the end for him and for us. It was a terrifying realization that sent me running out of the hospital in tears that day.

44

Our previous Christmas together, which had coincided with Adam's last depressive episode, had been a rough one for sure. After months of trying to cope with the doom and gloom generated by his depression—and his complete lack of effort to try to treat it—I was more than ready for a reprieve by the time my winter break rolled around. It probably wasn't a very merry Christmas thing to do, but I left for my parents' without him, a few days before he could get off from work.

I felt a bit guilty for leaving him behind, but I didn't regret the decision to do so. During those days that I was alone with my family, I felt better and more like myself than I had in a long time. Being around people who loved me and wanted to spend quality time with me was exactly what I needed, and it served as an important reminder that life doesn't always have to be so sad or so difficult.

But when Adam showed up with that same sullen, I-don't-care-about-anything attitude—an attitude I had grown so sick and tired of—the celebration was over.

"Adam, do you want to join us for a game? We could play Yahtzee or some euchre," I said.

"No, I'm good," he mumbled without looking up from his cell phone as he sat slumped in the corner of the couch.

"Adam, can I get you some dessert before we start the movie?" my mom offered. "I made this one especially for you."

"No. I'm tired. I think I'm just going to go to bed."

"Come on, Adam. Get dressed so we can take our family Christmas pictures. You know how much they mean to my mom," I told him.

"I'm not taking any pictures. I've put on so much weight because of these medications I have to take. Just go take the pictures without me."

I've heard it said that the Christmas season is one of the most romantic times of the year, but that Christmas, I felt nothing for Adam other than disgust. My parents had gone out of their way, as they usually did, to try to make our Christmas together special, and Adam ruined it for everyone with his bad attitude and total disinterest in being a part of the family.

Didn't he realize how important this was to me? Of course he did, but wallowing in his own misery always seemed to be more important to him than I was. I thought for sure that Christmas would go down in our family history book as being our worst one ever, but as it turns out, a Christmas spent with your manic husband in a mental health facility is worse.

While the rest of the world—or what felt like it to me—was surrounded by friends and family, enjoying the comforts of a warm home and making memories with the ones they loved, I was confined to our empty house alone, other than on the few short days that my parents came down to visit between Christmas Day and New Year's. While everyone I knew was concerning themselves with parties and family get-togethers, putting up holiday decorations and opening presents, I was concerning myself with hospital visits, completing short-term disability paperwork, and trying to figure out how to salvage what was left of my future with Adam.

Every day of Adam's holiday hospitalization was a struggle for me, but as expected, Christmas Day itself was by far the most brutal. After enduring another long, unpleasant visit with him that morning, I reluctantly accepted a dinner invitation at Emily's parents' new home, who had recently moved into town. The dinner was meant to be for her family. Her parents, her sister and brother-in-law, her brother-in-law's parents, and Greg and Judy made up the original guest list, but knowing I no longer had the option to go home for Christmas, she kindly invited me to join in.

I'm certain she thought a home-cooked meal and the distraction of other people would provide me with some comfort, but it didn't. I wanted to be home with my family, with my perfectly healthy and doting husband by my side. I didn't want to spend Christmas Day horning in on someone else's family dinner. I didn't want to pretend like I was happy or that it wasn't completely awkward for everyone because I was there. And I didn't want to make small talk with people I hardly knew either, people I could tell knew more than enough about me and my mess of a life, but that's exactly what I attempted to do.

And everyone played their parts in the whole charade as best as they could, taking turns trying to engage me in conversations that didn't in some way involve Adam, but my whole life was wrapped up in him. His illness impacted everything I did, everything I had, and everything I felt, so it didn't take long for those safe topics of conversation to run their course. Once they did, everyone became lost inside of their own lovely world, and I sat silently inside of mine. They reminisced about old family memories, laughed at the inside jokes they shared, and oohed and ahhed over every little thing that my niece and nephew did while I fought hard to hide the envy I was feeling over the joy they were so fortunate to have.

After a while, most of what was being said around the dinner table sounded like nothing more than white noise to me, until someone finally got up the courage to come out and ask me about Adam.

"So, Sydney, how is Adam doing? He's been in the hospital for a few days now, right?"

The atmosphere in the room instantly changed at the mere mention of his name, putting everyone on edge as they waited to see how I would respond.

"He has, and thank you for asking, but it will take a while before we see any real improvement. They've made some changes to his medications, and it takes time for them to build up in his body and become fully effective."

I was thankful someone had asked about Adam. I wanted to have the elephant in the room brought to the forefront so it could be addressed and then forgotten.

"And how are you doing? I can't imagine how hard this must be on you."

"I'm hanging in there, the best I can I guess."

Truth was I was barely hanging on, but it felt nice to have someone asking about me for a change, particularly in front of Adam's mom and dad. They made me feel as though I couldn't talk honestly about Adam's problems, and certainly not about how those problems impacted me. I can hardly remember a time they even asked how I was doing. Maybe that's because they didn't want to know.

From what I could tell, their strategy in dealing with Adam's illness had always been to push it, and all the hardships that came with it, under the rug. I think they told themselves that they were protecting him by doing so, but I think avoiding any real conversation about it just made it easier for them to believe that his issues weren't as severe, and that wasn't helpful or healthy for anyone.

Sometimes you need to talk things out, especially the hard things. I know I needed to. So I welcomed the questions.

"Have you ever considered leaving him?"

Whoa. That wasn't a question I was prepared for. It was an insensitive one to ask, especially considering the company we were in, but most people who had even an inkling about what it was like to be married to Adam would wonder if staying with him was wise or even safe. And of course I had. I had thought about it on more occasions than I could count, but I wasn't going to admit that in front of Adam's family on Christmas Day.

"Why would she leave him?" Judy interjected. "You wouldn't expect her to leave him if he had cancer, would you?" Then she looked to me, wanting me to affirm her proclamation, but I sat silently, appalled by her insinuation that Adam's illness was anything like cancer.

Cancer is a horrible disease, and since I don't have firsthand experience caring for a spouse with cancer, I have no idea how difficult it is. But what I do know is that being married to someone with cancer—an illness that others can understand and sympathize with—is not the same in the least.

People with cancer generally accept that they are sick. They don't disrupt society, threaten the safety of others, or make life-altering decisions based on whims, fantasies, or figments of their imaginations.

As far as I know, people with cancer don't have to deal with the same negative stigmas that the mentally ill do. They don't have to fight tooth and nail just to convince a hospital that they need medical treatment. They don't have to become psychotic or dangerously unpredictable in order to be taken seriously.

I'm not saying that being a caretaker for someone with cancer is any easier than being one for someone with bipolar disorder, but I am saying that it is different. The most significant difference being that caring for someone with cancer is not in and of itself dangerous. All one has to do is look at the statistics of how many people with bipolar disorder commit violent crimes.

I don't believe that Judy thought that they were the same either. What I do think is that she was trying to communicate to me, and everyone else there, that I had no right, under any circumstances, to leave Adam. As if that kind of decision was even hers to make. She was trying to tell me that it was my responsibility to care for him, whether he accepted that care or not, and that if sticking by him meant ruining my life, or even losing it, then, well, that was just the risk I had to take.

I think it had been well established, years before then, that I took our marriage vows very seriously, even though I'd entered our marriage under false pretenses. And despite all of Adam's failures to care for himself and all the unnecessary hardships he had placed on me, I was still there loving him, fighting for him, and sacrificing for him.

But that heinous ideology of hers, that somehow I owed him more of me, that I owed him my literal life, was ludicrous. And it drew a deep line in the sand between us that day.

45

One of the only good things that came out of Adam's hospitalization was the stress center's agreement to pursue another court commitment for him. During his last stay there, the hospital's lawyers wouldn't even attempt to go to court to seek another commitment, claiming they didn't have a strong enough case considering the language of the new, stricter mental health care laws. But with more documentation added to his medical file, which clearly demonstrated a pattern of noncompliance with his treatment plan, they felt they had a fighting chance to win this time around.

I was far from looking forward to testifying in court again. The last time had been somewhat traumatizing, to say the least, but I did feel more equipped to handle the pressure, having gained plenty of experience dealing with stressful situations and a much better understanding of why obtaining a court commitment for Adam was so important. He had proven time and time again that he couldn't, or maybe wouldn't, do what he needed to do to care for himself, at least not without some legal accountability. So I would've put myself through the process a hundred times over if that meant getting Adam the court commitment he needed.

I felt confident that a judge would see his need for one too, and having another court commitment put in place, one that would give us an entire year to get his mindset straight and his illness under control, gave me a bit of hope. I'd always thought that if Adam could just hang in there long enough, we could find the right combination of medications for him that would not only be effective at stabilizing his mood and behavior but wouldn't come with any significant side effects either. Then maybe he'd see for himself how much better his life was when he took his medications, and he'd choose to stick with them after the year of commitment was over.

That hope was viciously ripped away from me on the last day of my Christmas break, however, when Adam was released to come home the very night before we were scheduled to appear in court, thereby nullifying the hospital's request to seek a commitment for him.

"Hi, babe," Adam said. "I'm calling to let you know that I'm being released from the hospital tonight."

"What? No, that wasn't the plan," I said without trying to hide my bewilderment.

"Don't you want me to come home?" he asked.

No, I don't. I want to go to court. I want that commitment!

"I'm sorry. I'm just a bit surprised, and of course I do. When should I pick you up?"

No one from the hospital ever bothered to call and explain why they released Adam early. If I had to guess though, I'd say it was about saving on lawyers' fees—so Adam was ripped away from the safety and structure of the stress center before he was ready and without any extra support than when he had gone in, leaving us, mostly me, to figure things out on our own once again.

I doubted that things would be any different than they had been without the power of the legal system behind us to motivate him into strictly adhering to his treatment plan. Why would they be? Chances were he'd just slip right back into his old habits, like he had after every other hospitalization.

It was likely that he would continue to ignore the professional advice he had been given, overlook the desperate pleas of those who loved him, and do whatever he wanted to do, whenever he wanted to do it, without any regard for his bipolar disorder at all. The only thing that was even slightly different about his release was that he had made an appointment with a new counselor for the following afternoon, no doubt a chip he had played to help him secure an early release and avoid going to court. *How clever.*

This appointment did in some ways seem promising to me, because this counselor had been recommended to Adam by Tanya on the day she terminated our sessions with her, and even more so because he had quite an impressive résumé. He was a practicing physician with multiple professional degrees, including a master's degree in counseling. He was the executive director of a ministry geared toward helping women with issues ranging from eating disorders, unplanned pregnancies, and abuse. He was a well-respected Christian man with a leadership role in his church, who also volunteered his time to counsel in their free program, and he had written a book about depression and bipolar disorder, which is why he traveled the country to speak as an expert on those very topics too.

Frankly, I couldn't have dreamed up anyone better. On paper at least, he appeared to be the perfect match for us, uniquely capable of handling Adam's specific set of needs. Yet I knew that no matter how outstanding his credentials were, when it came to Adam, he'd still have his work cut out for him.

Even so, I wanted to take full advantage of the opportunity, however small or implausible it might've been. So without even a full day's notice, I found another teacher willing to cover the last fifteen minutes of my final class that Monday, and I went with Adam to his first appointment.

"Hello. I'm Doctor Henderson," he said as he offered us both his hand. "Please come in and take a seat."

"Thank you," I said for the both of us.

I could tell immediately that Doctor Henderson was the real deal, and everything about him naturally commanded Adam's respect. He was physically fit, kind but quick-witted, medically and theologically trained, and more than willing to challenge Adam on his faulty ways of thinking. He was exactly what Adam needed. He was a professional who understood the nitty-gritty of bipolar disorder, who was well versed in the best forms of treatment, and who wouldn't easily be fooled by Adam's charismatic personality or sly tactics.

But ultimately, Adam had to decide for himself if he was going to accept the help that was being offered, and just two days after that first counseling session, I received an email from Adam that made his decision quite clear.

Subject: Discussion Tonight

Sydney,

I mentioned this morning that I would like to talk with you tonight. I wanted to write you an email first to prep our conversation.

Since I got out of the stress center on Sunday I have been experiencing a lot of side effects from the medications I'm on. My brain feels like it is foggy and going back to the gym the last few days I've only been able to do about ⅓ of my workout. I have also noticed that I am hungry all of the time. I believe strongly that my mental health and physical health are closely tied together and currently the meds I'm on are sabotaging my workouts and making me feel like a zombie. This is understandable because the drugs are meant to suppress dopamine, serotonin, and oxytocin in my brain.

Since my diagnosis in 2006 the longest and most successful period of time that I was stable without a hospitalization was from January 2007–June 2012 (5.5 years). During that entire time I did not take medication but was very diligent in how I took care of my body and mind with exercise and good nutrition.

I would like to try managing my illness again without medication. I believe the best way to treat my illness would be for us to closely monitor my sleep patterns and behavior and keep a supply of the meds at home and if symptoms start to appear then begin taking the meds on an as needed basis. This is how pretty much all other medical conditions are treated, when you see symptoms you take medication until the symptoms are gone. Here is a recent article I found about Bipolar meds. Please give it a read with an open mind.

I love you so much and I want us to work together to beat this so we can have a happy, healthy, successful future.

Adam

It should go without saying that I didn't want Adam's quality of life to suffer as a result of any unreasonable side effects—*unreasonable* being the key word here. Even though I didn't think a little weight gain was a big deal in the short term, I understood that in the long term it could be. But his plan for treating his illness was ridiculous. It had so many holes in it, so many flaws that were destined to throw him right back into full-blown mania, that I couldn't approve of it.

He may have been right in saying that some medical conditions are treated with medications until their symptoms are gone, but probably not most and certainly not all. There are plenty of chronic conditions that require a long-term or even lifelong regimen of medication—diabetes, epilepsy, heart failure, organ transplantation, multiple sclerosis, Parkinson's disease, rheumatoid arthritis, just to name more than a few—and bipolar disorder, whether he liked it or not, is yet another illness to be added to that list.

Even if it wasn't, and somehow he could suddenly stick to monitoring his sleep patterns and start listening to those who tried to warn him of any hypomanic symptoms they were noticing—two things he had never been able to do before—he couldn't just take one dosage of medication out of nowhere and expect all his symptoms to disappear by the next day. Bipolar medications don't work like that. They take time to build up in the body and become effective.

And as to his claim that he was at his healthiest and most stable while he was in the military, despite not taking any prescribed medications, even if that was true, it clearly wasn't working for him any longer. He had been in pristine physical shape and still in the military when I experienced my first manic episode with him, and that did nothing to prevent it from coming. Exercise, nutrition, consistent sleep patterns, and other healthy habits help, but without medication, they simply aren't enough on their own. So I responded to his email.

Adam,

I understand how difficult it must be to deal with side-effects, but in my opinion going off meds is not an option. You have not even had a chance to normalize yet, and you don't yet know what medication changes can and need to be made. I believe God protected you during that time in the military, but it's clear your episodes are now getting closer together. All of the doctors you have seen have greatly emphasized the need for meds. I am very willing to talk to you about this tonight, but I'm letting you know now that if you do not want to take meds, or only partially listen to your doctor, counselor, and those around you, that I cannot stay married to you. I have already been through so much chaos with you that I'm not willing to place myself in an even more dangerous situation. I would be crushed if you choose to go your own way, but I am willing to end things if you are not going to put in the hard work.

Sydney

Just twenty minutes after I hit the send button, he sent a reply.

You can't even begin to imagine all that I have gone through. If that is your position, then you should go ahead and start the paperwork.

46

Neither of us started any paperwork, as Adam had bitterly suggested, but we did fight hard to get each other to see things from our own point of views. I used every trick in the book I could think of to keep Adam taking his medications, and he continued to argue against his need for them with his faulty logic and an occasional unsubstantiated website. Other than pushing me dangerously close to my own version of madness, my efforts proved to be nothing but pointless. As a result, Adam descended rapidly back into full-blown mania, losing all the progress he had made while in the hospital in just a few short days without medication.

He became more and more obsessed with working on his far-fetched business ventures and less and less concerned with anything else; his health, his job, his family, and his responsibilities went by the wayside—until eventually I snapped. I was fed up with his priorities being so backward. He should've come out of that hospital focused on nothing other than his treatment plan, knowing full well that any attempt he had tried on his own to control his illness had been nothing but an epic failure, but no. All he cared about was becoming an entrepreneur. Who cared if our life was crumbling in and around us?

He didn't, but I did. So I walked into his home office one evening and let all that pent-up frustration I'd been holding inside of me for so long out and into the open.

"I need you to stop goofing around on your computer and listen to me," I said firmly. "I cannot possibly comprehend why you are spending any of your time right now worrying about these business ideas of yours when you should be committing all of your time and energy toward managing your illness and repairing our relationship."

"I'm not—"

"Don't interrupt me. I'm not done. I don't think you have any idea how much you've ruined things for me. I'm constantly exhausted and stressed out because you refuse to take care of yourself, which is why I no longer have a life of my own. All I do is work and clean up your messes. And you don't seem to care at all about how your manic and depressive episodes are affecting me or our relationship, which is in complete shambles if you haven't noticed. I don't trust you and don't feel safe with you because time and time again you fail to do what's right. And I know how badly you want to have kids, but that's *never* going to happen."

"What?" he said loudly.

"That's right. We can never have children together. Not with all the chaos you create. I don't have any romantic feelings left for you anyways. I can't even stand to have you touch me. It's time you realize that your poor choices are destroying everything, and I'm telling you that if you don't take action to correct them right now, then the very thin thread I've been holding onto is going to break. Then our marriage will be over, and it will be your fault."

Talking to him like that was risky. I typically tried to deescalate emotionally charged situations when Adam was manic, not instigate them. And as a general rule, I didn't believe that a heated argument would lead to positive change, but in this case, I was willing to take the risk because I was desperate. I was desperate to pull his attention away from his fantasies and onto what was real: us. I was desperate to strike a chord inside of him and willing to do whatever it took to make him hear me.

And he heard me loud and clear all right, especially the parts about lacking any sexual interest in him and refusing to ever bring children into our home, but he didn't hear my underlying message. He just got angry and bitter, which blinded him from seeing the truth.

"I don't have to listen to any more of this. I'm getting out of here."

"No. You need to stay and hash this out with me, Adam."

"No I don't. I'm leaving."

"You don't need to do that, Adam. You can sleep in the spare bedroom or on the couch downstairs, and we can talk through this after we both calm down. This is important. Don't run away from me."

But without another word, he ran out into the darkness of the night, refusing to admit that his reckless mismanagement of his illness had inflicted harm not only on him but on me. He opted to flee from the truth rather than acknowledge that his selfish actions were responsible for ruining us, and he squandered the opportunity I had given to him to finally own up to his mistakes and begin fixing them before it was too late.

I don't know where he ended up sleeping that night, if he slept at all, but he did return in seemingly one piece early the next morning, just long enough to present me with a copy of some signed divorce papers that he had hastily printed off the internet.

"Here," he said as he pushed the papers in my face. "Now you've got what you want. Oh, and you should check your email."

As soon as Adam left, I opened my email account on my phone and found that he had sent an email at 5:35 a.m. to his family and closest friends.

Subject: Divorce Announcement

Family,

It is with a sad heart that I have to tell you that Sydney and I are getting a divorce. She has been through so much with my porn and tobacco addictions that I had (praise God he has rescued me from them now) and 3 hospitalizations that we both feel that the hard but right choice is to end our marriage. She said last night that she doesn't even feel like she can touch me anymore. We also have stark differences of opinions on theological issues. It is truly my hope that after a few years our marriage can be repaired and we can get remarried but only the Lord knows if that is in His will.

We appreciate your prayers and support during this time of transition for both of us. Sydney will continue to live in our house until the end of the school year and most likely will move up to Michigan with Max to start a new life up there close to her parents. I will be buying a modest house across the street from my office and most likely will try to find another single brother in Christ to rent a room from me. Fortunately God has blessed us both with great incomes and no debt except the house so all of our physical needs will be more than met. I am planning to continue biblical counseling for the next 4-6 weeks with Dr. Henderson or however long he wants to see me for. We would very much appreciate if you did not judge us because of this decision but show us Christlike love and pray that if it is the Lord's will for us to be brought back together after a time of healing that it will happen.

With love and a heavy heart

Adam

Wow! What a low blow. It was hard not to be embarrassed by his public proclamation that we were getting a divorce, especially since I didn't know we had decided on one. I was still waiting to finish the conversation we had started the previous night, thinking there was still a chance Adam would choose his love for us over his addiction for feeling a manic high, but his actions said otherwise.

His tasteless email and dramatic delivery of divorce papers, divorce papers that were not legally certified by any means, may have been more of an emotional outburst than an actual decision to end our relationship, but they still got me thinking. How much more of my life was I willing to waste waiting for Adam to change? Was I going to put myself at risk forever, waiting for something that was probably never going to happen?

I had intentionally placed Adam at a crossroads when I started that argument with him, forcing him to choose between the road of healing and the one that would lead to his demise, knowing neither one of us could go on as we had been for much longer. I had given him everything I had. I had tried everything that I could possibly think of to help guide him onto the right path, but I could no longer deny that Adam had made his choice. But could I accept that he had made the wrong choice, and was I strong enough to let him travel down that path of destruction alone?

47

A flurry of chaos, like I had never seen before, was set into motion from the moment that Adam gave me those divorce papers and walked back out of our door. From then on, he became completely unreachable to everyone—in mind, because his perception of reality had been entirely ravaged by an especially powerful and unprecedented kind of lunacy, and in body, because he couldn't seem to stay put in the same place for very long.

For the next three days, I hardly laid my eyes on him and was only vaguely aware of his whereabouts from the limited information I gleaned from his cryptic text messages and bizarre emails. From what I could gather, his brain seemed to be fixated on only one thing, and it wasn't us but yet another new business venture, which he described as his life's calling. Consequently, he traveled haphazardly all over the city and then outside of it, doing whatever he deemed necessary to get the support he needed to get his nonprofit missions organization off the ground.

At 1:41 a.m., on Saturday, January 16, I received one of his strangest emails yet, along with another forty people—family, friends, church leaders, former coworkers, and even an army colonel. This email, which was all of two single-spaced pages in length, was specifically addressed to his counselor, who he had nicknamed the Great Physician. And it illustrated quite colorfully how Adam's mind always connected his business ventures with biblical prophecy. A connection that served to build up the significance of those ventures in his mind even more so, blurring out everything else going on in and around him.

Subject: Name Change | Memorization | Gratitude | What's in a name? | MOVIE

Dr. Henderson, MD the great Physician,

Thank you for the homework. It was beneficial, however very elementary. I learned this when I was 8 years old and accepted Christ as my Savior. Instead of counseling I would like you to transition to being my mentor and health coach since you are a doctor and I am not. The Lord has put on my heart a name change much like Abram to Abraham and Saul and Paul. My new name is Martin Luther CS Lewis Sr.

I encourage you to memorize Isaiah 49 and Acts 2:17. The Lord revealed to me in 2012 that this chapter was written 3000 years ago by Isaiah about me and my family. Generation X + Generation Y = Christ's Second Coming. The Millennial generation was the thousand years and this new generation is called the Centennial Generation. Please pray for Sydney to conceive our sinless son Emmanuel Peter during our 6 months of Abstinence we are currently undertaking and will complete in June when I will go to Jerusalem to be baptized in the Jordan River as our older brother Jesus was. Also please pray earnestly for the resurrection as the Lord has not fully revealed to me when that will happen.

Is the divorce off then?

For further in depth reading on the mind of God please read Francis C. Collins book "The Language of God" which will explain the Holy Spirit at the cellular level.

I feel so honored, humbled and blessed to have been selected as YAHWEH's Chief Information Officer and Chief Technology Officer. I am very thankful for global warming which has turned our planet into Eden once again.

Please only share this message with believers that have the spiritual maturity to understand. Welcome to the new heavens and the earth. Thy Kingdom come, thy will be done on earth as it is in Heaven which is One nation under God, INDIVISIBLE, with Liberty and justice for ALL.

Following that, Adam thanked just about everyone on the sender list for how they had positively impacted his life, specifically in a spiritual sense. One of those people was Myra, his former girlfriend, the one he was engaged to before we met and had since been married to someone else:

Your name means God's Gift and that is what you truly are to me. I have never stopped loving you and think of you often.

It wasn't exactly something I was thrilled to read, but he didn't leave me out of the email either.

Finally, and most importantly to my beloved bride Sydney. You are the light that guides my path. Everything I do, I do for you. You are the purest, most spotless bride the world has ever known and how I was able to win your heart amazes me. You are Christ to 140 7th graders every day making them into little Christs learning to be obedient. They get to learn science from the most amazing teacher the world has ever known who also has a degree in theology.

I guess the animosity he had for me when he thrust those divorce papers in my face is gone then?

229

Then, after sharing the history and original meanings behind his first and middle name, my first and middle name, and both of our family names, he closed the email by addressing his former girlfriend's father:

> I think we should recreate the wedding from 2006 but more elaborate with riding in on elephants and make it more like 25,000 people. Let's do it big. The name of the film can be 'Two Countries Get Married' Micah and Sydney, you will have to be ok with Myra and I kissing one last time as actors in a movie. The power of this film will unite the entire world in love and usher in the Kingdom.
>
> Eternally yours, The Commander of the Lord's Army, Martin Luther CS Lewis Sr.
>
> PS - I am the ALPHA and SYDNEY is the OMEGA and the Government will rest on our shoulders forever and ever, Amen!

The obvious oddity and senselessness of the email certainly caught the attention of those who received it, so it came as no surprise to me that I spent most of that next morning fielding phone calls, emails, and text messages in between those I was receiving from Adam. But it was the horrified response of one of Adam's friends in particular—a friend who was more of a mentor to Adam because he was a successful, self-made businessman like Adam wanted to be—that helped me open my eyes a bit further to how serious of a situation I was in.

Although I had always considered Adam's illness to be a serious matter, which is why I had been pushing so hard for so long for Adam to manage it better, I had become somewhat desensitized to just how outlandish it all was. The turmoil, the uncertainty, and the insanity had become a normal part of my life, even though it was tearing me apart. Behavior that would be described as psychotic and terrifying by most had begun to lose its shock value for me. And granted, this dulling effect did make it easier for me to handle it all, but it wasn't healthy, because it often prevented me from protecting myself like I should have.

Adam's friend, however, had been completely unaware of his illness up until that email was sent to him. Because of this, his shock was completely unencumbered; it wasn't jaded by anything anyone else had told him, or watered down by years of living side by side with Adam as I had done. For this reason, his reaction was probably more befitting of the severity of the situation. And his God-given instincts were telling him my safety was in jeopardy, which prompted him to get involved.

So after conducting some recon of his own and discovering that Adam was heading toward his alma mater to meet with a former business professor, he asked me to consider staying with his family for a while, worried that Adam might drop by the house on his way up and that I'd be all alone. I did consider it, but I still declined. I had Max, I had work, and I didn't want to be chased out of my own home *again*.

And that's when he suggested I get a gun. *A gun? Has it really come to that?* Maybe it had. There was no telling if and when Adam would become violent, but even though I was a firm supporter of gun rights, there was no way I was going to get one. I couldn't use a gun to harm or even threaten Adam, and introducing a weapon into an emotionally charged situation, with someone who was mentally ill and twice my size, didn't seem like a wise thing to do.

Thankfully, Adam never dropped by that day—and wouldn't be able to for another week after that—because the campus police had been lying in wait for him. They had been tipped off by another off-the-wall email that Adam had sent his professor and a phone call this friend had made to them. The contents of the email, which I wasn't privy to, coupled with his behavior when he arrived on campus, ultimately got him banned from campus forever and placed under a seventy-two-hour involuntary hold at another hospital.

48

Although the chief of campus police had been kind enough to escort Adam down to Anderson to be treated—having remembered Adam from his suicide attempt back in 2006—he was still far enough away that neither I nor his parents went to visit him. Moreover, I think we all thought it would be beneficial for Adam to bear more of the weight of his poor decisions on his own for a while. So with the Anderson Center's tougher restrictions on making outgoing phone calls, I finally had some time alone to think. Time I used to process all that had happened since Adam's last hospitalization, without fearing for my own safety or for his.

Deep down, I knew then what I needed to do next, but I couldn't quite bring myself to say it aloud until his parents sent me an email with an attached document I didn't know existed. It was a fifteen-page document outlining Adam's medical history that his mother had been privately recording since 2006. They sent it to me so I could forward it onto Adam's newest social worker, in the event that the Anderson Center might be willing to pursue that highly desirable court commitment we always seemed to be chasing.

When I read it, the depravity of their deceit came into full view for me, and I was sickened by it. At the prompting of Tanya, a year and half prior, I sat in their living room and confronted them with Adam sitting by my side.

I asked them calmly but candidly, "Why didn't you tell me about Adam's illness? Why didn't you make me aware of his past before he proposed?"

"We didn't believe it was our place to say anything," Greg said cautiously. "It was Adam's responsibility, and we told him to talk to you about it."

"You're right, Adam should have told me, but when you learned that he didn't, why didn't you step in?"

"Well, we didn't think it would happen again. Especially since he made it through boot camp and officer candidate school without a problem."

What? Of course it was their place to tell me. They were his parents for heaven's sake and my future in-laws, and whether they thought "it"—I assume by *it* they meant another bipolar episode—would ever happen again, I still had the right to know. I told them that too, but then I dropped it. I decided to take them at their word, because not doing so would've made my marriage to Adam tougher, and I couldn't handle it being any tougher.

But when I opened that medical file, I knew they had lied to me. It contained a whole slew of things I wasn't aware of, and the picture it painted of Adam's mental health was absolutely grisly. It certainly wouldn't have given anyone the impression that his problems were only temporary.

From April 2006 to December 2006, Adam was hospitalized ten times at various institutions in multiple states, before he became stable enough to live back at home. And it took an additional year after that—a year in which he battled depression, abused alcohol, and struggled to stick with a job for very long—before he could move forward on his own, leaving six months late, due to a DUI offense, for basic training.

More outrageous than that, however, was the erratic and inappropriate behavior he displayed during and in between his hospitalizations. Behavior that resulted from going off his prescribed medications every single time he was released. *Boy did that sound familiar.*

The day after his first hospitalization—a two-night stay at Cornerstone Behavioral Health Center—he attempted suicide by purposely flipping his car on his drive back home to Springfield. I was aware of that already, but seeing it displayed so directly on my computer screen made my stomach churn.

> All Dates are in 2006
>
> April 24–26 - admitted to Cornerstone Behavioral Health Center, Marion, IN.
>
> (taken there by personnel at Health Services on campus after going there saying he was afraid he was going to hurt himself)
>
> April 27 - car accident (suicide attempt)
>
> April 27–29 - admitted to Marion, IN. General Hospital for tests and observations
>
> June 16–18 - St. John's Hospital, Springfield, IL.
>
> July 10–24 - St. John's

During his fourth hospitalization, at St. John's, he became aggressive, injured a nurse, and had to be restrained. Then ten days after his two-week stay, he set out on a road trip to Indianapolis, which under normal circumstances was a three-and-a-half-hour drive, but it took him a whopping ten hours to complete, only after his brother came to his rescue and led him to his house.

The following morning, Adam attempted to drive off again before anyone noticed, but Eric intervened, and with the help of the police, he took him to the Psychiatric Pavilion at Community North Hospital. It was his fifth hospitalization in just four months, lasting a total of three weeks.

A few days following his release from Community North, he flew to India, in search of his ex-fiancée, and didn't return to the States until eight days later, by way of Chicago, where he caused a public disturbance at a hotel and claimed to be the owner. It was then that his father pretended to have a heart attack so Adam would accompany him to Northwestern Hospital. Northwestern transferred Adam to Provena St. Joseph Hospital in Joliet, Illinois, for his sixth hospitalization, and then Provena transferred him back to St. John's Hospital, his seventh hospitalization.

Two and a half weeks after his release from St. John's, he went to the county courthouse dressed in Indian attire to change his name to Malkizedek Aslan Lee, not wanting to share a name with a man who had recently been strangled to death in his hometown. He got as far as completing the legal forms and paying the $193 fee, but while attempting to place a legal ad at the local newspaper office—a requirement for completing his name change—a security guard stopped him and convinced him to leave. This led to his eighth hospitalization, an additional week back at St. John's.

Three weeks after hospitalization number eight, he took his wildest road trip yet. It was one that lasted several days and had his family and numerous police units searching across multiple states for him. His original intention was to spend the day traveling down and then back again from his grandfather's house, who lived in a small, rural town 130 miles south of Springfield. But he drove to New Orleans instead, to see the new levees that were being built following Hurricane Katrina.

From there, he drove back into Arkansas, spending the night in a motel in Marion, where he stopped by the front desk numerous times throughout the night, because he kept misplacing his room key. Then the next morning, he drove on to Tennessee but left his cell phone behind. While eating at a restaurant in Brownsville, a police officer was called in, because Adam was acting strangely and claiming to be a police officer himself.

Suspecting that Adam was mentally ill, even though he vehemently denied it, the police officer escorted him into a local hospital after confirming his illness with Adam's father over the phone. As soon as the police officer left the hospital, however, Adam did too, and he managed to escape the clutches of treatment as he drove away toward Memphis. His parents were notified that he had fled the hospital, so they contacted the police again, hoping that they could intercept him and bring him home safely, but somehow Adam eluded them.

Later that day, Adam borrowed a cell phone from a stranger and made a call to his dad, telling him that he was on I-55 and heading back home. Of course, Adam wasn't headed home at all, nor was he on I-55, but the woman who had kindly allowed Adam to borrow her phone told Greg that he was on a two-lane road in Arkansas, heading west.

So Greg contacted the police a third time, knowing the general direction that Adam was moving, and arranged to have them check him into a motel room located in Augusta, Arkansas. This time, the police were able to successfully apprehend him, but soon after they got him checked into his motel, he walked out of his room completely naked and was taken to the local jail.

Not wanting Adam to sit in jail until Greg could make the drive to Arkansas to claim him, Greg called an old high school friend of Adam's—who lived only twenty-five minutes from the jail—and asked that he go to retrieve him. This friend took him directly to the White County Medical Center in Searcy, his ninth hospitalization, and Adam remained there until his father arranged to have him transferred to the McFarland Mental Health Center, back home in Springfield. This was his last hospitalization in 2006, and it lasted an entire eight weeks.

After reading all of that, I couldn't fathom how his parents could think that his mental health issues were just over. No amount of perceived normalcy, for any length of time, could negate all that madness. How could they possibly believe his problems were just a fluke, brought on by stress and sadness over his broken engagement?

People who are mentally healthy don't get hospitalized ten times when they are sad or stressed. They don't dress up in Indian attire to legally change their name or walk out into public stark naked. They don't drive all over the country for no apparent reason or fly to an entirely different country altogether to chase down their ex-fiancée. And if they did, why hadn't I done any of those things? I had certainly experienced more than my share of stress.

But for argument's sake, even if I could understand it—even if they really did believe Adam's problems were a thing of the past—how could they think that I didn't have a right to know what had happened? Two years of significant mental health issues dramatically impact a person, whether they experience them again or not, so it's only logical to assume that those impacts will also affect their relationships, especially one as intimate as a marriage.

By withholding the truth from me, they sent us both into a marriage with our hands tied behind our backs, and marriage is difficult enough without starting out at such a great disadvantage. There isn't anything that anyone could say to me that would ever make me believe that I shouldn't have been told everything. I deserved to know it all, every gruesome detail, so that I could've made my own, fully informed decision about whether I wanted to marry him or not.

By lying to me, they stole that right from me. They fooled me into thinking I knew exactly who Adam was. They made me believe that I'd be safe with him and that I would be loved by their family, but after reading that document, it was clear to me that neither of those things were true. And that's when I finally gained the courage to admit that my relationship with Adam had to come to an end.

49

After setting up an initial consultation with a divorce lawyer downtown, I called and asked Adam's parents if I could drop by for a visit so I could tell them about my decision in person. Telling your in-laws that you intend to file for divorce isn't something that's normally done, and telling them before you tell your own husband, that's unquestionably even more out of the ordinary. But there had never been anything normal or ordinary about our marriage, and since Adam was set to be released from the Anderson Center the next afternoon, I felt it would be best for everyone, especially Adam, if his parents knew. He would need the support of his family more than ever, and I wanted them to know what they needed to know, in order to give it to him.

As I walked into their home that afternoon, I was understandably nervous, but I knew breaking the news to them was necessary so that we could properly prepare for Adam's return. I had thought long and hard about how I would tell them, but I hadn't been able to come up with the words, aware that there wasn't any easy way to inform them that our marriage was over. I expected that it would be hard for them to hear no matter how I went about phrasing it, but deep down, I thought they might know it was coming and might even understand that it needed to, considering all I had endured with him.

"Can we sit down and talk a bit?" I asked.

"Of course. Let's take a seat in the living room," Greg replied warmly.

"Would you like something to drink?" Judy offered.

"No ... thank you," I said, eager to get our conversation over and done with.

The two of them sat together on one couch, and I sat on the other, holding tightly to Max's leash and wondering how to breach the subject. Then I took a deep breath and said, "You both know that Adam will be released from the hospital soon, and I want to make sure we are fully prepared for it."

They both smiled and nodded.

"So although there isn't any good way to say this, I thought I better let you know that I'm filing for divorce. I just can't—"

"What?" Greg interrupted loudly. "You can't file for divorce!" Then he stood up and grabbed his Bible from one of their living room side tables. "Divorce is a sin!" he said aggressively as he pointed to the Bible. "How could you even think about giving up on Adam? You made a commitment to him. A sacred commitment."

I could feel my blood pressure rise and my heart thud against my chest. I was rattled. I was completely bewildered by Greg's malicious response. *How could he say that to me? How could he believe that divorcing Adam was sinful?*

I'll admit that divorce isn't pleasant. It hurts and devastates everyone involved—no one more so than the couple themselves—so it goes without saying that divorce doesn't please God because He loves us and doesn't find any joy in seeing us in pain. God designed marriage to be a representation of the relationship Christ wants to have with us. A relationship that brings goodness into our lives and is built on the purest kind of love, which is why the commitment one makes to a spouse should be highly regarded and protected whenever possible.

But being married to another human being isn't easy, because unlike Christ, humans are flawed. They are self-serving, impatient, prideful, quick tempered, and unforgiving, among other things, so holding a marriage relationship together takes a lot of hard work and self-sacrifice from both sides.

And there are plenty of perfectly valid and biblical reasons for seeking divorce—abandonment, abuse, and infidelity, just to name a few—and I was fully justified in my decision to dissolve our marriage for at least the first two of those reasons. Every time Adam chose to go off his medication, or skip a doctor's appointment, or treat his body poorly, or lie to me, he was putting himself at a greater risk for having another manic episode, despite how much those manic episodes hurt me. I had suffered greatly at the hand of his mania, in ways most will never understand, and yet time and time again, he chose to indulge himself instead of doing what he should have done to love and protect me.

Adam had hardened his heart well before I decided to end our marriage, and after ten long years of struggling with his bipolar disorder, after reaping consequence after consequence, and hurting those closest to him over and over again, he still refused to manage it. In fact, I couldn't see that he had made any progress toward accepting it, let alone treating it. I had played my role as his loyal wife since the day I said, "I do"—not perfectly but to the best of my ability—but despite all the work I had put into him and our marriage, I couldn't force him to do the same. I couldn't force him to change. Even God doesn't use his infinite power to do that.

I had done everything I possibly could to help Adam, so God had made it clear to me that the time had come for me to save myself, before saving myself was no longer an option. If Adam's parents genuinely couldn't understand that, then their blindness to the truth was even worse than I thought.

I pulled Max closer to me, for his safety and for my comfort. "Adam is the one that broke that commitment," I replied firmly but in a calm tone. "He's done so over and over again for years. And I entered our marriage under completely false pretenses. But I'm not here to argue with you or ask for your permission. This is happening, and we need to work as a team to help Adam deal with this transition."

"I can't believe you're doing this," Judy added.

"I'm sorry, but I can't continue to put myself in harm's way. Adam is getting worse and worse, and after everything we've been through, he still hasn't accepted his illness. It's not safe for me to be with him any longer. But please, let's just sit down and work out a plan for him, together."

As Greg and Judy continued to berate me, trying to guilt me into changing my mind, it became clear that working together wasn't going to happen. From the very second I revealed my intention to end my marriage with Adam, a switch seemed to flip inside of them, and they immediately saw me as their enemy, not the woman who had been killing herself to care for their son the past three and half years.

"It's obvious we aren't going to accomplish anything now," I said to them. "So I'm going to go. Come on, Max."

Although I didn't go into their home that day thinking they'd be delighted by my decision, the cruelty they unleashed on me hurt. I had put myself in an intentionally uncomfortable situation, to demonstrate my love for Adam, but they couldn't show that same kind of love toward me. I walked into their home that afternoon knowing that my safety and well-being took second place to theirs and that of Adam's, but I left it certain that it didn't mean a thing to them at all. And that fact was further magnified by the phone call I received from Greg just a few minutes after I arrived home.

"Hello?" I said with a cautious amount of hope that he might be calling to apologize.

"Hi. We've been talking about it since you left, and if you insist on filing for divorce, we'd like you to wait on telling Adam about it for a while."

"How long is a while?"

"Two weeks."

"Two weeks! Why?"

"Because Judy and I are headed down to the Florida Keys for a vacation."

You've got to be kidding me. Why would they even think about going on a trip—especially one that would take them so far away from Adam when he's still so manic?

"You're still going?"

"Yes. We can't get the deposit back, and we really need a break."

They need a break? No, I need a break. I was the one who had been living in Adam's manic world for the past three and half years. I had been his primary caretaker and the leading recipient of the agony that came with it. I had a stressful, full-time job, and they were both retired. I had no family living in the state, and they had each other, along with Eric and Emily. The hypocrisy of it all was infuriating to me.

"I can't do that, Greg. Not after I've already told you and Judy. And I've spoken with Adam's social worker about it too. She advised me to tell him immediately, before he's released from the hospital. That way, he'll be somewhere safe if he has a hard time accepting the news. So that's what I'm going to do."

Before Greg had the opportunity to protest, I hung up and immediately called the hospital to talk to Adam.

"Hello," Adam said unassumingly.

"Hi, Adam. It's me. How are you?"

"I'm good. Will you be able to pick me up tomorrow afternoon?"

"Actually, I think it would be best if your dad did."

"Oh, okay. I'll ask him then."

"I do have something important that I need to tell you though." I paused, readying myself for whatever outburst was sure to follow. "Tomorrow morning, I have a meeting with a lawyer, and I'm going to start the process of filing for divorce."

There was silence.

"Did you hear what I said, Adam?"

"Yes," he said quietly.

"Okay, so are you all right? We can talk about it if you need to."

"No. I'm all right."

"Good."

Is this good? Does he really understand what I'm saying?

"Then I'd really appreciate it if you could start making plans to stay somewhere else after your release. Maybe you could ask your brother?"

"No problem. Would it be all right if my dad and I swung by tomorrow afternoon to pick up some of my things then?"

"Of course it would. Thanks for being so understanding. I'll see you then."

50

Ding-dong. I jumped to my feet at the loud sound of the doorbell echoing through the house. And my dad, who had come to accompany me to my first meeting with the divorce attorney that morning, quickly followed behind. I pulled open the door to find Adam and Greg standing there.

"Hi, Adam. Come on in."

Then he and Greg stepped inside. I didn't greet Greg.

"I have some things I'd like to talk to you about, but let's go upstairs so we can discuss them *alone*." I looked directly at Greg when I said *alone*.

"Sure. We can talk as I pack," Adam replied.

"I'll be down here if you need anything," my dad interjected assertively as we climbed the stairs to the second floor.

"I will, thanks."

"So did you decide where you're going to be staying?" I asked Adam.

"For now, I'm going to stay at my parents' house. They'll be leaving for Florida tomorrow anyway, so I'll have the whole place to myself."

"Are you sure it's wise for you to be staying there alone? You just got out of the hospital."

"Of course it is. I have plenty I want to do anyways. I'll hardly notice they're gone."

I bet.

"Right, well I wanted to ask you to call or text before you drop by the house from now on. I know you'll need things from time to time and that this is just as much your house as it is mine, but I'd still like to know when you're coming. Can you do that?"

"Yeah, I can do that. It makes sense."

I was amazed—somewhat—by how well Adam had been taking my decision to file for divorce, and skeptical of it. Did Adam really understand that I was serious about getting a divorce? If he didn't, how would his attitude change when he realized that I was?

From my brief interaction with Adam, I could tell that his mental state had improved during his five-day stay in the hospital but only slightly, so I knew it was a terrible idea for him to be staying anywhere alone, giving him the unsupervised freedom he'd undoubtedly use to get himself into more trouble, but that didn't stop his parents from leaving. And so the steady stream of poor decisions and wild behavior continued to rage onward—just as it had before he was placed in the hospital by campus police—from the very moment they left.

At first, it was mostly more of his typical manic behavior—an overabundance of activity and communication centered predominantly around his big plans for his business ventures, as well as his own self-proclaimed prophetical insights. And that was coupled with a constant need to call me, text me, or stop by the house to pick something up, drop something off, talk to me in person, or just pet the dog. But it didn't take more than a few days before his erratic and increasingly temperamental behavior began to scare me.

Although he had dropped by the house every single day since his discharge, noticeably more frenzied and irritable than the time before it, it was his first unannounced visit on the Monday after his release that truly got me worried. So much so that I didn't feel comfortable serving him the divorce papers myself, as originally planned.

"Adam, what are you doing here? Why didn't you tell me you were coming by?"

"I need my blender bottle and a corkscrew," he said as he pushed his way past me.

"But you promised you would let me know before you drop in."

"Yeah, yeah," he said sarcastically. "This is my house too."

"I know it is, but we agreed."

He ignored me.

"How are things going at your mom and dad's house?"

"Good actually. I'm getting so much work done, and since I stopped taking my medications, I have way more energy."

"Adam, you really should keep taking your med—"

"I'm going to take these two blender bottles. That leaves you two," he interrupted as he pulled the bottles from one of our kitchen cabinets.

"That's fine." *Not important but fine.* "Is there anything else you need? Think about it for a minute. That way, you won't have to keep making the trip over."

"No," he said abruptly.

Not only was I uncomfortable with him just popping in without warning, but his matter-of-fact admission that he was no longer taking his medications cemented in my mind that danger was coming. And a few days later, early on Thursday morning, at 4:25 a.m. to be exact, that danger presented itself.

My mom—who had been staying with me for the week—Max, and I were all asleep upstairs in the same bedroom for added safety, until I heard a noise that woke me out of a dead sleep. For most of my life, I had been a sound sleeper, but living with Adam had changed that dramatically, so even the slightest of noises sounded like a warning shot echoing through the house.

I reached toward the bedside table frantically, until I found my glasses and put them on. Then I sat straight up in bed and listened intently for a moment or two, certain that the noise I was hearing wasn't a typical house noise but one generated from someone who was downstairs but shouldn't be. If I had been thinking more clearly, I would have called the police right then and there, but instead, I jostled my mom awake and whispered to her.

"I think someone is in the house."

"What?" she whispered back.

"Someone is in the house. It doesn't sound like they forced their way in, so it's got to be Adam. Stay here and lock the door behind me while I go check it out. If you hear me scream, call 911."

I got out of bed and snuck as silently as I could down the hallway and to the top of the stairs. Then, creeping ever so slowly, I descended one stair at a time, praying to God that I wouldn't run into Adam on my way down. When I reached the landing, just two steps above the main floor, I peeked timidly around the corner and saw him standing in the kitchen with his back toward me, fiddling with something he had laid on the counter.

A wave of nervous energy rushed over me as I questioned if approaching him was really a wise thing to do, but I decided that it didn't matter. All I could think about was getting him out of the house and away from us, and the quickest way to make that happen was for me to handle him myself. So without another thought, I gently called out to him from the stairs, "Is that you, Adam?"

He spun around so abruptly that I flinched. *Is it too late to run back to my room and call the police?* No longer having the element of surprise, I believed that it was.

Before making a move, I zeroed in on what he had placed on the kitchen counter, which turned out to be his military dress uniform and a coffee mug he had filled with wine. *Perfect, now I have to talk him into leaving peacefully while he's both manic and intoxicated.* But what really got my attention was the large kitchen knife he held conspicuously in his right hand.

"It's okay. It's just me," I said softly.

With one eye on the knife and the other focused on his facial expressions, I took a few small steps toward him, leaving enough room between us in case I needed to make a quick escape. I tried to appear calm, but on the inside, I was completely terrified.

What if I can't convince him to leave? Or worse, what if I agitate him somehow? Things could get real ugly real fast for me. Why does he have to have a knife?

"What are you doing here so early?" I asked him.

"It's not early."

"It's four thirty in the morning, Adam. My mom and I were both asleep. I have to go to work in a couple of hours, and you scared us half to death."

"You sleep too much anyways." He laughed. "I haven't slept at all since Sunday, and I feel better than ever."

Sunday! That was four days ago. It was no wonder that his mania was accelerating at such a rapid pace.

"So what are you doing here?"

"I'm going to the men's group that meets at the church at six thirty this morning, and I want to wear my uniform, so I came to get it."

Strange. It was not only strange because wearing a dress uniform to a casual, civilian event is in and of itself odd, especially when that uniform is at least a couple of sizes too small, but also because his discharge from the military had been so hard on him. *Wouldn't wearing it only stir up bad memories for him?*

"So why do you have the knife?"

"I'm trying to fix one of the brass buttons with it."

"Oh, I see." I didn't see; there was nothing wrong with any of the buttons. "Would it be all right if I helped you with it? It might be easier for me since I have smaller hands."

He grinned and nodded in agreement.

I carefully took the knife from his hand and pretended to fix each one of the brass buttons. Then, after placing his uniform back into its garment bag, I made a suggestion.

"You know, if you're trying to look your best for this meeting, why don't you get a workout in at the gym before you go. If you leave now, you should have just enough time."

He stared at me, clearly pondering whether he liked my idea or not.

Oh no. He knows I'm trying to get rid of him.

"That's a great idea, babe. Thanks."

51

It was a big relief to see Adam go without a fight that morning, but I knew it wouldn't be long before he'd show up again, and when he did, there was no telling what his mindset would be or whether the outcome would turn out so well either—if you can consider his barging into the house early in the morning, with a sharp knife in his hand, while drunk, manic, and sleep deprived, a good turnout.

So while I went off to work that day, I sent my mom out of the house with a friend of mine, so she'd be safe while I couldn't be there. And then, once my school day was through, we made the decision to spend the night away from the house, with a couple I'd met through our small group, Alex and Christina. I was certain that staying somewhere else for the night—somewhere Adam would be less likely to look for me—was necessary, due to our harrowing morning encounter and another large group email he sent with the subject line of "D-Day (2.0) | SITREP | MISSION EXECUTION | Reverse Revolutionary War | Bloopers."

He sent this email at 3:24 a.m., about an hour before he had come to the house for his uniform, and then added to it, ten separate times, between 6:50 a.m. and 11:39 a.m. In it, he included pictures of the British royal family, a photo of the two of us on our wedding day, an image of the Thirty-Third Infantry's shoulder sleeve insignia, a picture of the Millennium Falcon—a new nickname he gave himself—numerous YouTube links and emojis, and all kinds of nonsensical text that spoke even further to the high level of insanity going on inside of him.

Following are examples of the texts:

> Enjoy the flow and clarity of this Word. Sorry that it has taken some of you a while to catch up. Generation Gaps are never fun. This should get us all on the same sheet of music and put many of you at ease.

> I think the best form of combat was the REAL old days of King David when he was guarding sheep and a bear comes up and he has to go ALL MMA style and snap the bear's neck. I always wanted to do that ;) But instead I got to exorcize demons in hospitals since 2006.

> Also, please confirm when NASA finds the "Asgard" Planet where all those like the Apostle Paul are hanging out with Thor and Odin because they weren't fortunate enough to have our fully sanctified genetics.

> Please do not ask me how I have been sleeping because I have bio-engineered through proper supplementation, diet, meditation, prayer, and worship to no longer require sleep.

But it was the small portion of this email that he directed toward me, along with a text I received from him telling me he was on his way home and bringing dinner, that made it clear that I was on his mind and that if I didn't find a place to hide, I'd likely be seeing him soon.

> Princess Sydney - Please make sure your wedding dress still fits your perfect body. You do resemble duchess Kate but of course you're the definition of perfection in my eyes. Plus we have well more advanced genetics. Heck Prince Max (our

lion/lamb hybrid dog) might even start talking soon since we have more degrees than Fahrenheit 451 between the two of us.

My cheeks flushed with embarrassment when I read it. In fact, one of the dozens of recipients to receive this email replied to Adam by writing, "It is advisable to not reference Sydney in any more emails. I believe it is embarrassing to her and not a loving thing to do."

Yes. Thank you!

So this email was strange and humiliating for sure, but was it threatening in nature? It was difficult to fully decipher but probably not. Yet Adam's mentality and disposition could change for any rhyme or reason, and since he got fired from his high-paying job at a well-known insurance company that afternoon—*surprise, surprise*—I couldn't take the risk of staying at home.

And I'm glad that I didn't, because the next morning, when I took my mom back to the house before going to work—upon her request but against my better judgment—I found that the front door had been left ajar.

"Look. The front door is cracked open," I said to my mom. "I know we didn't leave it that way. I'm going to go look through the garage door window and see if Adam's car is here."

"Okay."

It wasn't.

"His car's not in the garage, and I don't see it parked anywhere on the street, so I'm going to take a look inside the house. Stay here."

As I walked up onto the front porch, I took a deep breath in, trying to mentally prepare myself for whatever horrid scene I might be stepping into. *Why does Adam keep putting me into these frightening situations?* Then I pushed the front door open swiftly, but with my eyes only slightly opened, half-expecting to see Adam standing, or if I'm being honest, hanging there.

But he wasn't, so I stepped inside to look around. I moved from room to room quickly and quietly, keeping my back against the walls and my head on a constant swivel, while I checked every nook and cranny. There was clear evidence that he had been there all right—our bed had been laid in, the kitchen had been used and left a mess, and most of the lights in the house were on—but for the time being, it appeared that Adam was gone, probably causing havoc elsewhere.

I returned to the car and said, "The coast is clear. He's not here, but he was. Do you want me to take you somewhere else for the day?"

"No. I don't want to stay somewhere I'm not comfortable with. I'll be all right here."

"Are you sure? What if he comes back? You won't have access to a car if you need to get away."

"Yeah. I'm sure."

"All right. If that's really what you want, but promise you'll always keep your phone close by. I'll check in as often as I can."

"I will."

"And if he does drop by, call me immediately. I'll pick up no matter what. Okay?"

"Okay."

So at my mom's insistence, I left her there, but I worried about her every second of that day. I could only imagine what it would be like for her if he showed up while I was out. *What would he do? What would he say? How would she handle it?* She had no experience dealing with Adam when he was manic, nor did I ever want her to, but without a vehicle at her disposal, I was afraid she wouldn't have a choice.

52

With only fifteen minutes left in the school day, the longest day of work I've ever had to suffer through, I finally started to relax, thinking we had made it and were completely in the clear. That was, until my mom called and said, "Adam's here. He just opened the garage door, and he's pulling in now. What should I do?"

"What? He's there. Okay listen to me. All you need to do is stay out of his way if you can, and go along with whatever he says even if it doesn't make sense. Avoid arguing with him at all costs, and if you feel unsafe, run to the neighbor's house next door for help."

I remained calm as I told her what to do, but as soon as I hung up the phone, the thought of her being alone with him for even a minute or two filled me with a sickening kind of fear for her and a strong animosity toward him. If he laid a hand on her or threatened her in any way, I'd never forgive myself for leaving her there in such a vulnerable position. So I called Christina and asked if she could send Alex over to the house, since he worked just up the road at our church. Then I arranged for my teaching partner to monitor my last class so I could leave.

When I got home, my mom met me at the front door. I could tell by the look on her face and the hammer she held in her hand that things had already gotten interesting, for lack of a better word.

"Are you okay? Isn't Alex here?" I asked frantically as I looked her over to make sure she was still in one piece.

"No, he isn't, but Adam's upstairs, and I've never seen him this bad before."

"What do you mean, and why do you have that hammer?"

"He's been moving all around the house with this hammer, swinging it around carelessly. I'm not sure why he picked it up in the first place, but when he threatened to hit Max with it, I coaxed him into giving it to me. Then he began telling me all kinds of inappropriate things that no mother-in-law would want to hear, so I left him upstairs and brought the hammer and Max down here with me to wait for you."

"I'm sorry, but you did the right thing. I'll deal with him now. I have to get him out of here."

I climbed the stairs to the second floor quickly and found him darting around his office from place to place, rifling through drawers and pulling things off shelves, lost in whatever imaginary world his mind had created for him. His body movements were sharp and jarring, as if his limbs had a mind of their own, and while he moved, he rambled on and on to himself. About what, I really couldn't tell.

"Adam ..." I said from the hallway. He didn't respond or even seem to notice that I was there.

"Adam ..." I said a bit louder as I stepped into the office and reached out gently to touch him.

He turned toward me when he felt my hand on his shoulder. Then he smiled sweetly when he realized it was me there. I didn't know how long it would last, but at that moment, I felt safe enough to come close to him, so I placed my hands on each side of his face to hold him still. I looked deep into his eyes, which appeared unfocused and hazy, for any sign that the man I had fallen in love with was inside of him somewhere.

I remembered how I had done the same in that very room just a couple of years prior, while I begged and pleaded with him to check himself into the hospital. I remembered how I had cried out in desperation, sobbing uncontrollably in his arms. I remembered the agony I felt when I realized just how ill he was, how much he needed help, and how incapable I was of forcing that help upon him.

My heart broke a little more every time I had to watch Adam fall apart, and this time was no different. It didn't seem fair that someone who could've given so much good to the world, someone I loved and cared for, had to suffer at the savage hand of mental illness. But it wasn't fair that I had to either, and so it was time to set aside that sympathy I felt for him, the sympathy I had let supersede my common sense, and do what was necessary to protect myself.

"Adam, what are you doing here?"

"The gold they keep in Fort Knox. That's the gold we will use to pave the streets in heaven, starting with our own estate."

"That's great, but why are you here? Are you looking for something?"

He turned away from me and began pulling more papers from the closet. "President Obama will be landing here soon in his helicopter, right in our front yard. I already told our neighbor."

Wonderful.

My efforts to try to understand why he had come to the house were obviously futile. His attention span was too short to hold any kind of conversation, and anything I did get him to say to me came out of his mouth as a muddled and delusional mess. He was too far gone, possibly more so than I had ever seen him, to seek help or just leave the house under his own volition, so I had no choice but to take a more aggressive course of action.

"Okay, I'll leave you to it then." Then I ran back downstairs to talk to my mom.

"I'm not going to be able to talk him into leaving this time, and I want him gone before Dad gets here. I think it's time for me to call the police."

I didn't want Adam anywhere close to us or the house when my dad arrived. Like my mom, his experience with Adam when he was manic was limited, and I was certain that if he saw him in the extreme state he was in, his protective instincts would override his self-control, and a fight would begin. So once Alex and Christina showed up, I had them sit in the family room with Adam while I snuck away to call 911.

"Hello, I need some help. My husband, who has bipolar disorder, is here but shouldn't be, as we are going through a divorce. He's extremely manic, off his meds, and hasn't slept in at least five days. Please come quickly and make sure your flashing lights and sirens are off; otherwise, he might run."

Four minutes later—which felt like an entire lifetime to me— the first set of police officers arrived. When I saw their patrol cars pull up, I walked out onto the porch with my hands in the air, before they could alert Adam by knocking on our front door.

"Hi," I said timidly. "I'm the one that called. My husband is inside, along with some—"

"Who's there?" one of the police officers yelled as he reached for his gun and the other two officers followed suit.

I whipped around backward to see if Adam was standing behind me, but he wasn't. No one was.

"Who are you talking about?" I replied.

"There, in the window. And what's in their hand?"

I could see they were pointing to a silhouette of my mom.

"It's okay! Don't shoot! It's my mom, and she's holding onto my dog's leash. It isn't a weapon."

Their sudden change in demeanor and quick response to seeing a possible threat was impressive, but it scared me, and it made me even more aware of how serious bringing the police into my home really was. Maybe I should've known to tell my mom to step away from the window before I walked out, but honestly, it never crossed my mind. And why would it? Why would someone who hadn't even received a traffic ticket know what to say, do, or how to behave when three armed police officers approached their front door?

But that's how it always was when it came to Adam. I was constantly being thrown into situations that I had no idea how to handle but had to muddle through somehow. It wasn't my fault that we had inadvertently made the officers nervous, but it sure put me on edge. I wasn't going to make that same mistake again, but how would Adam respond when they suddenly appeared? My stomach was in knots at the thought of them having to use their weapons.

Oddly enough, though, Adam didn't seem to be phased at all by the sight of three police officers entering our family room unannounced. Instead of questioning why they were there or getting defensive, he welcomed them in as if they were old friends.

Don't tell me that Adam is going to fool these officers into thinking he's fine. If they leave without him, I'll be right back at square one, wondering how in the world I'm going to get him out of here.

But then Adam started talking about the military rather than answering any of the questions the officer in charge asked him about his mental health. And after he asked the lead officer, "Is the powder in your bullets dry?" he was quickly ushered into our attached garage for a more private conversation.

After a few minutes of what sounded like silence from my side of the door, followed by some brief but loud scuffling noises, the officer returned to the family room and asked me to join him.

As I stepped out of the mudroom and into the garage, I quickly scanned the space for Adam, but he wasn't there.

"Ma'am, we've arrested your husband, and he's on his way now to the stress center. We will be placing him on a seventy-two-hour hold since he gave us reason to believe that he's a danger to others as well as himself."

"Thank you."

"I strongly suggest that you consider filing for a protective order. Here is my contact information." He handed me his business card. "I would be happy to testify in court on your behalf."

"You think I need a protective order?"

"I do, ma'am. I think you should contact your lawyer right away."

He didn't offer up any specific details of his interaction with Adam, and because I was so shaken up by what had happened, I didn't press him for any, but from the dirt covering his uniform and the noticeable scrapes on his right knee and left hand, I knew that Adam had become violent.

A few days later—after the dust had settled and the shock of the whole ordeal wore off—I asked the police officer stationed at my school to send me a copy of the official police report. As I read it, the true details of the incident came to light, and suddenly any hesitation I had about seeking a protective order disappeared. Below is an excerpt from the Incident Narratives section of that report.

> Out in the garage Mr. Adam would talk about multiple things and wouldn't make any sense about what he was talking about. During the conversation he asked me about my father and I told him that my father was deceased and Mr. Adam said good, you will be seeing him soon. At that time I asked him to place his hands behind his back and I grabbed his left wrist. As I was telling Mr. Adam to place his hands

behind his back and I was grabbing his wrist, he pulled his wrist away and hit me with his right hand with an open palm across the left side of my face. He then dropped down into a fighting stance by lowering his center of gravity and bending his knees and holding his hands in front of his face, his palms open facing out. At that time I grabbed his left arm and the inside of his right leg and started to lift his legs and him off the ground to take him down and ran into the side of a blue car that was in the garage. As soon as I started to take him to the ground Officer H. grabbed Mr. Adam's right arm and pinned it on the ground. Mr. Adam ended up on his back with both of his arms pinned down, I had his left arm and Officer H. had his right arm. Officer G. jumped on Mr. Adam's legs to keep him from kicking us. Myself and Officer H. began telling Mr. Adam to stop resisting and to roll on his stomach and place his hands behind his back. Mr. Adam rolled to his stomach but still resisted along the way and was resisting to place his hands behind his back. Officer G. assisted myself and Officer H., rolling Mr. Adam onto his stomach. Myself and Officer H. had to force his hands behind his back in order to secure him. Once his hands were behind his back Officer G. placed him in handcuffs. After Mr. Adam was secure on his stomach, he then stated to us that he was going to kill us and was going to end our lives by putting a bullet in our hearts.

53

As frightening as my experience with Adam and the police had been, some good things did come from it. For one, I was able to forward the police report onto Adam's brother, which played a significant role in getting him that yearlong court commitment, and secondly, it led to a judge granting me a two-year-long protective order, which legally allowed me to change the locks on the house, even though both of our names were on the deed. Yet I can't say that things got any better with Adam, or any easier on me.

The months of February and March were particularly difficult, as Adam bounced into and right back out of the hospital numerous times, all the while remaining in a severely manic state, and so he continued to spiral, making one bad decision after another.

He spent exorbitant amounts of money on all kinds of unnecessary expenses using several newly opened personal and business credit cards. He engaged in various risky behaviors involving drugs, alcohol, and possibly sex. And he disregarded the terms of his court commitment and those of my protective order as well, leaving me to feel unsafe no matter where I was but especially when I was home alone.

I can't even begin to describe how awful those two months were, nor could I possibly make note of everything that happened during that time, but there were a few moments in particular that tormented me more than others.

On February 16, I was granted my protective order by the courts. Although my lawyer and I, along with the officer who had arrested Adam in our home, had been prepared to testify, the judge granted the order without a word from any of us, since Adam never showed up for the hearing. We found out later that he hadn't been able to come since he had been forced back into the stress center after violating his court commitment when he missed a mandatory appointment. He missed that appointment because he took a spur-of-the-moment trip to Colorado, which he posted about on social media. On Twitter, he tweeted that he was snowboarding with Payton Manning and eating beer-flavored snow cones.

The following afternoon, I emailed Greg and Judy to make sure they were aware of all that had happened with Adam while they were vacationing in Florida, specifically regarding the knife incident and Adam's arrest. I also wanted them to know that I had been granted a protective order, so they could help Adam stick to it whenever possible.

They replied the next day with an email of their own. In it, they wrote that they "do not apologize" for going to Florida, as it gave them a "chance to retreat and prepare." And they downplayed the seriousness of Adam's violent behavior by stating, "one of the tools police use to justify apprehending someone in Adam's condition is to do their best to provoke the person, causing him to lash out and become combative. We believe the police did their job well."

Oh so it's the police officer's fault that Adam became violent.

That same day, Adam was tagged in a post on Facebook, which included a picture of a girl in her underwear and low-cut white tank top. I don't know if Adam was in the picture with her or not, but there was a man's arm shown resting next to her that could've been his. After doing an internet search using her Twitter handle, which she included in the post, I learned that she was from the same area in Colorado that Adam had just returned from. I also found some videos she had posted of herself on a pornographic website. When Adam's mom saw the post, she texted me to defend Adam.

> The post on Adam's Facebook page could not have been generated by him. He is in the Stress Center and was there when this was posted. Please inform those who are thinking Adam is responsible for this.

Clearly she didn't understand how Facebook posts and tags worked. I responded,

> Judy, he was tagged by a stranger. I know there could be an explanation for it, but it doesn't look good. Is this your only response to me? How do you think that post makes me feel?

She didn't respond. *Why do I even bother?*

I didn't think my view of Adam's parents could get much lower at that point, but on March 3, I received an email from one of the associate pastors at our church that changed my mind. I'm certain this email was prompted by Greg and Judy since the pastor wrote in the opening of the email that he was friends with them, and from the way I understood it, Adam's parents were attempting to use the church as a way of guilting me into staying married to him.

It was remarkable that Greg and Judy didn't think it was their place to tell me about Adam's mental illness before we were married but somehow believed it was their place to try to stop our divorce. And the notion that the church leadership thought they too had some say in the matter was almost as preposterous.

I had been begging for help from the church for years when it came to Adam, but I didn't receive any. Aside from one of the many elders in the church who happened to be a personal friend, I think everyone else was afraid to get involved because they didn't have the skill set to deal with Adam's bipolar disorder. It wouldn't have been hard for them to echo what his doctors were telling him, "Take your medication," "Prioritize sleep," "Stay up with your appointments," and "Listen to those who love you," but even that proved to be too difficult for them.

Yet as soon as the word *divorce* came into play, suddenly they were springing into action, since *divorce* is such a dirty word in the Christian faith. I personally think they felt more comfortable offering counsel when it came to divorce because divorce is a common occurrence these days. But the conditions that led to my divorce were far from being common. Any wisdom the leadership thought they might have had in hopes of saving my marriage would've been irrelevant and wouldn't have done a thing to change Adam's illness or his unwillingness to treat it.

So as far as I was concerned, they had long ago lost out on any opportunity they might have had to speak into my life, and so I told the pastor that I had every intention of following through with the divorce. I also attached a copy of the medical file that Adam's mother had been keeping and suggested that he, Greg, and Judy meet with my dad and me in person. After about a week of some more back-and-forth communication, they declined our invitation, and I stopped hearing from the church altogether.

I was relieved when the emails stopped because I didn't have the time or the energy to devote toward defending myself—nor should I have had to—but the whole situation angered me. The church should have come around me. They should have supported me, not jumped right into condemnation because they didn't understand my situation—which had been their choice all along—and Adam's parents never should have pitted the church against me. It was a shameless attack that had no hope of ending in anything but more pain.

The onslaught of mental and emotional assaults that Greg and Judy hurled upon me, however, weren't the only reasons why those two months were so difficult. Other than the obvious, it was the numerous ways in which Adam broke the conditions of my protective order as well, sometimes to frighten me and sometimes to demonstrate that he still loved me.

He showed up at my school to hand deliver a bouquet of flowers. He dropped a "Happy Anniversary" card off in our mailbox. He took a picture of our riding lawn mower, which was sitting in our backyard, and posted it on Facebook with the caption of "Free Tractor at the Estate … I must get going in case Law Enforcement arrive. Don't want to go to Leavenworth."

But the worst of it came on the day of March 14. After work that afternoon, I headed to the gym for a workout, as I normally did. I stopped at the front desk to check in and was greeted by one of the managers.

"How are you today?" she asked.

"Oh, I'm surviving. I have some frustrations to work out while I'm here."

"I wanted to let you know that your husband was here a few days ago. He was obviously intoxicated and smelled strongly of alcohol. He also changed the credit card on your account to his."

"Ugh, I'm sorry. Can you please change it back to mine?"

"Of course," she said as she took my credit card from me.

While she pulled up my account, I added, "I'd also appreciate it if you could keep an eye out for Adam. I've been granted a protective order against him, so he should be using another club. If you see him, please call the police."

"Sure," she replied sympathetically.

I placed my belongings in one of the cubbies behind the desk and then walked to the cardio deck.

For the next hour, I'm going to forget about Adam. I'm going to burn some calories and try to melt away some of my stress.

I stretched my legs, climbed onto an elliptical machine, and turned my iPod on, and within a couple of minutes, I was in my own world, lost in what I was doing for myself. But partway through my workout, I noticed a familiar figure standing at the front desk.

Wait. Is that … I focused on the figure, watching the way in which he moved. *It is. It's Adam!*

I watched closely as he checked in with a different manager than I had. Then he took a good look around the room until he spotted me. Once he did, he began circulating around the gym, intentionally passing in front of me several times, never even attempting to use any of the club's equipment.

Is he just here to intimidate me? If he was, it had worked.

Occasionally, he'd stop and talk to a person he knew but always with his body facing in my direction so he could stare over their shoulders at me.

If he doesn't leave before I'm ready to get off this elliptical, I'm calling the police myself.

But before my time on the elliptical was up, he left, telling the front desk that he better get going before the police arrived on his way out of the door. Later that day, I filed a complaint with the police department.

54

Throughout the second half of March, Adam's social media accounts exploded with highly inappropriate posts in which he made sure to tag me so that everyone I was connected to—my family, my coworkers, and my friends—could see them, at least until I was able to remove the tag. These posts contained profanity, references to drugs and alcohol, and sexually explicit language relating to prostitution, nudity, his body parts, and sometimes mine. So as soon as my spring break began, Max and I hopped into the car and drove north to Michigan.

Although I felt I needed to constantly monitor Adam's posts for anything I wouldn't want my name connected to, I still found some solace knowing that I was safe and far away from him for a while. But as the days passed, I began to get more apprehensive about going back home.

Do I really want to throw myself back into the chaos?

No I didn't, but I didn't see that I had much of a choice in the matter.

I don't know how much more of Adam I can take. The posts, the text messages, and the surprise drop-ins … I don't want to deal with them anymore.

Then on March 28, the day of my thirty-second birthday, Adam rented a room at the JW Marriott downtown, hoping I would join him there for the night, not knowing I had gone to my parents' house for spring break.

Even though I didn't respond to his request, I knew he spent a total of $598.53 on the room, $217.94 of which he spent on room service, since he provided the front desk with my email at check-in. I'm not aware of what he did throughout that night—although I think it's safe to assume he had a good time based on the amount of money he spent—but I do know that he gave himself up to hotel security the next morning, and that landed him back in the hospital, which made it a bit easier for me to return home when spring break ended.

Ten days later, he was transferred to LaRue D. Carter Memorial Hospital, one of the few mental health facilities left in the state that could treat him in the long term. So after dredging through the muck of Adam's mania for months, I could finally let my guard down, knowing that he was somewhere safe and I was too. For as long as he remained within the confines of LaRue Carter's walls, I no longer had to look over my shoulder everywhere I went.

At long last, after countless nights of restlessness, I was able to sleep soundly, feeling for the first time in a long time that I was out of harm's way. It was a good thing too, because I had more than enough on my plate to deal with. Other than school and my typical household responsibilities, I had an endless array of things to get done in order to push our divorce proceedings forward and get our house ready to sell, both of which had remained nearly stagnant since I filed for divorce near the end of January.

But even with Adam tucked safely away—finally stationed in one place for a while—and me functioning more normally again, nothing seemed to get done without a great deal of time and money being wasted. Since Adam was being held in a facility with limited ability to communicate with his lawyer, or any of the outside world for that matter, it made everything move more slowly. And his ever-changing attitude toward our divorce made any forward progression intensely difficult.

His feelings on the matter had oscillated at an extreme level since the very day I told him about it. Sometimes he felt angry about my decision, sometimes indifferent, and sometimes he acted as if our relationship wasn't ending at all.

For example, on January 24, he initiated a conversation with me via text in which he wrote the following:

> I'm sorry to have gotten nasty in front of your mom but you have been very disrespectful and ungrateful to me for all I have tried to provide and give you a great life where all your needs were met and give you great adventures like proposing at a private picnic at the Grand Canyon.

Later in the conversation, he also wrote this:

> Honestly it (the 4 years we'd been married) was the worst 4 years of my life.

But after that, he wrote the following:

> It hasn't been the worst 4 years of my life. I said that out of frustration. We had some awesome experiences together along the way and I am really sad, I just have my armor on so thick and tight it is easier to be the tough guy that feels nothing that the Army taught me so well to be.

Seven hours later, he asked me out to dinner, and two days after that, he sent me an email with our families Cc'd on it, titled "Proposed Marriage Reconciliation Plan." In it, he suggested that we "cancel the divorce immediately," "enjoy a year of dating," so he could continue to work on his business ventures at the apartment he planned to lease, and then head to Hawaii to renew our vows on the beach.

His emotions continued to fluctuate like that for months and only began to stabilize as he did. On April 29, exactly one month after his LaRue Carter hospitalization began, I received an email from him. Due to the hospital's internet restrictions, along with the protective order I had in place, it was the first time I had heard from Adam since he began his treatment there.

Sydney,

1. I apologize for contacting you directly and for all the things I wrote on facebook while I was manic.
2. I am doing a 60-90 day (dependent on treatment team) rehab program to get me to where I can manage my bipolar disorder / codependency / substance abuse issues. It is a bit like Army training which is great for me. I'm walking 5-15 miles a day and trying to lose the 45 lbs of marriage lazy complacency weight that I put on.
3. Please do not destroy any of our wedding photos or art from the house. I would like to take all of it and put it in storage.
4. I am working on LinkedIn through writing articles and making connections to raise $7.5 million for my company. I hope to accomplish this before the house sells so I can buy out your portion of the house.
5. I understand why you want a divorce and have accepted the cause of it is that I lost my rigid self-discipline that I had when you met me that was part of what you were attracted to. I went down a slippery sinful slope that I couldn't recover from until I crashed and burned. The purpose of the rest of my time here is to get all of that back so I can lead a healthy, happy, and productive life.

6. Thank you for picking up pieces like taxes and listing the house.
7. I still love and pray for you every day that at some point we can be reconciled.

All my heart,

Adam

In that email, he sounded more pleasant and mellow to me than he had in a long time, but he still hadn't accepted that our divorce was, in fact, happening and that he couldn't say or do anything to change my mind. So he dragged his feet on everything, especially when it came to signing the divorce agreement I proposed.

Coming to an agreement should have been a relatively easy thing to do. We didn't have kids, we didn't have many shared assets—except for the house and joint checking and savings accounts—and I simply wanted to split everything down the middle, while allowing each one of us to keep our personal belongings. The only thing I asked to keep that we had purchased together was Max, and there was no one on the face of the planet who would think Adam could care for him, since he hadn't been caring for himself.

Even with such a straightforward proposal on the table though, coming to an agreement proved to be anything but easy. And after the long and tumultuous months he had put me through, and then being forced to wait even longer for him to become sane enough to begin having such conversations, my patience for all his stalling tactics and flood of requested modifications, which typically only came in one at a time, began running thin.

First, it was that he didn't want to be responsible for any expenses related to Max since our separation began. *A little petty, considering Max was supposed to be a shared responsibility, but not that big of a deal.* Then it was that he wanted me to offer up all his furniture for sale to anyone interested in purchasing the house, but he still wanted to retain the right to accept or reject any offers made on said furniture, despite our inability to communicate with each other directly. *Right, like I don't have enough to do.*

After that, he refused to pay any portion of our mortgage payments, starting back in January, claiming he had no choice but to rent an apartment. *What! That's a bold-face lie!* He had been bent on renting his own place since his Christmas hospitalization, more than a month before I decided to file, because he wanted space to focus on his business ventures, and he could've continued to stay with his parents for free if he'd wanted to.

Still, after a tremendous amount of back-and-forth communication between myself and my lawyer and Adam and his lawyer—who described dealing with Adam as extremely difficult because he never knew which Adam he was going to get—we were able to come to an agreement. And Adam signed it, along with the divorce decree, on May 13. Then two weeks later, the court approved our settlement agreement, and I was finally granted permission to get our house on the market.

55

I wouldn't describe the moment when my lawyer told me that our divorce was final as a happy one. It felt strange and slightly insensitive to be given congratulations when it came to legally dismantling what had been the most significant relationship of my life, even if it had inflicted more pain on me than I thought was possible. Even so, that day was a significant turning point for me.

There were times throughout the process when I really questioned if Adam would ever choose to sign, leaving me to wait indefinitely for my freedom, preventing me from moving on by being stuck in the in-between. So when that pivotal day did come, I was grateful—grateful to have the biggest hurdle standing in the way of a fresh start behind me and ready to get to work on selling our house.

But like everything else had been since Adam came into my life, the house-selling process was an arduous one. I had to keep up with the yard, a large yard full of mature trees that constantly dropped sticks and branches every time the wind blew. I had to keep the inside of the house spotless and be prepared to get Max and I out of it at a moment's notice, in case someone requested a last-minute showing. I had to collect estimates on finishing our upstairs bonus room and screened-in patio so potential buyers could get a better idea of what they might have to spend if they bought the house. Plus there was the extra challenge of trying to communicate offers with Adam through the long chain of my Realtor to me, me to my lawyer, my lawyer to Adam's lawyer, Adam's lawyer to him, and then back again, before I could accept, turn down, or counter any offers. And in addition to all of that, the reality of my divorce, along with everything else I was going to have to leave behind, was starting to sink in.

I'd lie in bed every night, alone and immersed in near silence, staring at the blank spots on the walls that had been left slightly discolored by the pictures of Adam and me that once hung there, thinking about what should've been. I'd think about how much I loved the home we had built and how many hopes and dreams I had held for it. How I had planned to make a lifetime of memories with our family, friends, and future children in it and how all of that had been so horribly ruined.

Our home had been turned into a physical representation of the pain and tragedy brought about by Adam's illness and his and his family's deceit. Yet the thought of selling it to someone else, someone who would get to live in it and carry out those very dreams instead of me, was tough to accept. Still, I knew that it needed to be done.

And after a couple of all-day open houses, dozens of private showings, the disappointment of a good offer falling through, and even a strange claim that a Realtor showing the house heard footsteps upstairs, I received an offer on July 18 with a requested closing date of August 26, and I accepted it, even though the offer was a bit lower than the house was worth. I did so because every day that my move back to Michigan was delayed would've only made saying goodbye to what I still loved about our home, and Indianapolis, harder.

I knew that moving back to my home state was the best thing for me. If I had learned anything from my time spent with Adam, it was that I needed to be close to my own family, because my parents had been the only two people in my life who had always been there for me when things got bad. And it would have been impossible to move on from my turbulent past with Adam if everything around me constantly bombarded me with memories of him.

I couldn't have begun to heal in the very city where I fell in love with him and then had my heart so viciously broken by him. I couldn't have been happy trying to live a life that was *almost* the life I wanted, so I had no choice but to come up with a whole new set of dreams for my life and to do it somewhere far away from him and his family. But just because I knew all of that didn't mean it didn't hurt to leave my old life behind.

It hurt a lot actually, but I kept the sadness I was feeling hidden most of the time, only allowing small amounts of it to escape in private, sometimes in the form of tears and sometimes in the form of anger. And when I felt angry, embittered by the fact that everything I had worked so hard for had been decimated by selfishness and lies, I'd try to use it as fuel to get through those especially difficult moments, like sorting through an entire house full of things to get ready for the move. Things Adam and I had brought with us into the relationship and things we had collected as a couple, all of which we'd carefully arranged and fashioned into the rooms of our home together.

Almost everything held some kind of memory—both good and bad—forcing me to relive them as I packed the item into a box or threw it away. As anyone might guess, I had a particularly hard time letting go of my wedding dress, my engagement ring, our personal photographs, and the love letters we wrote to each other, but it was the things I didn't expect to bother me—the things I hadn't prepared myself for—that elicited such an intense kind of heartsick aching inside of me that I'll never forget how painful it felt to have to let them go.

One evening, I began filling cardboard boxes with Adam's clothes for him, and I came across one of his old, worn-out army sweatshirts. To the average eye, it would have looked like rubbish, well overdue for being tossed in the trash. But to me, it was a powerful reminder of when times with Adam were good.

I spread it across the bed in our guest room to look at it more closely, first circling around the Officer Candidate School Medallion in the upper-lefthand corner of it with my fingers and then feeling for the tiny holes in the cuffs left behind by Max, who loved to play tug-of-war with the sleeves.

Adam had first offered it to me on a cool summer's night soon after we started dating.

"You look cold, Sydney," he said. "Let me find you something to put on." Then he pulled that sweatshirt from his closet and offered it to me. "Here, this should help keep you warm."

Being a men's size large, it hung sloppily from my body, hiding any and all shape of my petite female frame, but I adored wearing it. I loved having his sweatshirt wrapped around my body, smelling of him as we snuggled closely together on the couch. And after that night, I never brought a sweater or jacket of my own to his apartment again, eventually wearing it so often that he gave it to me.

Throughout our years together, I continued to wear that ratty gray sweatshirt anytime I needed comfort or to be reminded of the man I fell in love with, so it was hard to let it go.

What should I do with this? I can't just throw it away.

I knew I couldn't keep it, even though a small part of me wanted to, but it took me days to decide to give it back to Adam. And once I decided, I shoved it into one of his cardboard boxes, piled a bunch of his other clothing on top of it, and sealed it shut with numerous layers of packing tape. Then I tossed it into the garage to get lost among all the others.

I wonder what Adam will think when he opens that box. I hope he remembers how good things used to be when he sees it.

56

Two weeks before the day of the house closing, after my parents and I had successfully emptied every square inch of my home, I traveled back to Michigan to begin fitting the things I had left following the divorce, a two-day garage sale, and a Salvation Army purge back into my childhood home. I'm not sure if it was a coping mechanism or merely the result of the physical and emotional exhaustion that had been compounding over the past several years, but I don't remember feeling sad or sentimental when we left, just numb, and that numbness stuck with me for several days, becoming an odd source of comfort at the time.

But with no plans to speak of and nothing substantial to keep me occupied—only loads of free time to sit and think—eventually my detached layer of protection began to melt away, and I was terrified to face what was hiding underneath. So on a whim, I downloaded a job search application onto my phone, knowing I couldn't take an entire school year off to rest and recover like my parents had suggested.

I didn't think I'd find anything of interest to me anyway, considering the start of the next school year was only a couple of weeks away, but after just a few days of casual browsing, a secondary science position at a charter school popped up on my feed. I wasn't particularly interested in teaching at a charter school—I have always been a public school teacher at heart—but

I didn't see any harm in applying for it, thinking that an interview would give me a good reason to get out of the house. And since the school was in Traverse City, one of Northern Michigan's most popular vacation spots, I figured my mom could come along, and we could make a day of it.

But after a few days passed, without hearing a word from the school, I assumed the position had been filled and that teaching for the year wasn't in the cards for me. Teaching was an emotionally demanding job anyway, and I was far from being in tip-top shape in that regard.

I suppose it's just as well, but I do need to find something meaningful to do with my time. And until I do, I'm going to try to be thankful that I have a safe place to live with a family who loves me. I can be patient until something comes along. Right?

Soon after I wrote that charter school off, however, I received a request for an interview, asap. And a few days later, I made the drive over to Traverse City, feeling uncharacteristically confident in myself.

With all the free time I had, I had done everything I could do in advance to prepare. I had researched the school's history, educational philosophy, and core values. And I brought along enough highly organized, color-coded folders for everyone on staff containing my résumé, letters of recommendation, example lesson plans, and pictures of former students' work. But I think most of that confidence came from my new mindset: *nothing, including botching an interview, could be nearly as scary as living with Adam.*

As soon as I walked into the secondary office, I was greeted by a man who peeked his head out of the backroom.

"Hi, you must be Sydney. Thank you for coming. We aren't quite ready for you though, so do you mind taking a seat?"

"I am. And sure I can sit. I'm in no rush."

"Great. We won't be long," he said before he ducked back into the room from which he came.

While I waited, a little boy came into the office and sat down next to me. I noticed he had some sort of trinket in his hand.

"Hi," I said to him. "What do you have there?"

"It's a keychain that I 3-D printed," he said as he held it out for me to see.

"You made it with a 3-D printer? That's so cool. Do you have one at home?"

"No, but we just got one here at the school. You can make all kinds of things with it."

"Really? Can you tell me how it works?"

"Sure!" he said enthusiastically. "There are a lot of things already programmed into it, but you can add your own code in as well. And you can get lots of different colors of filament for it too."

"Wow! You seem to know a lot about it. I'm impressed."

He smiled.

We continued to chat for a while longer, until the man from the back room reappeared.

"We're ready for you now."

"Okay," I replied. Then I turned back toward the little boy and said, "I've got to go now, but it was nice talking with you."

"Good luck," he said with a grin.

Forty-five minutes later, my interview concluded, and I rejoined my mom, who was sitting in the car out in the school parking lot.

"How did it go?" she asked.

"I know this sounds a bit overconfident, but I think I'm going to get the job."

"You do?"

"You know that I'm not an overly optimistic person, but yeah, I do. Maybe I'm wrong, but from my point of view, the interview went well. I was prepared for all their questions, and I think they were impressed by the folders I made too."

"That's great," she said.

"Yeah, but we'll see what happens. I'm sure they'll be letting me know one way or another soon. Let's go find a place to get some lunch."

Three hours later, I received another call from the school.

"Hello," I answered.

"Hi, Sydney. It was nice meeting you today. We've been talking since you left, and we have all agreed that you'd be a great fit here. So we'd like to offer you the job. What do you think?"

Wow! That was fast.

"Yes. I'd love to accept. Thank you. I'm just a bit surprised that you called so soon."

"Well, if I'm being honest, we were ready to offer you the job before you even interviewed."

"What do you mean? Was I the only one to apply?"

"No, but we were listening in on your conversation with Cameron. He's the son of one of our science teachers here, and she was part of your interview today. We place a high priority on building positive student relationships here, and we can tell that you do too."

57

Initially, I was a bit astonished that I had been offered a job due to a chance encounter with a little boy, but the more I thought about it, the more I became certain that it was God who brought Cameron into the office that day. Maybe I would've been given the job without Cameron, and maybe I wouldn't have, but either way, I know that God orchestrated it, giving me a leg up on the competition before a single interview question was asked.

God knew I needed that job—not necessarily for what it provided me with financially but what it allowed me to do. It allowed me to move out of my parents' house, far enough away from them to have the privacy I needed to work through all that had happened to me but still close enough that I could go home on weekends when I wanted to. It allowed me to start a new life in a place where no one knew who I was or what I had been through, so I could begin to figure out who I was myself and what I wanted to do with my future, without the uninformed opinions and unfairly imposed labels of others messing with my mind. And it allowed me to hold my head up a little higher when my dad and I left—the very next day, I might add—to close on my house and say goodbye to the last piece of my old life.

I firmly believe that God wanted to make His presence in my life abundantly clear to me. I think He wanted to show me that He was still there, rooting me on as He had always been, even if others in my life had betrayed me. Looking back now, I can see countless ways in which He provided for me, protected me, and showed me love when I needed it most. If it hadn't been for God's gracious protection, I could've come out of my marriage in much worse shape than I did, or not come out of it at all. But while I was going through it, and for some time afterward, it had been hard at times not to question where He had been and what He was doing.

In some of my darkest hours with Adam, it felt as though God was a million miles away from me, as if He had intentionally turned His back while Adam and I both writhed in pain. Why hadn't He done something to help us? Why hadn't He done something to help me?

Why didn't He reveal the truth about Adam's illness to me before we got married? Why had He allowed me to cross paths with Adam at all? Why did the man I fell in love with have to suffer from a mental illness, and if there was a good reason for it, then why didn't He force Adam to stick to his treatment plan? Was there any kind of purpose or greater good behind my torment, or was God using it as some kind of cruel punishment for something I had or had not done?

I struggled with those questions a lot over the course of that school year, and although I didn't find the answers to all of them, and may not until I meet the good Lord face-to-face, I did come to some conclusions that helped me make it through that first year after Adam. For one, even though God is unquestionably good, has an infinite amount of power and wisdom, and could have forced Adam to stick with his treatment plan just like He could have forced Adam's family to tell me the truth, I believe He didn't exercise His power in that way because of the gift He gave us all, free will.

Even though I believe God prompts us to choose what is right, just like I'm sure he did with Adam and his family an innumerable number of times, it is ultimately up to us to make the right decisions for ourselves. But we don't always make the right decisions, and because none of us live in a vacuum completely devoid of other people, we will be impacted by the decisions of those around us, just as we are by our own.

So I wasn't being punished by God. Instead, I was being hit by the fallout generated by a long series of poor decisions that Adam had made regarding his mental health, and since I was the closest to him, it only made sense that I would suffer the most damage, excluding Adam himself. Which is exactly why ending our marriage became my only option. I had to put an end to our relationship so I could step out and away from the danger zone and stop the flood of negative secondary consequences from overtaking me.

And as for Adam, I don't think he was being punished by God either. It may not seem fair, but I think he was simply the unfortunate recipient of faulty, disease-producing genes—the type of genes that came into existence when sin and death entered the world via Adam and Eve—and his unwillingness to surrender to them, to do whatever it took to minimize their sting, made it exponentially more difficult on him. That was his fault, not God's.

But that still begs the question, why didn't God urge me to run the other direction when I met Adam, or at least before I fell in love with him? I can't say that I ever remember feeling as though I should've. As a matter of fact, I was quite certain that building a life with Adam was a part of God's plan for me.

Did that mean then that God wanted me to marry Adam even though He knew it would end in heartache? Did that mean that there was some kind of purpose to our relationship, even though it brought about so much sorrow and pain? Did that mean Adam's illness, as horrible as it was, was part of a greater plan? Yeah …
I think it does.

Of course, I can only guess as to what that plan is. I know God used me to give Adam a reason to stay healthy and to provide him with numerous opportunities to follow through with doing so, even though he chose not to much of the time. I know that my experiences with Adam have changed me into someone who is stronger, more empathetic toward others, and thankful to have true friends, a loving family, and a sound body and mind. And I think my story has and will continue to impact others, in ways I hope will help them gain a better understanding of mental illness, encourage them to make better decisions in their own lives, and fight through the challenges they face with the strength of Christ.

But I admit that I don't have the ability to see the whole picture like God does, and I can accept that my thoughts are not as high, or smart, or good as God's thoughts (Isaiah 55:8–9). So I have chosen to trust that whatever purpose God had in mind for leading me to Adam, it must have been worth the cost I paid, and believing so has freed me from much of the bitterness I harbored inside of me for so long. That doesn't mean I don't struggle or battle with those same questions from time to time, but ultimately, that faith provides me with the peace I need to keep moving forward.

58

I may have been able to reconcile that God loves me despite the hardships I faced, and even accept that good things could come from them someday, but I had a harder time letting go of the anger and resentment I harbored toward Adam and his family, particularly when it came to his parents. For the longest time, I had a banner hanging in the front of my classroom that said, "Knowledge is Power," and although I hung it there to inspire my students to take their academic studies more seriously, its sentiment holds true outside of the classroom as well.

Adam's parents had possessed all the knowledge they needed, and thus all the power too, to steer me away from Adam and prevent me from suffering through a marriage riddled with heartbreak, yet they chose to keep silent. Then, despite having a front-row seat to witness how their deception hurt me, and after watching me take blow after blow for their son's sake, they still didn't have the decency to admit that they had wronged me. How could anyone do what they had done and continue to stand behind it?

No matter how I looked at it, it didn't make sense to me. And knowing it never would, and thinking I'd never be able to forgive them for it either, I pleaded with God to help me put them out of mind. But that didn't happen. For the better part of that school year, I found myself thinking about Adam and his family often.

Everything I did, everywhere I went, and every new person I met had a way of conjuring up old memories of them, and ninety-nine times out of one hundred, they weren't the good ones.

Those memories then led me to think about them even more ... *What are they doing with their time? How are they handling Adam on their own? Do they regret the damage they did to my life, my parents' lives, and their own lives, or are they pretending like nothing happened? Do they feel guilty for lying to me, or are they still holding tightly to the falsehood that they haven't done anything wrong?*

And Adam. *Is he finally taking care of himself? Is he still lost in mania or struggling through another bout of depression? Is he living back in his overpriced apartment, locked away in a hospital somewhere, or, worse, wandering the streets? Does he think about me as often as I think about him, or has he already moved on to someone else? Please, God, tell me he wouldn't destroy the life of yet another unsuspecting person ...*

Ugh! Why can't I make it stop? Why are they always on my mind in some way or another?

Adam and his family had been the center of my world for so long, and almost as soon as he entered it, I hardly had the time or the energy to think about anyone else. My brain had been conditioned to think about them. And because their actions had greatly altered who I was and where I was headed in life, training my mind to focus on other things, better and more future-oriented things, didn't happen overnight.

Even my dreams were inundated with thoughts of Adam. Sometimes those dreams forced me to relive the most frightening moments I had with him, and sometimes they were just fabrications of horrible things that never actually happened, but at one time or another I feared they might. For months after I moved to Traverse City, for example, I had the same recurring dream of Adam violently pushing me down a flight of stairs.

Occasionally though, my dreams took me back to the good times we shared, before I knew anything about bipolar disorder, tricking me into believing that my life with Adam had been everything I'd ever wanted it to be. Until the dream was over, and I'd wake up reaching toward the other side of the bed, expecting to feel him next to me, then realizing why he wasn't. And there I'd be again, thinking about him, thinking about his family, and thinking about all the ways in which they had hurt me.

But with the passage of time, a lot of hard work, and even more prayer, some healing did come. So by the time the end of the school year drew close, my heart—which had been shattered into thousands of tiny pieces—started to feel almost whole again. I knew that it would never be the same as it was before Adam. It would always have the scars left behind from him, but as it began to strengthen and reassemble itself, it also freed my mind from the unrelenting stream of negative thoughts, which allowed me to look forward to a future that was suddenly full of possibilities. A future that might have been extinguished all together if God hadn't granted me the strength to walk away before it was too late.

From time to time though, I still wondered how Adam was doing. I wondered if he had used the year, as I had, to heal and try to move on. I hoped that he had. I hoped that everything he had thrown away, especially our life together, had finally been the motivation he needed to do what I asked him to do on the day I left Indianapolis for good—to take care of himself, to forgive himself, and to push himself to do better. I didn't imagine I'd ever really know though, for sure.

On the Saturday before the school year was set to end, I spent the day hiking with my family through the old growth forest of

Hartwick Pines State Park. Before heading home, my mom and I ran into a local grocery store, while my dad stayed in the car to make a phone call to a friend, who was still in the hospital following a rather complicated heart surgery. After fifteen minutes or so, we returned to the car, and I got an immediate sense that something was wrong.

At first, I feared that his friend had taken a turn for the worse, but when I saw the look of heartrending concern on my father's face—the kind of look that a father holds in reserve for his children—I knew it had to be something else.

"I don't know how to tell you this," he said cautiously, "but—"

"Adam killed himself, didn't he?" I interrupted.

A look of bewilderment flashed across his face. "Yes. Eric just called and wanted me to tell you. How did you know?"

"I didn't know, but I do know Adam."

Deep down, I had always been waiting for it to happen. I had been praying that it wouldn't, but when I made the decision to file for divorce, I did so knowing that Adam was headed straight into the depths of his own self-made destruction and that only an aggressive, yet highly unlikely, 180-degree turn would save him. Knowing that, however, still didn't prepare me for the way I felt when it did happen.

"Are you okay?" my dad asked. "Do you want to talk about it?"

"I'm fine, and not really."

I wasn't fine, but I wasn't ready to talk about it either, so I just sat in silence on the way home, while I had my own conversation in my head.

How do I feel about this? How should I feel about this? Is there an appropriate way I should be feeling about this?

I don't know. I divorced Adam, and he's my ex-husband, so am I even allowed to be sad?

But I didn't want to divorce him. I simply had no other choice. I still loved him when I filed, and I still loved him when I left.

Our relationship had always been complicated, and the way I felt about his death was too. I felt relieved because I knew that Adam was in a better place, that his suffering had ceased, and that I no longer had to worry about him making an unexpected reappearance in my life. I felt grateful because I didn't have to personally witness Adam's suicide, or answer the door when the police came to break the news of his death, or have my life tragically taken away alongside his.

I felt a bit of regret because I never got the chance to tell Adam I loved him and that I forgave him, not in person anyway. About three weeks after our divorce was finalized, he sent me an email from the hospital titled "Please Read." In it, he apologized for all that he had put me through and said he wished he could turn back time and follow through with his treatment plan. Toward the end of the email, he wrote this:

> One request I have is to see you again. I don't want our last memories of each other to be when I was manic. Would you consider dropping the protection order so we could communicate back and forth now that I am stable? … I want you to know that you'll always be the love of my life and I'll never give up hope on us being reconciled to each other to live a happy, healthy life.
>
> All my heart,
>
> Adam
>
> PS: Please give Max a big hug and kiss for me. I miss him like crazy and wish I could go back to the days of taking him to work with me every day. Sometimes you don't appreciate how great things are until they are all taken away.

It took me two full weeks to respond to his email, and although every bit of it made my heart ache for him, I decided not to drop the protective order. It was the right decision, but I might've agreed to meet up with him if I'd known I wouldn't get another opportunity. I would have liked to have had one more chance to touch him, to hug and kiss him, and to officially tell him goodbye.

But it was the deep sadness along with the red-hot anger I felt that affected me the most—that temporarily knocked me back a few steps, and then a few steps more, when I learned more of the details behind his death.

Adam had taken his own life with a gun he had rented at a shooting range while he was out on a twenty-four-hour release from the hospital, signed into the care of his parents. While his parents were busy elsewhere, a friend of his agreed to take him out for breakfast and then was told to drop him off at his apartment when they were done. After his friend left, Adam hopped into his car, which he shouldn't have had access to, and drove himself to the shooting range, a shooting range he had visited before, despite having a mental illness and a history of attempting suicide. It was there he found a quiet place alone to take his own life.

He never should've been at that shooting range or been permitted to rent a gun. *How could the hospital have been so foolish in granting him a temporary release? Didn't they have access to his medical records? Weren't their so-called medical experts supposed to be adept at recognizing the warning signs?*

And why hadn't his parents watched him like a hawk, especially considering he had attempted suicide earlier that year by purchasing some toxic seeds online? The friend he had breakfast with that morning told me about that. *It was only twenty-four hours of their time. Didn't anyone understand how ill Adam was?*

When I thought about Adam with a gun in his hand, preparing to pull the trigger, and then falling to the ground when he built up the courage to do it, my heart broke all over again. He must have been at his lowest of lows, crushed under the weight of the sorrow he felt when he thought about all he had lost, and defeated by an illness he couldn't control, to have taken his life in such a violent way. He must have been so tired of it all to decide that death was a better choice for him than life was, and he must have been entirely void of all hope to be willing to put his family and friends through the agony of losing him, or at least convinced that they would be better off without him.

And then I started to ask myself the hard questions. *Did I have something to do with this? Was leaving him what sent him over the edge? Would he still be alive and fighting if I was still fighting alongside him too?*

I think those kinds of questions are normal to ask when one loses a loved one to suicide. I'm sure Adam's death made his family question every decision they ever made and every conversation they ever had with him, especially over that last year of his life, but those kinds of questions, albeit normal, are not good, or healthy, or fair.

The fact is Adam had a severe mental illness, and there was nothing that anyone could do about it. We all tried to help him deal with it, and we all made mistakes in the process, but ultimately, Adam's illness was just too much for him. No one could've stopped his suicide. No one had that kind of control over him—not me, not his parents, and not the medical professionals who were treating him—so there was no point in looking for someone to blame and no reason to feel guilty for being unable to do the impossible.

Epilogue

Although I wish I never would have been introduced to the horrors of Adam's illness, and I wish someone would've told me the truth to spare me from it all, that's simply not what happened. And there's nothing I can do to change that either. I can't go back in time, or wish it all away, or go on blaming others in hopes that it will somehow rewrite my past. So what can I do? It's a question I've contemplated repeatedly since Adam's death.

I heard it said once that you have to choose not to live your whole life wounded. That only you have the ability to cooperate with God and live as He intended you to. That you have to move past the what-ifs, let go of the what-could-have-beens, and forgive those who wronged you so you'll be able to see and take hold of the good things God places in your life. Of course, that's all easier said than done, and *how* does one do that exactly? For me, it's been by writing this book.

About two months after Adam's death, I started writing. At first, I did it solely for myself. Up until then, I survived by living day by day, never letting myself gaze too long at the entire picture, but by putting it all down on paper—or should I say a computer screen—I was finally able to process everything and how I felt about it as a whole.

But throughout that second school year in Traverse City, as I added here and there to what was nothing more than a digital journal at that point, I started to feel like my story needed to be shared. I got more comfortable talking about it with others—friends, acquaintances, even strangers—and I couldn't believe how many of them were not only interested in it but also knew someone who had a severe mental illness too.

So when that school year concluded, I quit. I did what I never thought I'd do, and I moved back home to give writing this book a real shot. There was no guarantee that it would become anything worth publishing, but it was the choice I made to begin living my life unwounded.

My greatest hope is that it will touch everyone who reads it. That it will inspire you to be more compassionate toward others, especially the mentally ill and their caretakers. If you yourself have a mental illness, I hope it will help motivate you to manage it appropriately with counseling, doctors' visits, and prescribed medications. And if you're going through your own season of suffering, I hope it will encourage you to reach out for help. There's no one better to turn to than Jesus Christ.

> And we know that in all things God works for the good of those who love him, who have been called according to his purpose. (Romans 8:28 NIV)

> "For I know the plans I have for you," declares the Lord, "plans to prosper you and not harm you, plans to give you hope and a future." (Jeremiah 29:11 NIV)